BECOMING FREE, REMAINING FREE

BECOMING FREE, REMAINING FREE

MANUMISSION AND ENSLAVEMENT IN NEW ORLEANS, 1846–1862

JUDITH KELLEHER SCHAFER

LOUISIANA STATE UNIVERSITY PRESS

BATON ROUGE

Cloth

12   11   10   09   08   07   06   05   04   03

5   4   3   2   1

Paper

12   11   10   09   08   07   06   05   04

5   4   3   2

DESIGNER: Andrew Shurtz
TYPEFACE: New Caledonia
TYPESETTER: Coghill Composition Co., Inc.
PRINTER AND BINDER: Thomson-Shore, Inc.

ISBN 0-8071-2862-7 (cloth); ISBN 0-8071-2880-5 (paper)

The paper in this book meets the guidelines for permanence and durability
of the Committee on Production Guidelines for Book Longevity of
the Council on Library Resources. ∞

For Tim, again

And for Bennett H. Wall

CONTENTS

ILLUSTRATIONS

ACKNOWLEDGMENTS

During the fifteen years that I have researched and written this book, I have piled up a large number of debts to those who have helped me in one way or another along the way.

My colleagues at the Murphy Institute of Political Economy, especially Richard F. Teichgraeber III and Ruth A. Carter, have provided encouragement and financial support throughout the years. I am also grateful to the former deans of Tulane Law School, John Kramer and Edward Sherman, and the present dean, Lawrence Ponoroff, for their support and encouragement. It is an indication of how long I have been working on this project that I have three deans with five-year terms to thank.

Wayne Everard and Irene Wainwright of the New Orleans Public Library are archivists of great talent and dedication who work under almost impossible conditions but have fabulous materials with which to seduce the researcher. They cheerfully and efficiently retrieved my long lists of cases from the New Orleans district courts and played an invaluable role in helping me find the materials upon which this book is based. David Combe of the Tulane Law Library and Wilbur Meneray from Tulane's Special Collections found materials for me that I might otherwise have missed. Marie Windell, archivist extraordinaire, gave me her expertise in the records of the Supreme Court of Louisiana. Katie Nachod of Tulane Law Library expertly helped me obtain copies of state slavery statutes from the 1840s and '50s, not the usual work of a modern law librarian. All of these archivists were amazingly generous with their time and knowledge.

Bennett H. Wall, friend, mentor, and drinking companion, has read the manuscript several times. His thoughtful critique has been invaluable to me, as has his friendship. We have had wondrous times together. This book is quite appropriately co-dedicated to him.

Heartfelt thanks to my fellow members of the Juniper Society of New Orleans: David Combe, James Gill, Henri Schindler, and Tommy Tucker. Although the Juniper Society has no intellectual agenda—we just drink gin together—the camaraderie and good wishes of its members has always served as an inspiration to me.

Special thanks also to the members of TUFF (Tulane University Fishing Fanatics), who have provided much-enjoyed moral support with their weekly fishing reports. Most of these are true (although by necessity they are "fish stories").

Others who deserve thanks for assorted reasons include: Warren Billings, Catherine Clinton, Ginger Gould, Bob Kerachuk, Ray Diamond, Paul Finkelman, Perry Jamieson, Kent Newmyer, Jonathan Prichett, Glenda Stevens, and Helen Ulrich. None of these good people should bear blame for the shortcomings of this book. I did not always follow their advice.

Chris Waldrep improved this book immensely with his helpful suggestions, although he is not responsible for any errors and omissions the reader may find. His insistence that I read the New Orleans newspapers proved invaluable, even if it added three years to the project. A quick glance at the footnotes shows how important the newspapers became as a source.

Sylvia Frank Rodrigue is a great credit to the LSU Press family. Along the road to getting this book in print, she handled all matters adroitly, and we became friends in the process. I was fortunate to have Alisa Plant as my copy editor. She makes me look like a better writer than I am.

My dear friends Margaret Kessels and Fr. Terry Davis continue to be anchors in good times and in bad. So are Suzanne and William Hammel, Suzanne and Ted Reveley, Marky and Uwe Pontius, and Kay and Paul Lapeyre. My good friend Ed Haas constantly renews my faith that there is someone on earth more sarcastic than I am.

To my family I owe my largest debt of gratitude. My favorite (and only) brother Cody Kelleher is a treasure to me. My children, Ashley Schafer and T. Gregory Schafer, are the best of the best (of course). Ashley expertly photographed all of the illustrations that came from Tulane. She made a tedious task fun. I am also very glad that their spouses, John T. Suttles Jr. and Elizabeth Billings Schafer, joined our family. But it is to the best spouse in the world, Timothy G. Schafer, that I feel the greatest thanks. He has made me the luckiest woman in the world. This book is for him, again, for all the reasons he knows best.

INTRODUCTION

"Life, Busy, Puffing, Smoking, Precious Life"

This book tells a story about the quintessential human longing for freedom, a quest that knows no color or culture. The inhabitants of New Orleans in the 1850s included thousands of people of color, from black to near white, who longed for their liberty; a significant number of them resorted to the city's courts to sue for their freedom on various grounds, and many used the legal system successfully and became free people. Other persons of color, already free, struggled mightily to keep their liberty. Runaway slaves passed themselves off as free; free people of color who had entered the state illegally tried desperately to blend in with the native-born free people of color. Louisiana law supported the institution of slavery, but some slaves found ingenious and remarkably sophisticated ways to use the law, lawyers, judges, and the local courts to gain their freedom. In doing so, they found a way to make the law act as an autonomous force in the contravention of slavery. While human bondage owed its very existence to laws that established it as an institution, slaves found ways to use the law to their own advantage, bringing to light the tension between the law and freedom. Slaves used the law designed essentially to keep them as slaves to win their freedom, and free people of color used the law to maintain and often to fight vigorously to safeguard their liberty.

What did freedom mean to a person of color in the antebellum South? Did it mean, as James A. Garfield would later ask, the "bare privilege of not being chained"? Did freedom simply mean an end to the restrictions of bondage without conferring any rights that would make freedom worthwhile? Even in a city and state where a patchwork of laws and ordinances controlled many aspects of the lives of slaves and free people of color, freedom meant not always being under another's control and supervision every hour of the day. Freedom also meant being able to keep the fruits of one's labor and the path to financial autonomy. Although city ordinances and state law conspired to deprive free and freed people of color from social, political, and economic equality, being able to function as an autonomous individual and keep one's own wages represented tremendous advantages over being a slave. In New Orleans society, as in any place and time, freedom constituted the most important issue next to life itself. As Judge John Ferguson said some forty years later when he ruled against Homer Plessy by refusing to allow him a seat in a "whites only" train car, Plessy "was not deprived of his liberty. . . . He was simply deprived of doing as he pleased."[1]

Inevitably, this book not only chronicles slaves suing for their freedom, but free people of color forced to prove their status in an increasingly hostile legal and social climate. At any moment their freedom might be snatched away and their lives changed forever. The meaning of freedom for them was inextricably chained to their ability to defend their liberty at law. Free people of color often found themselves using the very laws that supported slavery as a creature of the law to maintain their own liberty. Failure to understand and use the law properly could result in freedom forever lost. In an instant their lives could spin out of control.

Free blacks constituted what one historian has termed "leaks in a system which logically should have been watertight." Any change in the laws governing free people of color could threaten their freedom and security. They saw people of color being kidnapped, others ordered to leave the state, and some forced into slavery. Free people of color found themselves forced to prove their freedom at every turn. As the law prevented them from acquiring political rights, they had no share in making, challenging, or changing the laws that governed them, except by their very presence. Even the most stable and legally secure segment of the black community, the native-born free people of color, lived in a more or less precarious position between slaves and whites. These creoles of color, considered by whites the most re-

---

1. Eric Foner, "Rights and the Constitution in Black Life during the Civil War and Reconstruction," *Journal of American History* 74 (December 1987): 867. See also Hendrik Hartog, "The Constitution of Aspiration and 'The Rights That Belong to All of Us,'" *Journal of American History* 74 (December 1987): 1,013–34. I am much in debt to Hartog and Foner for their views on freedom. Also Keith Weldon Medley, "When Plessy Met Ferguson," *Louisiana Cultural Vistas* 7 (winter 1996–97): 59.

spectable part of the black community, nonetheless often had to struggle to prove their freedom. By the eve of the Civil War, as the issue of slavery came to a full boil on the national level, white hostility to the free colored population in New Orleans had escalated to the point that some creoles of color immigrated to Haiti and Mexico. Others chose to enslave themselves voluntarily rather than grapple with the dangers of an increasingly menacing environment. In many instances, free people of color found themselves a people under intense pressure. Despite these formidable disabilities, free people of color used the law and the courts in quite ingenious ways to maintain their liberty.[2]

A great city provides the setting for this story: New Orleans, the largest city in the Deep South in the 1850s. The Crescent City, which one visitor called "this splendid bedlam of a city," reached a height of commercial and cultural achievement at midcentury that it never surpassed. The location of the city, situated in a great looping curve of the Mississippi River, was the basis for its wealth, estimated in 1857 at $95,744,927—a figure that included real estate, slaves, capital, income, stock in vessels, horses and carriages, and furniture. The total wealth of the city grew by more than $8 million each year during the 1850s. The bustling port of the New Orleans, situated along the Mississippi River levee, formed the heart of the city's commercial prosperity. During the six-month-long "business season" from mid-October to mid-May, thousands of ships cleared the port of New Orleans, depositing their goods and acquiring new cargoes bound for ports all over the world. In 1856, a local newspaper described the levee scene:

> Our levee presents a most animated and busy appearance. Cotton, boxes of merchandise, sacks of produce, barrels, hogsheads, drays, et. cetera, are strewn or piled all along the levee. The drays and other vehicles hurrying to and fro with their inanimate or living loads raise a cloud of dust (not to talk of noise) which envelopes the forests of masts at the upper part of the levee in a dim, misty veil, and gives their complicated rigging (to a landsman) a phantomlike appearance. . . . The bosom of the

---

2. Winthrop D. Jordan, *White over Black: American Attitudes toward the Negro, 1550–1812* (Chapel Hill: University of North Carolina Press, 1968), 108. The word "creole" indicates a Louisiana-born person of European or African ancestry, or a combination of both. See Joseph G. Tregle Jr., "Early New Orleans Society: A Reappraisal," *Journal of Southern History* 17 (February 1952): 20–36.

river is troubled with life, busy, puffing, smoking, precious life. The fruit
and book vendors, with their baskets, pass hurriedly from boat to boat.
Captains on hurricane roofs vigorously ring bells; mates curse and "tear
around"; clerks hurry to and fro; the retail stores along Front street pick
up customers . . . strangers move off of newly arrived boats into the city;
strangers leave the city on departing boats. The levee of New Orleans is
a panorama of life to look at by anybody.

The nearby French Market provided another hub of frantic activity. Im-
mense crowds of people listened to peddlers hawking their wares, as one
observer noted, in "English, French, Italian, Spanish, and in lingoes which
have never been reduced to grammatical rules. . . . [E]ach proclaimed the
cheapness of his or her goods. . . . [E]very article which a man may require,
from spoons to spectacles, can be had in this famous market."[3]

The city's bustling international trade ensured that New Orleans would
have a remarkably diverse population of many ethnicities, cultures, and lan-
guages. Benjamin Latrobe, a visitor to New Orleans in the 1820s, commented that the city's inhabitants spoke a "gabble of tongues" that sounded
as the "issue from an extensive marsh, the residence of a million or two
frogs, from bull frogs to whistlers." Frederick Law Olmsted, a tourist in the
city in the 1850s, observed, "I doubt if there is a city in the world, where
the resident population has been so divided in origin, or where there is such
a variety in the tastes, habits, manners, and moral codes of the citizens."[4]

A huge influx of immigrants contributed to the diversity of the city. Made
up mostly of German and Irish people fleeing famine or political unrest in
their own countries, the newcomers often numbered more than six thousand a month during the 1850s. The flood of immigrants meant that native-
born New Orleanians barely outnumbered the foreign-born. Arriving with

3. Frank de Caro, ed., *Louisiana Sojourns: Travelers' Tales and Literary Journals* (Baton
Rouge: Louisiana State University Press, 1998), 70; *New Orleans Daily Picayune*, 22 February
1857, 12 October 1858. The business season lasted only during the cooler months, as fear of
yellow fever caused thousands of New Orleanians to leave the city in May or June and return
after the first cool weather in the fall. *New Orleans Daily Picayune*, 27 April 1850, 24 October
1851, 18 November 1856 (block quote), 16 February 1852.

4. Benjamin H. Latrobe, *Impressions Respecting New Orleans: Diary and Sketches, 1818–
1829*, ed. Samuel Wilson (New York: Columbia University Press, 1951), 18; Frederick Law
Olmsted, *The Cotton Kingdom: A Traveller's Observations on Cotton and Slavery in the American Slave States*, ed. Arthur M. Schlesinger Sr. (New York: Random House, 1984), 235.

little but the clothes on their backs, their health weakened by long voyages and poor diets, these new arrivals often fell prey to the diseases that periodically ravaged the city. Epidemics and many kinds of illnesses—especially the dreaded yellow fever—stalked the citizens of New Orleans. Between September 1852 and August 1853, 6,705 people (nearly 10 percent of the city's population) died of yellow fever, while over 900 people died from other types of fever, 503 from cholera, 820 of consumption, and over 600 of diarrhea and dysentery.[5]

The filthy condition of the city no doubt contributed to its high mortality rate. Without a sewage system or any form of sub-surface drainage, human and animal waste and rotting garbage of all descriptions piled up in the streets. The city dealt with stray animals by setting out poisoned sausages, but it made no provision to remove their dead and decaying bodies. Households and hotels discharged their cesspools into the gutters. In 1852, a local newspaper complained that the city's servants had a habit of throwing their slop water from second-floor balconies into the streets, and the city council passed an ordinance prohibiting this practice. Opening the sluices and letting the river water clean the gutters provided some relief, although the filth washed down to a putrid swamp at the back of the city, which provided a fertile breeding ground for mosquitoes.[6]

The New Orleans police wrestled mightily to keep the peace. The city's recorders' courts offered daily scenes of dozens of people brought in for drunkenness, brawling, mayhem, disturbing the peace, vagrancy, being "dangerous and suspicious," or being "lewd and abandoned women," the polite term for prostitution. People caught carrying concealed weapons, from knives and metal knuckles to handguns, often appeared before the recorders and attempted to justify this practice by claiming self-defense. Piles of merchandise and produce on the levee provided numerous opportunities for theft, and the local newspapers reported on loosely organized groups of thieves. In one instance, police conducted "an examination of about twenty women and children who were yesterday arrested for being in the habit of daily pilfering about the levee. The worst part of this habit is that the par-

5. *New Orleans Daily Picayune*, 15, 16 June 1852, 22 September 1853; Joseph Tregle Jr., "Creoles and Americans," in *Creole New Orleans: Race and Americanization*, ed. Joseph Logsdon and Arnold Hirsch (Baton Rouge: Louisiana State University Press, 1992), 164–6.

6. *New Orleans Daily Picayune*, 19 March, 19 June 1854, 18 September 1851, 1 June 1853, 16 February 1852, 17 May 1853.

ents oblige their children to follow this unlawful means of gaining a livelihood, thereby training them up to a life of robbery." In one six-month
period, police arrested 10,833 persons on charges that included murder,
manslaughter, rape, assault with a deadly weapon, stabbing, mayhem, duel-
ing, assault and battery, larceny, burglary, vagrancy, keeping a brothel, and
drunkenness.[7]

The Louisiana Constitution of 1845 authorized the formation of five district courts for New Orleans, and the Supreme Court of Louisiana continued to hold most of its sessions in the city. In 1846 the Louisiana legislature
created the five district courts, and they began to operate in April of that
year. They continued to hold sessions until the city fell to Union forces in
April 1862. A sixth district court, authorized to hear cases from the newly
annexed city of Lafayette (now the Garden District), began to hear cases in
1853. Until that year, the Presbytere, the building next to and downriver
from St. Louis Cathedral on the Place d'Armes, held all of the district
courts, the Supreme Court, and the conveyance, mortgage, and court records of the city from the colonial period onward. A visitor to the city, A.
Oakey Hall, who would later become the mayor of New York, described the
courthouse in 1851:

> I cannot forget the curious scenes I occasionally saw when in the
> New Orleans court-house. It fronts on a scraggy-looking square termed
> the Place des Armes [now Jackson Square], with a front and side the
> classifications of whose architecture would puzzle the most learned in
> the art. The Cathedral darkens its entrances and obscures its windows.
> Lazy looking priests and greasy garçons rub the whitewash from its base.
> Applewomen take possession of its lobbies. Beggars besiege its vault like
> offices. The rains from heaven sport among its rafters. It has everywhere
> an ancient, fatty smell, which speaks disparagingly of the odor in which
> justice is held. And yet in the building . . . are held from November until
> July, six courts, whose officers brave damp and steam enthusiastically
> and perseveringly. You turn out of Condé Street into a narrow alley and
> brushing past a greasy crowd, are soon within the criminal court, where

7. Ibid., 7, 8 December 1858, 8 December 1852, 13 September 1853. The city had a recorder's court for each district. Recorders were committing magistrates who disposed of minor
criminal matters themselves and sent people accused of more serious crimes to stand trial in
criminal court.

a judge, perched in a high box, wrangles hourly with half-crazed witnesses;—here you behold jurymen, who of themselves constitute a congress of nations; zealous, full-lunged lawyers; and audacious criminals ranged in boxes, very much to the satisfaction of a moustached district attorney and the merry-looking keeper of the Parish jail.[8]

Hall's vivid description of the courthouse also took note of a "weary flight of stairs" leading to a "dreary room" and a series of "clerky offices." He inquired of a "round-shouldered red-faced clerky-looking personage," "Is litigation around here attended with much formality?" The answer: "We do it up here as brown as they do it anywhere." One of the clerks actually kept a baby alligator in his desk drawer. Hall's rollicking description of the court echoed more earnestly in the editorials of local newspapers, which noted the unsafe condition of the galleries, the fallen brick chimneys on the roof, and the piecemeal repairs to much of the building. One reporter noted the "present courthouse is wholly insufficient to accommodate so large a business; neither is it secure enough for the safe keeping of records." City official contemplated building a new "fireproof" courthouse or moving the courts to the area of Lafayette Square, especially after the building's roof caught fire in 1851, but nothing came of these plans before the Civil War.[9]

Editorials complained of poorly cleaned offices, "extreme disorder," furniture of a "most wretched character," and the lack of an allowance of ice, so necessary in the steamy subtropical New Orleans climate. In the winter, jurors complained that the building was cold and drafty, with no stoves for heat and wind whistling through broken windowpanes. A huge volume of legal activity took place in this cramped and dirty building. In 1853 the five

8. "Constitution of the State of Louisiana" (1845), in James O. Fuqua, ed., *Code of Practice in Civil Cases for the State of Louisiana* (New Orleans: Bloomfield and Steel, 1867), Sec. 75, p. 20 (hereafter *Code of Practice);* "An Act to Organize District Courts in the Parish and City of New Orleans," Act of April 30, 1846, *Louisiana Acts, 1846,* pp. 32–4; "An Act to Organize District Courts for the Parish and City of New Orleans," Act of April 28, 1853, *Louisiana Acts, 1853,* pp. 190–3; "An Act Relative to District Courts for the Parish and City of New Orleans," Act of March 4, 1855, *Louisiana Acts, 1855,* pp. 315–7; A. Oakey Hall, *The Manhattaner in New Orleans; or, Phases of "Crescent City" Life* (1847; reprint, Baton Rouge: Louisiana State University Press, 1976), 78.

9. Hall, *The Manhattaner in New Orleans,* 79, 82. *New Orleans Daily Picayune,* 22 April 1852, 7, 10 October 1856; *New Orleans Bee* (*L'Abeille de la Nouvelle Orleans*), 29 May 1851; *New Orleans Daily Picayune,* 31 January 1851.

district courts in operation heard 5,073 cases. The First District Court alone, which had the criminal docket, heard 1,154 cases. Civil suits filled the dockets of the other district courts. The Presbytere also contained over 100,000 original records, including case files, successions (estates), conveyances, mortgages, and other miscellaneous documents. One reporter noted, "One-half [of] the property in the State, and every particle of the real estate in the city and parish of Orleans, pass [sic] through these courts once in every generation. . . .Yet these buildings had already caught fire twice, and the merest chance had prevented their entire destruction." The dampness of the New Orleans climate posed as great a danger to the court records as did the threat of fire. One journalist reported, "The papers of the court being exposed to the damp of the walls, are rapidly accumulating mould and undergoing decay. Nothing can be kept with security in the little, dingy, dark, damp back room on the ground floor of the old courthouse."[10]

The Presbytere also housed the Recorder's Court of the First District. An 1861 grand jury reported that the

> building of the Recorder's office of the First District [is] insecure and unsafe, the courtroom too small, the ventilation very bad, and the air fetid and unwholesome from the near connection of the privies underneath. The lockup of the second story is also considered very insecure, and the ground floor to be particularly unwholesome and offensive, being covered several inches with accumulated water, mud, and filth, the accommodation is too small for the number of prisoners and the privies in the cells making it infamous.

The recorders' courts operated six days a week, and each morning a new set of vagrants, prostitutes, wife-beaters, drunkards, brawlers, and other offenders against the public peace came to the court from jail via the "Black Maria," an open cart that transferred prisoners from the parish jail to the court. Often as many as a hundred offenders crowded into the courthouse, adding to the bedlam and confusion of a building already housing the district courts and the Supreme Court until that court moved to the Cabildo (the building next to and upriver from the St. Louis Cathedral and the former city hall) in 1853. The newspapers seemed to enjoy describing the

10. *New Orleans Daily Picayune*, 13, 20 November 1855, 3, 7 November 1858, 3 July 1853, 12 May 1851, 4 February 1858.

scenes in the recorders' courts; as one reporter wrote, "A greater crowd of creation's fag-ends no one could desire to look upon. One glance at the wretched dock full afforded a blended picture of ugliness, filth, poverty, intemperance, wickedness, fear, grief and stupidity such as the art[ist] might ever hope to transfer to canvas. . . . For the concentrated extract of human ugliness and degradation, there is no place like Recorders Court on a Monday morning."[11]

According to the U.S. Census, 116,375 people lived in New Orleans in 1850; ten years later, the city's population had risen to 168,675. Of these, free people of color numbered 9,905 in 1850 and 10,698 in 1860. These numbers reflect an undercount, as free people of color tended to avoid the census takers and the compilers of the city directories. Some free people of color who lived in Louisiana illegally understandably avoided census takers, whose job included asking each individual for his or her place of birth; laws designed to prevent non-native-born free people of color from entering the state existed during much of the antebellum period. As the social and legal climate hardened against them in the 1850s, many free persons of color might well have felt it prudent to avoid being listed. Often free people of color with addresses in the city appear in court records but are absent from the census and the city directories. The city's slave population numbered 7,011 in 1850 and 13,385 in 1860. African Americans, free and slave, who resided in the city personally generated hundreds of lawsuits seeking freedom or striving to maintain their liberty between 1846, when the district courts began to operate, until the courts closed after Federal troops took over the city in 1862.[12]

The original manuscript records of the six district courts, housed in the City Archives at the main branch of the New Orleans Public Library, provide the primary source for this study. Incredibly rich and varied, these handwritten records have never been systematically used in an analysis of this nature. They present a new and unexplored body of evidence about slavery, freedom, and manumission, as well as a vivid picture of the gritty day-to-day operation of the local courts. My other principal primary source, the New Orleans Daily Picayune, supplied many details not contained in the

11. Ibid., 24 January 1859, 29 June 1861.

12. Richard Wade, Slavery in the Cities: The South, 1820–1860 (New York: Oxford University Press, 1964), 326.

trial transcripts. During the district court terms, the *Picayune* reported, albeit sporadically and often incompletely, on some of the cases I discuss in this book. I chose the *Picayune* because it existed during the entire time frame of this study and because the paper reveled in gossipy details, which helped to flesh out the case records. Accordingly, in a three-year endeavor, I read the morning and afternoon editions of the *Picayune* from April 1846, when the district courts began to operate, to the summer of 1862, when the courts ceased to function because of the surrender of New Orleans to Union forces.

This book is about how slaves and free people of color used the judicial system in New Orleans to gain, maintain, or surrender their freedom. It is not a social history of slaves, slaveowners, and free people of color, although the cases reveal much about all three. Its chief focus is the decisions of the local trial courts of New Orleans that manumitted or failed to bestow liberty to slaves and free people of color, and in the end, assisted in enslaving them.

Subject indexes do not exist for any of the courts, and unlike appellate court cases, there are no printed law reports of these local trial courts. The only way to find cases in which slaves sued for their freedom or free people sued to maintain their freedom proved incredibly time-consuming, daunting, and tedious: a page-by-page examination of the Minute Books of the courts (huge and unwieldy books in which the clerks wrote down the daily business of each court). When I found a case that might contain a petition for freedom, I noted the docket number (cases are only accessible by docket number) and retrieved the case. Finding a significant number of cases proved a difficult task, and it is my hope that future researchers will find the list of cases in the bibliography of the book a valuable research tool.

The Mormons microfilmed many of the Second, Third, Fourth, and Fifth District Court records that they considered genealogically significant, but they apparently did not consider freedom suits important, because few appear on microfilm. Fortunately, the City Archives of the New Orleans Public Library has most of the originals. Many of the trial transcripts of the Sixth District Court no longer exist, leaving the researcher with only the Minute Book of that court as a rough guide to its operations.

The trial transcripts of the First District Court provide special insight into New Orleans politics and customs. Housed for many years in the attic of the Criminal Courts Building at Tulane Avenue and Broad Street (along with the judges' Mardi Gras costumes and other nonjudicial items in space not blessed with any sort of climate control, not to mention archival management), neither the general public nor historians had access to these records. Pigeons flew into the open attic windows and the Minute Books often rested on old-fashioned radiators.

I began trying to get in to see these records in 1984, when I first undertook this project. I wrote the court's judicial administrator, who ignored my letters and refused to take (or return) my telephone calls. I had nearly lost hope of ever gaining access to the court's records when my then-fourteen-year-old son began to date the daughter of one of the criminal court judges. My son told the good judge of my frustration with the judicial administrator, and the judge said I should contact him on Monday morning. Not only did I get into see the records, but the judicial administrator allowed me to work in his office, brought me coffee, and generally "Dr. Schafered" me to death. My son's "relationship" (if a fourteen-year-old can have such) did not last the month, but I was in. The moral of this story is that having a charming and handsome son is a fabulous, although quite unexpected, research advantage. Incidentally, the judicial administrator subsequently lost his position as a result of embezzlement. He waits tables now at a local restaurant.

The records of the First District Court have subsequently been relocated to the City Archives of the New Orleans Public Library, where even ordinary people who do not have handsome sons can use them. The Mormons filmed most of the records of the First District Court (but few manumission suits) from 1846 to 1855, when the court's docket became exclusively criminal. The library has the originals of the suits after 1855. Before 1855, the majority of suits involving slaves suing for freedom originated in the First District Court. After 1855, slaves suing for freedom resorted to one of the other five district courts.[13]

---

13. Although antebellum Louisiana attorneys and judges used the terms "emancipation" and "manumission" interchangeably, most modern historians use "manumission" to mean freeing a slave during a time in which slavery existed under the law and "emancipation" to denote the general freeing of slaves following the Civil War. Louisiana civil law further complicated the issue, as the term "emancipation" also meant freeing a minor child from the legal and civil disabilities associated under the *Civil Code* with being under the age of twenty-one. To avoid confusion, I will follow modern usage. *A Digest of the Civil Laws Now in Force in the Territory of Orleans* (New Orleans: Bradford and Anderson, 1808), Arts. 87–97, pp. 74–6 (hereafter *Digest of 1808*); *Civil Code of the State of Louisiana* (New Orleans: J. C. de St. Romes, 1825), Arts. 367–81, pp. 54–6 (hereafter *Civil Code*); "An Act Relative to District Courts for the Parish and City of New Orleans," Act of March 14, 1855, *Louisiana Acts, 1855*, p. 316.

The Louisiana Constitution of 1864 officially ended slavery in Louisiana. In its very first article, the constitution declared that slavery was "forever abolished and prohibited throughout the State" and forbade the legislature to pass any law "recognizing the right of property in man." Although social, economic, and political equality did not accompany emancipation, the need for freedom suits no longer existed.[14]

14. "Constitution of the State of Louisiana" (1864), in Fuqua, ed., *Code of Practice*, Title 1, Arts. 1–2, p. 68.

BECOMING FREE,
REMAINING FREE

PROLOGUE

Laws Governing Manumission, 1807–1857

O n the morning of March 6, 1857, Chief Justice of the Supreme Court
Roger B. Taney began to read his opinion in the case of *Scott* v. *Sandford*. Over eleven years earlier, a slave named Dred Scott had sued for his
freedom on the grounds that his master had taken him to free soil. When
Taney finished reading, two hours later, Dred Scott remained in bondage.
On the same day, eleven hundred miles away from Washington, D.C., the
Louisiana legislature passed a one-sentence act that totally prohibited slave
manumission in the state from that day forward. The passage of that law
represented the final blow to freedom for Louisiana's slaves.[1]

Throughout the antebellum period, Louisiana law reflected an ongoing
ambivalence and growing hostility toward slave manumission. Although
Louisiana remained the easiest Deep South state in which to free a slave—at
least until 1857—lawmakers fretted over the consequences of increasing the

---

1. Scott v. Sandford, 19 Howard 393 (1857); Don E. Fehrenbacher, *Slavery, Law, and
Politics: The Dred Scott Case in Historical Perspective* (New York: Oxford University Press,
1981), 3–4; Kenneth Stampp, *America in 1857: A Nation on the Brink* (New York: Oxford University Press, 1990), 93–4; "An Act to Prohibit the Emancipation of Slaves," Act of March 6,
1857, *Louisiana Acts, 1857*, p. 55. The *New Orleans Daily Picayune* praised the *Dred Scott*
decision, writing, "It is settled to be the law of the land that the constitution recognizes and
guarantees to every State the right of the master to property in slaves." Realizing the significance of the ruling, the paper editorialized, "Generally the government of the United States
was made for free whites, and Africans and descendants of Africans are not part of the 'people'
of the United States, and cannot constitutionally become citizens. The really considerate and
patriotic in the free States cannot fail to see the hopelessness of effecting anything legally and
constitutionally." *New Orleans Daily Picayune*, 20 March 1857. A nearly identical editorial appeared in the *Picayune* on 22 March 1857.

population of free people of color. Nevertheless, throughout most of the antebellum era, many New Orleans slaveholders voluntarily and legally freed their slaves with permission to remain in Louisiana. District courts in New Orleans also freed a number of slaves who claimed their freedom on the same basis that Dred Scott had—that they had been taken by their owners to free soil. As the decades passed, however, the state legislature gradually placed more restrictions on owners wishing to free slaves. As the law made manumission more difficult, demands for individual exceptions increased. Petitions to police juries, judges, juries, and even lawmakers often succeeded in bypassing legal restrictions on manumission. Finally, after juries of the New Orleans district courts freed hundreds of slaves in 1855 and 1856, the legislature slammed shut the door to freedom for the state's approximately 300,000 slaves. While the total prohibition of manumission in Louisiana was a direct response to this sudden and dramatic increase in emancipations, it also reflected the heightened political crisis over slavery in the 1850s.[2]

Slaves in American Louisiana had two unique rights. State law allowed

2. Laurence J. Kotlikoff and Anton J. Rupert, "The Manumission of Slaves in New Orleans, 1827–1846," *Southern Studies* 19 (summer 1980): 172–81. Kotlikoff and Rupert found that the Orleans Parish Police Jury allowed each slave whose manumission they approved between 1827 and 1846 to remain in the state. In 1846 legislators abolished the Orleans Parish Police Jury and transferred responsibility for hearing petitions for freedom to the newly created Emancipation Courts of the Councils of the Three Municipalities of New Orleans. "An Act to Abolish the Police Jury in the City of New Orleans," Act of May 27, 1846, *Louisiana Acts, 1846*, p. 104. Each petition requested that the slave have permission to remain in the state, and the councils allowed these requests. "Slaves Emancipated by the Councils of Municipality No. 1, No. 2, and No. 3, 1846–1851." City Archives, New Orleans Public Library, Main Branch. For examples of slaves freed by New Orleans courts, see: Marie Louise, f.w.c., v. Marot, No. 2748, 8 La. Ann. 475 (1835); Smith, f.w.c., v. Smith, No. 3314, 13 La. Ann. 441 (1839); Arsène, alias Cora, f.w.c., v. Pignéguy, No. 459, 2 La. Ann. 620 (1847). These cases originated in the First Judicial District Court of New Orleans. In each case the slave won at trial, the owner appealed, and the Supreme Court of Louisiana affirmed the decision of the lower court freeing the slave. For discussions of these cases see Paul Finkelman, *An Imperfect Union: Slavery, Federalism, and Comity* (Chapel Hill: University of North Carolina Press, 1981), 210–4; Judith Kelleher Schafer, *Slavery, the Civil Law, and the Supreme Court of Louisiana* (Baton Rouge: Louisiana State University Press, 1994), 271–7. See also Ira Berlin, *Slaves without Masters: The Free Negro in the Antebellum South* (New York: New Press, 1974), 188–9 n. 139; Kenneth Stampp, *The Peculiar Institution: Slavery in the Antebellum South* (New York: Knopf, 1956), 232–4.

them to contract for their freedom and to initiate a lawsuit for their liberty. Article 174 of the *Civil Code of the State of Louisiana* (1825) allowed slaves to enter into only one form of contract—for their freedom. Although quite limited, this right was unknown in other slave states. Slaves could not compel their owners to sell them when they managed to acquire their appraisal price, but if their masters or mistresses consented to the contract, slaves obtained the price their slaveholders set, and the proper contract was prepared for the transfer of real estate (slaves were considered real property in Louisiana), the parties entered into an enforceable contract for the slaves' freedom.[3]

The *Civil Code* also permitted slaves to sue directly for their freedom. In most common-law states, those who wished to sue for freedom had to proceed through the use of a legal fiction. Some states prohibited slaves from suing for their freedom directly without the aid and support of a free person, a court-appointed guardian *ad litem*—a "Near Friend" (as it was called in Tennessee), or "Next Friend," as some other southern courts termed it. In these suits, southern states often required that either the slave or the guardian of the slave begin an action of trespass or a charge of assault and battery against the master or mistress, who would respond that the plaintiff was a slave and therefore that no injury had taken place, whereupon the plaintiff would claim to be free. The court would then ignore the fictitious trespass or assault and battery and agree to rule on the issue of freedom.[4]

Slaves' right to sue for their freedom constituted an exceptional legal act in antebellum Louisiana. Article 177 of the *Civil Code* held that slaves could not be parties in any civil action, either as plaintiffs or defendants, except to claim their freedom. Although the French *Code Noir* deprived slaves of legal capacity in civil suits, Spanish law granted slaves the right of self-purchase (*coartación*). Slaves in Spanish Louisiana obviously had to possess legal capacity to bring self-purchase petitions against their owners. Although

3. *Civil Code,* Art. 174, p. 27, Art. 461, p. 68.

4. Stampp, *Peculiar Institution,* 197; Arthur Fletcher Howington, "The Treatment of Slaves and Free Blacks in the State and Local Courts of Tennessee" (Ph.D. diss., Vanderbilt University, 1982); Paul Finkelman, *The Law of Freedom and Bondage: A Casebook* (New York: Oceana Press, 1986), 97–9. In Dred Scott's case in federal court, the defendant claimed that Scott could not sue because of his race. Paul Finkelman, *Dred Scott v. Sandford: A Brief History with Documents* (Boston: Bedford/St. Martins, 1997).

the right of *coartación* did not survive the Spanish period, the *Digest of 1808* and the *Civil Code,* which constituted the civil law for the antebellum period, maintained this capacity of slaves to sue directly for their freedom. The Louisiana *Civil Code* also explicitly permitted owners to free their slaves: "A master may manumit his slave in this State either by an act *inter vivos* [during life] or by a disposition made in prospect of death, provided such manumissions be made with the forms and under the conditions prescribed by law."[5]

Although the "conditions prescribed by law" became increasingly more complex and difficult as the national crisis over slavery intensified, the procedure to free a slave at first appeared fairly simple. An 1807 Louisiana law required slaves to have exhibited "honest conduct" for four years before manumission—specifically, that they had not run away or committed a criminal act—and to have reached the age of thirty years. If the slave had saved the life of the slaveowner or a member of the slaveowner's family, such restrictions did not apply. Yet the age requirement presented a formidable obstacle to manumission. Often this qualification prevented an owner from freeing a slave woman over thirty and her children. It also prohibited a free man or woman of color who purchased an underage spouse from effecting an emancipation until the slave reached the specified age. Because the child took the status of the mother, children born to slave women while owned by their free black husbands remained slaves by law for at least thirty years. Although free black purchasers would not have treated their spouses and children as slaves, if the free parent died, the spouse and children fell into the succession as did any other property and faced judicial sale to satisfy the deceased's debts if the estate proved insolvent. Even if the deceased did not die in debt, the spouse and children became the property of the legal heirs.[6]

Slaveowners often successfully petitioned the legislature to make indi-

---

5. Barry Nichols, *An Introduction to Roman Law* (New York: Oxford University Press, 1962), 72–3; Hans Baade, "The Law of Slavery in Spanish Luisiana," in *Louisiana's Legal Heritage,* ed. Edward F. Haas (Pensacola, Fla.: Perdido Bay Press, 1983), 65, 70; *Digest of 1808,* Tit. IV, Chap. 3, p. 30; *Civil Code,* Art. 177, p. 28, Art. 184, pp. 28–9.

6. "An Act to Regulate the Conditions and Forms of the Emancipation of Slaves," Act of March 9, 1807, *Orleans Territory Acts, 1807,* pp. 82–8; *Civil Code,* Arts. 183, 185–6, pp. 28–9. The Louisiana Supreme Court stated that if slaveholders could free their slave children, it would "flood the community with a class of persons who are totally incapable of supporting and taking care of themselves." Carmouche v. Carmouche, No. 243, 12 La. Ann. 721 (1857).

vidual exceptions to the age requirement for manumission. In 1823 the legislature granted permission for a free woman of color to free her two children, aged twenty-six and twenty-four. In 1824 lawmakers permitted seven slaveowners to free fifteen underage slaves; in the same manner, five slaveholders freed eight more slaves the following year. Thirteen slaves under thirty gained their freedom from seven owners during the legislative session of 1826. Of the thirty-eight slaves who received their freedom from twenty owners by legislative process, eleven slaves gained their freedom from seven free women of color, usually their free black mothers. Most of these acts stated that the manumission take place "as if the slave had attained the age required by law." A few required that the manumitting owner provide maintenance until the age of thirty years. Tired of the stream of petitions for exceptions, legislators made the age requirement less rigid in 1827. Persons wishing to free a slave under thirty could petition the parish judge and the police jury (the governing body of a parish) to allow an underage manumission, provided that the slave at issue was born in the state.[7]

7. "An Act to Authorise the Manumission of Certain Slaves," Act of March 7, 1823, *Louisiana Acts, 1823,* p. 36; "An Act to Dispense Certain Slaves Therein Named with the Age Required by Law for the Emancipation of Slaves," Act of February 25, 1824, *Louisiana Acts, 1824,* pp. 42–6; "An Act to Dispense Certain Slaves Mentioned with the Age Requirement by Law for the Emancipation of Slaves," Act of December 20, 1824, p. 22; "An Act to Dispense Certain Slaves Therein Mentioned with the Time Prescribed by Law for the Emancipation of Slaves," Act of February 17, 1825, *Louisiana Acts, 1825,* p. 132; "An Act to Emancipate Certain Slaves Therein Mentioned," Act of February 18, 1825, p. 150; "An Act to Authorize the Emancipation of the Slaves Therein Mentioned," Act of February 19, 1825, p. 198; "An Act to Authorise the Emancipation of Certain Slaves," Act of February 14, 1826, *Louisiana Acts, 1826,* p. 32; "An Act to Dispense Certain Slaves Therein Mentioned with the Age Required by Law for the Emancipation of Slaves," Act of February 22, 1826, p. 40; "An Act Supplementary to the Act Entitled 'An Act for the Relief of Catherine Moreau,' Approved March 18, 1820," Act of March 14, 1826, pp. 64–6; "An Act to Authorize the Emancipation of the Slaves Therein Mentioned," Act of March 22, 1826, pp. 110–2. It cannot be determined whether the legislature rejected any petitions to free underage slaves or how many petitions came before the legislature. The journals of the Louisiana legislature in the 1820s either have not survived or might never have been published. The legislature did not grant manumissions before 1823 except in one instance, when lawmakers freed two slaves as a reward for revealing an insurrection plot. The act also provided financial compensation for the owners of such slaves. "An Act to Emancipate Certain Slaves and for Other Purposes," Act of February 13, 1813, *Louisiana Acts, 1813,* p. 100. See also Henry Campbell Black, ed., *Black's Law Dictionary,* 1st ed. (St. Paul, Minn.: West, 1891), 907; "An Act to Determine the Mode of Emancipating Slaves Who Have

The statewide population of free people of color grew by 53 percent between 1820 and 1830, from approximately 10,000 to 16,000. Alarmed, Louisiana legislators responded with a draconian measure against free people of
color in 1830, which was intended not only to limit their numbers but to
expel some of the new arrivals. This act required all free persons of color
who had come to Louisiana after 1825 to leave the state within sixty days or
face a sentence of imprisonment at hard labor for one year. Failure to depart within thirty days after the jail term imposed a penalty of imprisonment
for life at hard labor. These provisions also applied to free blacks who came
into Louisiana after passage of the act. The law required those wishing to
free slaves to post a $1,000 bond to guarantee that the newly freed slave
would leave the state within one month of manumission. The statute also
ordered all free people of color legally allowed to remain in the state to register themselves in the office of their parish judge, recording their ages, gender, color, occupation, place of birth, and the date they arrived in Louisiana.
It cost fifty cents per person to register. Failure to do so could result in a
fine of $50 and one month's imprisonment. The 1830 law also established
penalties against white people who wrote or printed statements that served
to "destroy that established line of distinction . . . between the several classes
of this community." Whites who used language that might engender slave
discontent or even rebellion could receive a sentence of six months to three
years in jail and a fine of $300 to $1,000. Free people of color violating this
provision faced hard labor from three to five years and afterwards perpetual
banishment. The First District Court of New Orleans tried a number of
cases in which free people of color failed to record themselves. The court
usually sentenced those convicted to one hour in jail, a $25 fine, and pay-
ment of court costs (usually around $8).[8]

Not Attained the Age Required by the Civil Code for Their Emancipation," Act of January 31,
1827, *Louisiana Acts, 1827*, pp. 12–4.

8. "An Act to Prevent Free Persons of Color from Entering into This State, and for Other
Purposes," Act of March 16, 1830, *Louisiana Acts, 1830*, pp. 90–6. This violation of the First
Amendment right of free speech was not as egregious as it might seem. In Barron v. Baltimore,
7 Pet. 243 (1833), and Permoli v. The City of New Orleans, 3 How. 589 (1845), the Supreme
Court later ruled that the Bill of Rights did not apply to laws enacted by the states. For a free
person of color's conviction for "failure to record," see State v. Powell, f.w.c., No. 10,876, First
District Court of New Orleans, 19 May 1846. A conviction for contravention (being in the state
in contravention to the law) resulted in an order to leave the state within sixty days for Mary
Ann Martin, f.w.c. Martin did not leave as ordered, and on October 4, 1846, the First District

The following year, lawmakers softened the rule that required slaves to leave the state within thirty days after manumission, although they kept the harsh penalties regarding those who had entered the state after 1825. With a three-fourths vote, parish police juries could now permit newly manumitted slaves to remain in the state, and any slave freed for "meritorious conduct" could bypass all restrictions. A study of parish police juries from 1831 to 1846 indicates that the Orleans Parish Police Jury did not apply the law, however, not making even one freed slave leave the state as a condition for manumission.[9]

The clash between the native-born French-speaking population and the more prosperous Anglo-Americans resulted in a division of New Orleans into three separate municipalities by 1836. Each municipality established their own manumission courts. Surviving records—all in French—indicate that without exception the manumission courts that freed slaves in Orleans Parish between 1846 and 1851 did not force them to leave the state (*sans qu'elle/qu'il soit obligée/obligé de quitter l'état*).[10]

Beginning in the late 1830s and throughout the 1840s, Louisiana lawmakers passed various acts granting legislative manumission that required some newly freed people of color (whom police juries had allowed to remain

---

Court sentenced her to one year in the state penitentiary at hard labor. State v. Mary Ann Martin, No. 299, 4 October 1846. For cases in the First District Court in which free people failed to record themselves, see: State v. Eddington, f.m.c., Nos. 3112, 3122, 20 December 1848; State v. Coffee, f.m.c., No. 4244, 20 October 1849; State v. Jannings, f.m.c., No. 4910, 6 April 1850.

9. "An Act to Amend an Act Entitled 'An Act to Prevent Free Persons of Color from Entering This State,'"Act of March 25, 1831, *Louisiana Acts, 1831,* pp. 96–8; Kotlikoff and Rupert, "The Manumission of Slaves in New Orleans, 1827–1846," 172–81. In 1839 the legislature passed an act allowing the police juries of West Feliciana and Livingston Parish to free several slaves owned by free persons of color but required a bond to ensure that those freed would not become a public charge. "An Act to Authorize the Police Jury of the Parishes of West Feliciana and Livingston to Emancipate Certain Slaves Therein Mentioned," Act of March 14, 1839, *Louisiana Acts, 1839,* p. 78.

10. "An Act to Amend the Act Entitled 'An Act to Incorporate the City of New Orleans Approved February the Seventeenth, Eighteen Hundred and Five,'" Act of March 8, 1836, *Louisiana Acts, 1836,* pp. 28–37; *New Orleans Daily Picayune,* 25 July 1846; Conseil de la Municipalité No. Un, 1 July 1846–7 July 1851 (Emancipation Court), City Archives, New Orleans Public Library. In Louisiana parlance, the French-speaking creoles referred to the English-speaking Anglo-Americans as "Americans," despite the fact that the creoles had also been Americans since 1803.

in the state) to post bond to ensure that they would not become public charges. Legislators continued to make exceptions to the age requirement for manumission; they also allowed some free people of color to remain in the state who were required by law to leave it. By the early 1850s, however, Louisiana legislators no longer took such a charitable view of manumission or the resulting increase in the population of free people of color. By this time slavery had moved to the center of the national political stage. The publication of *Uncle Tom's Cabin* by Harriet Beecher Stowe in 1852 whipped up antislavery sentiment in the North, and southern fears of abolition grew accordingly. The willingness of supposedly respectable people to stop enforcement of the harsh Fugitive Slave Law of 1850 infuriated and frightened southerners.

Early in the 1852 Louisiana legislative session, Representative François Arceneaux of Lafayette Parish introduced a bill to prohibit all slave manumissions, and Francis DuBose Richardson of St. Mary Parish sponsored a bill that required all liberated slaves to depart the state for Liberia. In the initial debate over these acts, Richardson cited the need for change in the manumission law of the state. Arceneaux stated, "The constant increase of free negroes in this State, and their intercourse with slaves, tending to corrupt and poison them, was a crying evil, and in fact an absolute nuisance." He further asserted that no benefit could possibly come to slaves by freeing them, thereby "condemning him to drag out an irksome and precarious existence." Africa, he continued, could prove to be the only place on earth "compatible with [a slave's] mediocrity of intellect."[11]

In reply, Representative Uriah Burr Phillips of West Feliciana argued that although he understood the "evils accompanying a free negro population," he believed that Richardson's bill would cause an "entire prohibition of all emancipations." Representative E. Warren Moise of Plaquemines Parish accurately declared that Richardson's measure was aimed at New Orleans: "Its object was to take away from the Municipal Council the power to emancipate slaves with permission to remain in the State." Moise proposed an amendment requiring newly freed slaves to depart the state within ten days of their manumission. He pointed out that the 1850 census showed a

---

11. *Journal of the House of Representatives of the State of Louisiana* (New Orleans: G. W. Weisse, 1852), 18, 36; *Report of the House of Representatives of the State of Louisiana* (New Orleans: G. W. Weisse, 1852), 7. Gallic names such as Arceneaux and DuBose are evidence that country legislators' interests transcended ethnic loyalties.

huge increase in the population of free people of color in New Orleans, a rise that he blamed on a liberal policy toward manumission. Such a large number of free blacks, he stated, served to "corrupt the morals of the slave, tended to make him dissatisfied with his condition, and formed a constantly augmenting nucleus of mischief and evil."[12]

Despite the fact that the population of free people of color in New Orleans had actually declined dramatically from a high of 19,226 in 1840 to 9,905 in 1850, no one corrected Moise. This shrinking of the free black population might have resulted from the more stringent enforcement of the 1830 statute forcing free people of color to leave the state if they had entered it after 1825. No doubt this act deterred some free people of color from moving to Louisiana and inspired others to leave. During the same period the free black population of Charleston more than doubled, as did that of Louisville and Washington, D.C. Of ten leading southern cities, only New Orleans and Norfolk, Virginia, experienced declines in the population of free people of color, and Norfolk's population only declined from 1,026 to 956, a net loss of 7 percent. Furthermore, the percentage of free people of color in the total population of New Orleans shrank as Irish and German immigration swelled. Foreign-born persons comprised 49 percent of the city's population in 1850.[13]

Representative Tillinhurst Vaughan of Claiborne Parish suggested that legal complications might arise from the passage of Richardson's bill. He expressed a desire to see abuses of the present manumission law eliminated, without a wholesale deportation of freed slaves. He expressed concern for those slaves who had contracted for their freedom but who had not yet become free. Richardson's bill would, of course, leave such slaves without recourse.[14]

Representatives from New Orleans expressed the most opposition to Richardson's measure. In an impassioned speech, C. C. Lathrop stated that although he remained a staunch advocate of African colonization, he opposed the bill because it proposed "to ship off indiscriminately all emancipated slaves to Liberia. . . . By doing so we would foist vicious subjects on

12. *Report of the House, 1852*, 7–8.
13. Richard C. Wade, *Slavery in the Cities: The South, 1820–1860* (New York: Oxford University Press, 1964), 325–7.
14. Ibid.

that colony and thus tend to destroy its usefulness." Concerned with impos-
ing the "scum of the colored population of the United States on Liberia,"
Lathrop also questioned the logistics of the act, as the American Colonization Society in Louisiana had but one ship to send to Liberia annually. No
one challenged his argument, despite the requirement that slaves manumitted in Louisiana had to establish that they had been of "honest conduct" for
at least four years prior to their emancipation. And was Lathrop suggesting
that he wished freed slaves of bad character—the "scum of the colored population"— to stay in Louisiana?[15]

William S. Campbell of Orleans also expressed his objections to the provision requiring freed slaves to leave the state and the posting of a $1,000
bond, and he indicated that he would vote against the bill if these requirements remained. Campbell felt that masters should have the right to free a
faithful slave who had provided the owner with meritorious service. He also
recognized slaves' ties with their communities, reasoning, the "feeling
towards slaves is not of that hostile character which should compel them to
go abroad, for by doing so you tear them away from all kindly associations
and family ties." Campbell concluded by equating Richardson's bill with the
total prohibition of manumission. As he declared, "He could not vote for a
law taking away from the people the right to emancipate their slaves."[16]

Obviously feelings ran high in the House. Campbell's colleague from Orleans, J. G. Sever, recommended keeping the ten-day requirement for freed
slaves to leave the state. He warned the legislators that they should protect
Louisiana from "this fanatical notion of abolition at the North." Sever told
his fellow representatives, "It is no humanity, no favor, no mercy to set a
man free in a white community. If it was in his power, he would make every
black man in the country a slave and would engraft this on the Constitution
of the United States." Lathrop then gave a glowing account of the success
of the Liberia colony, and added that the "negro race would find a home in
that land; that for their own good and their safety, they must be removed to
Liberia."[17]

15. *Report of the House, 1852*, 8–9; "An Act to Regulate the Conditions and Forms of the
Emancipation of Slaves," pp. 82–8.

16. *Report of the House, 1852*, 8.

17. Ibid., 8–9.

Early in February 1852, the Louisiana House and Senate appointed a joint legislative committee to consider the "further protection of slave property in this State, for the greater restriction of the emancipation of slaves, and for the removal of emancipated slaves from the State." In March, Representative Richardson sponsored a successful resolution to turn over the House chambers to the Reverend J. M. Pease, a minister from New Orleans, who delivered a lecture on the benefits of African colonization. A few days following the lecture, the House passed a resolution supporting African colonization, a cause which "deeply involves the best interest of the State." The resolution called for an appropriation of state funds to aid in removing free people of color *with their consent* to Liberia.[18]

Even as the House debated restricting the emancipation of slaves to those who would go to Liberia after receiving their liberty, legislators continued to hear individual petitions for legislative emancipations. On March 11, lawmakers passed an act freeing the slave Nanny "for faithful and meritorious services during the long and painful illness of her said master, any law to the contrary notwithstanding." The act ordered Nanny to leave the state within three months of her liberation, "never to return," but did not require her to go to Liberia.[19]

Revealing the deep divisions in their views concerning emancipation and free people of color, lawmakers passed four important but conflicting bills between March 15 and March 18. The first measure clarified an 1842 act that required parish authorities to imprison all free black sailors who arrived in a Louisiana port until their ship departed. The 1852 act allowed them to remain on board their ships as an alternative to incarceration. Ship captains had the duty to register and describe free black sailors to the proper authorities. Discovery of a free black crew member on shore illegally resulted in imprisonment for the sailor and a fine of $1,000 for the captain and owners of the ship. The second act freed the slave Eloy Barabino with permission to remain in the state. The third act freed a slave family—Ben, his wife Clarissa, and their three children—with the requirement that they leave the

18. *Journal of the House, 1852*, 56, 144, 164. The 1850 census lists Pease as a minister, but he does not appear in the 1860 census. New Orleans city directories fail to list him or indicate his denomination.

19. Ibid., 30, 85, 121, 161, 166; "An Act to Authorise the Emancipation of the Slave Nanny for Meritorious Services to Her Master," Act of March 11, 1852, *Louisiana Acts, 1852*, p. 122.

state (but not necessarily for Liberia) within three months of the date of the act or risk reenslavement.[20]

The fourth act addressed the formidable obstacle of transportation to Liberia in the manumission procedure. Lawmakers required all persons freeing slaves to send them to Liberia within one year of manumission. The manumitting person had to pay passage of $150. Emancipated slaves who did not depart for Liberia, or who returned to Louisiana, forfeited their freedom. Now slaves whose owners might wish to free them faced a choice of liberty and banishment or remaining in slavery. This law made it necessary for more free people of color to hold their relatives as slaves, since freeing them meant certain deportation. It also made some whites reluctant to free their slaves, knowing they would have no place to migrate where they would be welcome. Slaveholders besieged the legislature with requests for individual exceptions, and the number of legislative manumissions with permission to remain in the state increased. Before the effective date of the act, many slaveholders rushed through manumission petitions that contained provisions for freed slaves to remain in the state. Lawmakers responded to slaveholders' complaints in the 1853 session by passing five acts freeing eleven slaves without forcing them to leave the state. In 1854, four legislative acts liberated seven slaves, all with permission to stay in Louisiana.[21]

20. "An Act to Amend an Act Entitled 'An Act More Effectually to Prevent Free Persons of Color from Entering This State and for Other Purposes, Approved Sixteenth of March, Eighteen Hundred and Forty Two,'" Act of March 18, 1852, p. 193. These acts were not unusual. Most of the Deep South states had similar acts. Carol Wilson, *Freedom at Risk: The Kidnapping of Free Blacks in America, 1790–1865* (Lexington: University Press of Kentucky, 1994). For the second and third acts, see: "An Act to Emancipate Eloy Barabino, a Slave Belonging to the Estate of the Late Stefano Barabino," Act of March 18, 1852, p. 198; "An Act to Emancipate the Slaves Ben, Clarissa, Edward, Susan, and Mary, for Meritorious Service Rendered Their Late Master, Samuel Estelle, Deceased, Late of the Parish of Carroll," ibid., p. 200.

21. "An Act Concerning the Emancipation of Slaves in This State," Act of March 18, 1852, pp. 214–5; "An Act to Emancipate Jane Mary, the Slave and Daughter of Patsy, f.w.c.," Act of April 28, 1853, *Louisiana Acts, 1853*, p. 162; "An Act to Enable Baptist Dupeyre, or His Legal Representative, to Emancipate the Slave Zoe, Without Removing Her from the State," Act of April 28, 1853, pp. 163–4; "An Act to Emancipate the Slaves Belonging to the Estate of the Late J. B. Cajus, of the Parish of Orleans," Act of April 30, 1853, pp. 273–4; "An Act to Manumit or Emancipate Marie Melandy, Slave of Moise Hébert, of the Parish of St. Landry," Act of April 30, 1853, p. 276; "An Act to Emancipate Henrietta, Slave of Rebecca Coleman, of the Parish of East Baton Rouge," Act of April 30, 1853, p. 277; "An Act Authorizing W. C. Wilson

On January 17, 1855, Governor Paul Octave Hébert addressed the issue of manumission at the opening session of the legislature. Citing a petition to free the slave Caroline and her children and allow them to stay in the state, Hébert asserted that the bill created an exception to the law of 1852, which reflected the policy of the state on manumission, and which he would enforce. The governor acknowledged that occasional exceptions might arise but added, "The cases, however, are few. . . . It is the settled conviction of the people of the southern States generally, that it is impolitic and dangerous to permit the increase, by emancipation or by introduction from abroad, of the free colored population."[22]

Before the end of January, members of the House introduced petitions to manumit several other slaves, and the bill to free Caroline and her children again appeared on the agenda. Early in February, Representative A. Slaughter of Caddo Parish introduced an act to allow a free woman of color, Mary Amelia, to remain in the state. Representative Dennis Cronan of Orleans introduced yet another bill to free a slave woman and her child. Representative D. E. Beecher of Orleans petitioned to allow a free man of color, Philip Claiborne, to emancipate his slave family. The House referred these acts to the House Judiciary Committee, which reported unfavorably on all of them or tabled them. In all, the judiciary committee heard and denied petitions for freedom of more than a dozen slaves, as well as petitions of three previously freed slaves to be allowed to remain in the state.[23]

Louisiana legislators made a sweeping revision of the laws concerning

to Emancipate His Slave David," Act of March 7, 1854, *Louisiana Acts, 1854*, pp. 34–5; "An Act to Authorize John Cousin, of the Parish of St. Tammany, to Emancipate the Slave Frances and Her Three Children," Act of March 7, 1854, p. 35; "An Act to Authorize Mrs. S. A. Withers, Wife of Joseph M. Kennedy, to Emancipate Her Mulatto Slave, Clarisse, With Permission to Remain in the State," Act of March 7, 1854, p. 36. Sterkx, *The Free Negro in Antebellum Louisiana* (Cranberry, N.J.: Associated University Presses, 1972), 143. On the effect of laws combining manumission with banishment, see Tommy L. Bogger, *Free Blacks in Norfolk, Virginia, 1790–1860: The Darker Side of Freedom* (Charlottesville: University of Virginia Press, 1997), 29.

22. *Journal of the House of Representatives of the State of Louisiana* (New Orleans: Emile La Sere, 1855), 9–10.

23. Ibid., 9–10, 15, 18–9, 29, 48, 53, 56, 69–70, 81, 100–1. The reason that the exact number cannot be ascertained is that one act involved "Certain Slaves" (no names given), one was for a free man of color's family (no number of children given), and one was for a slave woman's children (again, no number given).

manumission in 1855. Weary of having so much of their time taken up with petitions for exceptions to the 1852 act, lawmakers decided to turn manumission over to the district courts. This opened the door for hundreds of lawsuits for freedom with permission to remain in the state, as owners who wished to free their slaves without forcing them to leave the state rushed to take advantage of the new law. One of the most significant aspects of these manumissions is the spectacle of free people, white and black, using the law to free their human property. In an stark contrast to the national scene, in which southerners increasingly had to defend themselves against abolitionist agitation, hundreds of New Orleans slaves gained their freedom and the right to remain in the state. Frustration with this unanticipated turn of events would lead to a total prohibition of manumission in 1857, as Louisiana finally fell in line with her sister slave states that prohibited manumission entirely.

1

SUING FOR FREEDOM

Slaves in Transit

Between 1846 and 1862 the district courts of New Orleans heard hundreds of cases in which slaves sued for their freedom, owners sued to manumit their slaves, and free persons of color tried to prove that they did not have slave status. African Americans' rate of success in gaining or maintaining their liberty must be seen in the context of the deepening national crisis over slavery. Set against a backdrop of national events such as the passage of the federal Fugitive Slave Act in 1850 and escaped slave Frederick Douglass's withering criticism of slavery in his famous "What to the Slave Is the Fourth of July?" speech in 1852, the ability of Louisiana's slaves so often to win their freedom is all the more surprising. Clearly, Louisiana's jurisprudence fell outside that of traditional slave states.

In the late 1840s and the early 1850s, slaves suing for freedom in New Orleans district courts found a dramatically successful argument for asking the courts to declare them free: claiming that their owners had taken them to a state, territory, or country where slavery did not exist. Their twenty-seven suits claimed that the laws of the free state or country operated on them to free them, since no positive law existed to hold them as slaves. Once free, their return to Louisiana did not mean that they reverted to a state of slavery. Indeed, the *Civil Code* held that an "emancipation, once perfected, is irrevocable, on the part of the master or his heirs." From 1791, French law held that slaves became free as soon as their foot touched the free soil of France. During the late 1840s and into the 1850s, New Orleans district courts generally followed this rule in manumission cases. These rulings ran counter to two rulings by the Supreme Court of the United States in 1837. Both cases involved New Orleans women of color whose owners took them to France for an extended visit. The Supreme Court held that French law did not free the women and that their status remained unaffected by their visit to France. One of the slaves, Pricilla Smith, subsequently sued for her freedom in a state court in 1839. She lost at trial, but the Louisiana Supreme Court declared her free on appeal. In the decision, Chief Judge François-Xavier Martin did not mention the ruling in Smith's United States Supreme Court case. It is ironic that a slave would receive a more favorable decision from the highest court of a slave state than from the highest court of the nation.[1]

In 1846, the Louisiana legislature specifically enacted a law to close this avenue to freedom. This statute stated, "From the passage of this act, no slave shall be entitled to his or her freedom, under the pretence that he or she has been, with or without the consent of his or her owner, in a country where slavery does not exist, or in any other of the States where slavery is prohibited." Despite this law, the district courts of New Orleans continued to grant freedom to slaves who could prove that they had lived in a free territory before 1846. Women of color instituted all but one of these lawsuits; their owners had taken them to free countries (mostly to France) as personal servants.[2]

The First District Court of New Orleans heard the first of these suits, *Josephine* v. *Poultney,* in 1846. The slave Josephine had accompanied her mistress to New York and Philadelphia in 1841 and had remained on free soil for three years. Upon her return to New Orleans, she sued for her freedom on the basis of having lived in free states before 1846. She won her freedom in the First District Court, and her mistress appealed to the Louisiana Supreme Court. Chief Justice George Eustis wrote in the decision affirming her freedom, "The operation of the laws of Pennsylvania upon the personal condition of the plaintiff . . . by a residence acquired in that State . . . released the plaintiff from the dominion, which the defendant had over

---

1. U.S. v. *Garonne,* U.S. v. *LaFortune,* 11 Peters (U.S.) 73, January 1837; *Civil Code,* Art. 185, p. 9; Smith, f.w.c., v. Smith, No. 3314, 13 La. 441 (1839).

2. *Civil Code,* Art. 189, p. 29; Finkelman, *An Imperfect Union: Slavery, Federalism, and Comity,* 206; "An Act to Protect the Rights of Slaveholders in the State of Louisiana," Act of May 30, 1846, *Louisiana Acts, 1846,* p. 163; Sterkx, *The Free Negro in Antebellum Louisiana,* 138–41. Neither Finkelman nor Sterkx had access to the New Orleans District Court cases, and they therefore missed any suits of this nature that did not go up to the Louisiana Supreme Court.

the person of the plaintiff as a slave, in Louisiana. Her condition once being fixed [free on free soil], she cannot be reduced to the condition of the slave. . . . [Her] subsequent return to this State cannot restore the relation of master and slave."[3]

The following year the First District Court heard *Eugénie* v. *Préval,* in which a slave sued for her freedom on the basis of an eight-year residence in France in the service of her mistress. The First District Court rendered a judgment of non-suit on the basis that the Act of 1846 had destroyed Eugénie's capacity to sue for her freedom on the grounds that she had lived on free soil. The case went up to the Louisiana Supreme Court, which reversed the decision of the trial court because the slave's residence in France pre-dated the passage of the Act of 1846. In his decision, Chief Justice George Eustis again ruled in favor of freedom, writing, "It cannot be presumed that it was the intention of the legislature to strike at the past and divest a right acquired by a residence in a foreign country. . . . Could she hold the plaintiff in slavery in France? It is certain that she could not." The high court there-fore ordered that Eugénie "recover her freedom" and ordered the defen-dant to pay court costs, costs of the appeal, and wages to Eugénie of $146 (her salary from the institution of the suit to the day of judgment).[4]

A few months later a similar First District Court case appeared before the Supreme Court of Louisiana, *Arsène, alias Cora,* v. *Pignéguy* (1847). The counsel for the defense, Christian Roselius, argued that the slaveholder who had taken Josephine to France had only visited France for a brief time and had not established residence there. Thus, he argued, Arsène could not acquire her freedom on the basis of having lived on free soil. Represented by her attorney, Jean Charles (J. C.) David, Arsène won her freedom in the trial court, and the owner appealed. The Supreme Court affirmed the deci-sion of the trial court, saying that to hold Josephine as a slave in France was to "expect that foreign nations will consent to the suspension of the opera-

---

3. Louisiana law required free people of color to have the initials "f.w.c." or "f.m.c." (free woman or man of color) after their names in all legal actions. "An Act to Prescribe Certain Formalities Respecting Free Persons of Color," Act of March 31, 1808, *Orleans Territory Acts, 1808,* pp. 138–40. The courts sometimes allowed slaves suing for their freedom the courtesy of using these initials. At other times they only allowed the person to use "c.w." (colored woman) or "c.m." (colored man). Josephine, f.w.c., v. Poultney, Supreme Court of Louisiana, No. 5935, 1 La. Ann. 329 (1846).

4. Eugénie, f.w.c., v. Préval, No. 99, 2 La. Ann. 180 (1847).

tion of their fundamental laws, as to persons voluntarily sojourning within their jurisdiction. . . . [T]he plaintiff became free by remaining two years in France, and her former master ceased to have authority or dominion over her." The court ordered the defendant to pay Arsène wages of $8 a month from the date of the original lawsuit to the date of judgment, as well as cost in both courts.[5]

The First District Court heard another of these cases, *Sally* v. *Varney*, in 1847. Aimée Andry had purchased Sally, a thirteen-year-old slave girl, in 1838. The same year Andry had married a French citizen, Alphonse Varney. In 1845 Alphonse Varney decided to return to his native France, taking with him his wife and infant child. As Aimée Varney did not wish to nurse her baby, her slave Sally came along as a wet nurse. Sally remained in France for two years, at which time the Varneys sent her back to their agent in New Orleans with orders to sell her. Sally claimed that as a free person, she "cannot fall again in slavery." Through her attorney she petitioned the court to affirm her freedom and order the Varneys to pay the costs of the suit. Several persons aboard the ship that took the Varneys and Sally to France testified that the slave had indeed sailed on the ship. A free woman of color, Euphrosine, testified that Sally earned $12 a month for her services and could therefore support herself. Citing the Act of 1846, the Varneys objected to the suit. However, Judge John McHenry refused to make the law retroactive. In a telling choice of words, McHenry ruled, "It is therefore ordered and adjudged and decreed that the plaintiff be released from the dominion of the defendants and be *restored* to freedom" (emphasis mine). McHenry ordered the Varneys to pay the court costs of $18.55.[6]

The same year, in *Milky* v. *Millaudon*, a slave named Milky sued for her freedom based on a sojourn in France. Her wealthy owner, Laurent Millaudon, admitted that he had sent his wife, his three children, and Milky to France to visit relatives. Millaudon owned the vessel that had carried Milky and her mistress to France. They had arrived on June 30, 1839, and departed on October 27 of the same year. Millaudon denied that he had ever

5. Arsène, alias Cora, f.w.c., v. Pignéguy, Nos. 395, 434, First District Court of New Orleans, 4 November 1846; No. 459, 2 La. Ann. 620 (1847).

6. Sally, f.w.c., v. Varney, No. 906, First District Court of New Orleans, 28 June 1847. There is another No. 906, a larceny case that has nothing to do with Sally, f.w.c., v. Varney.

contemplated freeing Milky, and indeed denounced her character and health as being unfit for freedom: "I have never said that I would give this slave her freedom, nor did I ever think of doing so, but as she was one of my first slaves [slaves stricken out] servants she was always allowed greater privileges than others owned by me, being frequently sick she was not kept at any regular work." Furthermore, he stated in court, she constantly caused trouble among his other slaves by quarreling. Because of her poor health, he said, he felt that freedom would prove to be a burden for her. Now he claimed that he was too irritated by her behavior to even consider freeing her. Milky alleged that Millaudon had promised to free her upon her return from France, but that he had continued to hold her in slavery. She claimed the value of her labor at $12 per month since her return. At this point, Millaudon had his personal physician testify that Milky was "afflicted with disease," which greatly reduced the value of her services. Judge John McHenry declared Milky free but would not consider the issue of back wages, holding that she "can maintain no other action save for freedom." He did, however, order Millaudon to pay court costs of $21.20.[7]

The following month, in *Phany* v. *Bouny and Poincy* (1847), another slave woman sued for freedom on the basis of transportation to France. Phany stated in her petition that as a slave child she had traveled to France in 1822 with her mother and her mother's owner, Desdunes Poincy. Phany and her mother had remained in France with their owner for several years. After their return to Louisiana, Poincy had sold Phany to the widow Bouny, who owned a bakery. Poincy testified at trial that she did not know that taking Phany to France would have the effect of freeing her. Phany subsequently had three children, and she sued for her freedom, the freedom of her children, and wages of $20 a month since 1822. Phany had worked as a bread seller, driving a cart about the city to sell her mistress's wares. Several witnesses testified that bread sellers made between $20 and $30 a month. The widow Bouny disparaged Phany's character, stating that since Phany had filed her suit for freedom, she had acted as a free woman and refused to obey orders. The widow said she had purchased Phany from the Citizens Bank of Louisiana and that she knew nothing of the allegations in Phany's

7. Milky, c.w., v. Millaudon, No. 1201, First District Court of New Orleans, 11 November 1847.

petition. Both defendants asked Judge McHenry to dismiss Phany's suit with costs. However, Judge McHenry ruled to free Phany and her three children, ordering Poincy and Bouny to pay court costs of $27.90.[8]

Two weeks after the *Phany* decision, the First District Court heard *Lucille* v. *Maspereau* (1847). Lucille claimed that she had spent several months in France with her mistress, Anabele Charbonnet, in 1836 or 1837. Her mistress had remained in France, but in 1838 she had sent Lucille back to New Orleans to serve the widow of Pierre Maspereau. Lucille, an eighteen-year-old at the time she filed suit for her freedom, petitioned the court to appoint a curator to represent her, as persons in Louisiana could not bring suit in their own name until they became twenty-one. The court appointed Bernard Couvent, f.m.c., as her curator. The First District Court declared her free and awarded her $10 per month wages from the date of the lawsuit. However, the court ordered her to pay the costs of the suit. Her attorney, J. C. David, must have feared that Maspereau would appeal to the Supreme Court of Louisiana, because he agreed to pay court costs "provided no appeal shall be taken by the defendants."[9]

In *Tabé* v. *Vidal* (1847), the defendant admitted the claim of the slave, Tabé, suing for her freedom on the basis of having lived for three years on French soil. Tabé also sued for the freedom of her three children, born since her return from France. Perhaps the preceding cases convinced the defendant that she would lose the lawsuit; six days after Tabé filed her suit for freedom, Vidal filed a "confession of judgment" renouncing all claim to Tabé and her children. Article 196 of the Louisiana *Civil Code* stated, "The child born of a woman after she has acquired the right of being free at a future time, follows the condition of its mother, and becomes free at the time of her enfranchisement, even if the mother should die before that time." Therefore, the court never questioned the freedom of Tabé's children.[10]

Another slaveholder who took a slave to France tried subsequently to sell her to avoid losing his capital investment in her. In *Aimée* v. *Pluché* (1848), the slave Aimée based her freedom suit on travel with her master to

8. Phany, w.c., v. Bouny and Poincy, No. 1421, First District Court of New Orleans, 30 November 1847.

9. Lucille, c.w., v. Maspereau, No. 1692, First District Court of New Orleans, 7 January 1848; *Civil Code*, Arts. 367–81, pp. 54–6.

10. Tabé, c.w., v. Vidal, No. 1584, First District Court of New Orleans, 26 November 1847; *Civil Code*, Art. 196, p. 30.

France to escape a cholera epidemic raging in New Orleans. In her petition for freedom, Aimée stated that her owner admitted that she had acquired the right to her freedom because of her eight months in France, but that "he could not let her be free" and had sold her to his brother-in-law as a slave. Pluché admitted that he had taken Aimée to France but claimed that her petition contained "manifold errors, untruths & uncertainties." The judge of the First District Court ruled Aimée "to be released from the bonds of slavery" and ordered Pluché and his brother-in-law to pay court costs of $22.[11]

In 1848 a slave named Souri filed suit for her freedom on the basis of a few months' stay in France. She claimed that her owner, Louis Bordeaux, had remained in France but had sent her back to New Orleans to be sold. Joseph Vincent had purchased her for $765, although he later denied that he had bought her; he furthermore claimed that he knew nothing of her ever having gone to France. Souri won her freedom before the First District Court, and Vincent had to pay $2 per month in wages from the date of the suit to the date of judgment and $14.40 in court costs. The low wages for her services may have stemmed from Bordeaux's son-in-law's testimony that her services were not worth much as she was very young and spent her time selling callas (creole rice cakes) in the street.[12]

Bernard Couvent, f.m.c., served as the tutor (a civil law term for guardian) for another slave seeking her freedom on the basis of having traveled to France. The slave girl Mary went to France in the spring of 1847 with her mistress, Mrs. Guesnard. Her owner testified that she had never intended to keep Mary in France and had taken her on the voyage only because of an illness that had required her services. Guesnard said that she had sent Mary back to New Orleans at the earliest opportunity to have her sold. Mary's attorney, J. C. David, alleged that being on French soil had freed her and that her involuntary return to Louisiana could not reenslave her. David acknowledged that her stay in France occurred after the passage of the Act of 1846, but he termed the act unconstitutional because it impaired the contract of freedom obtained by Mary in France. Such law, he said, could not

11. Aimée, c.w., v. Pluché and Bosquet, No. 1650, First District Court of New Orleans, 4 May 1848.

12. Souri, c.w., v. Vincent, No. 2660, First District Court of New Orleans, 17 January 1850.

"render a slave a person who had been freed in France." Guesnard's agent testified that he had planned to sell Mary for $500 to a man who had intended to take her to Mobile, "where he was told he could sell her well." The prospective buyer had developed cold feet when he realized that the slave had traveled to France. Another witness in the case testified that, as a member of the Louisiana legislature, he had authored the Act of 1846 as a result of hearing of the case of *Arsène, alias Cora,* v. *Pignéguy.* This is an especially revealing example of how the string of manumission cases captured the attention of state legislators and prompted them to pass legislation designed to halt this kind of lawsuit. By using the courts to gain their freedom, slaves, supposedly rendered powerless by the law, influenced the legislative agenda and the actual making of law.

In his decision, Judge John McHenry stated, "If Mary became free by the operation of the laws of France for one moment, it was not in the power of her former owner or the legislature to reduce her again to slavery." But he ruled that the Act of 1846 compelled him to dismiss her claim to freedom. Mary's attorney appealed to the Supreme Court of Louisiana. Although the high court appeared reluctant to rule against her, the justices declared themselves forced by the Act of 1846 to declare that touching free soil did not free a slave: "There can be no question as to the legislative power to regulate the conditions of this class of persons." Robert Rogers, a free man of color and Mary's godfather, sued the Guesnards the following year, demanding that they pay $1,000 in damages and their agent pay $400 for holding Mary in slavery when she had become free by her stay in France. Judge McHenry ruled that the Act of 1846 "inhibited the court from giving her [Mary] the relief sought. . . . [T]he same woman is the real plaintiff in this case." The court held that Rogers had no standing to bring this suit.[13]

The same year the First District Court heard a similar case with an uncertain outcome: *Sarah* v. *Hagan and Guillaume.* Sarah, a slave hairdresser, had accompanied her owner, Mathilde Guillaume, a free woman of color, to France in 1833 and had remained there for four years. Guillaume, who had

13. Couvent, f.m.c., tutor of Mary, c.w., v. Guesnard, No. 1786, First District Court of New Orleans, 17 January 1848; No. 1063, 5 La. Ann. 69 (1850). Rogers, f.m.c., v. Guesnard, No. 2362, First District Court of New Orleans, 8 February 1849; No. 1507, Unreported Louisiana Supreme Court case (1850).

been living with John Hagan, a white slave trader, had sent Sarah back to
New Orleans with Hagan. Sarah eventually sued for her freedom, claiming
back wages of $30 a month from 1833, when she alleged she had become
free. She also claimed freedom for her child, born after she had supposedly
acquired her freedom. Judge John McHenry rendered a judgment of non-
suit because Sarah's owner received no notification of her suit for freedom.
As a result, Guillaume could not defend against the suit. Hagan denied that
Sarah had ever lived in France, and he asked the judge to order that Sarah's
owner receive notification of the suit in France. There is no disposition of
this case. Perhaps Guillaume could not be located and the suit never proceeded. In a worse scenario, perhaps Hagan sold Sarah out of the state to
prevent her from pursuing the suit.[14]

In 1848 the slave Aurore sued for her freedom on the basis of having
lived in France for five years, from 1818 to 1823. In 1828, her owner had
sold Aurore to her sister. Aurore bore five children after her return from
France, and she sued for freedom for herself and her children. Aurore
claimed that her present owner knew that she had lived in France. In fact,
Aurore testified, her new owner had asked her for news of France, had
asked whether she had liked Paris, and had jokingly termed her the "Paris-
ienne." The judge of the First District Court declared Aurore free and ordered her owner to pay the costs of the suit. He also ruled that Aurore's
owner could call her sister in warranty (meaning her title was not legal), as
she had sold Aurore after Aurore had already acquired the right to
freedom.[15]

A remarkable case heard by the Third District Court of New Orleans
the following year gives a rare insight into the relationship between slaves
suing for freedom and their attorneys. The slave Charlotte sued her owner,
Pierre Cazelar, for her freedom on the grounds that he had taken her to
France in 1838, where she had remained for two years. She had returned to
New Orleans with him and had continued to work as a slave, caring for Cazelar's children. She requested the court to declare her free and award her
$12 a month in back wages. Cazelar admitted that he knew that because of

14. Sarah, c.w., v. Hagan and Guillaume, f.w.c., No. 1898, First District Court of New
Orleans, 11 November 1848.

15. Aurore, c.w., v. Decuir, No. 1919, First District Court of New Orleans, 16 October
1848.

"certain court decisions" Charlotte could successfully claim her freedom upon her return from France. Yet he testified that Charlotte did not then claim her freedom, and that because of her young age "she naturally returned to his house as her natural protector." He stated that she had never demanded her freedom, and that when she had eventually left his house, he did not attempt to force her to return. He admitted that Charlotte had a right to her freedom and asked the court to dismiss him from the suit, as he did not contest her free status. At this point, Charlotte's attorney, J. C. David, filed a supplemental petition, alleging that Cazelar had treated Charlotte cruelly, had forced her to wear ankle chains while working in the fields, and had the sheriff whip her for an undisclosed offense. David also alleged that Cazelar had a slave on his plantation flog her.

David's allegations remained totally unsupported by the testimony that followed. Many witnesses asserted that Cazelar had treated Charlotte well and had never put her to hard work or treated her cruelly. One indignant witness for Cazelar inquired of Charlotte "whether she was not ashamed to give trouble to her master." She replied that "it was not her, it was her lawyer to whom she had already given $60 and that she was perfectly satisfied and did not know what her lawyer wanted now." Another witness stated that, to the contrary, he had seen Charlotte in David's office and she had told him to go on with the suit. To clarify matters, the judge questioned Charlotte as to her intent, and she did not deny that her attorney had her permission to prosecute the suit. The judge ruled in favor of Charlotte's freedom but did not award her damages. Obviously disgusted at both her attorney's solicitation of her business and at her pursuit of the suit after gaining her freedom, he also ordered her to pay the court costs.[16]

The same year a slave named Elvira Malotte sued for her freedom on the grounds that she had lived in Indiana for four years. She claimed that her owner, a citizen of Salem, Indiana, had purchased her with the intention of freeing her, and she claimed to have lived as a free woman in Salem. She also requested that the court allow her to "enjoy her freedom" pending the outcome of the suit, which the court granted. At trial, testimony cast doubt on whether she had ever lived in Indiana with her owner; indeed, witnesses alleged that she had run away to Indiana. One witness testified that her

16. Charlotte, c.w., v. Cazelar, No. 1078, Third District Court of New Orleans, 14 March 1849.

owner had placed Malotte in his hands for the purpose of hiring her out at the highest wages. In the power of attorney setting up the hiring, Malotte's owner specifically stated that she could not be hired on a steamboat that traveled to a free state "because it would afford an opportunity to abolitionists to run her off." He knew that she had thought of such an escape because she had implored him to hire her to a steamboat traveling to Pittsburgh. She had also escaped once from her owner's agent. Malotte's owner's personal physician testified that she had run away from Louisville to Salem, Indiana, but that her owner had sent her back to Louisville the following day. The court record indicates no disposition of this case, but as testimony supported the fact that Malotte had entered Indiana as a runaway rather than with the knowledge and consent of her owner, she almost certainly lost her suit for freedom.[17]

J. C. David, who had encouraged Charlotte in *Charlotte* v. *Cazelar* to sue for her freedom even though her owner did not contest it, followed the same practice in *Hélène* v. *Blineau* (1849). In 1838, the slave Hélène had accompanied her owner's daughter to France. She had remained there for several months and after her return made what the record called an "amicable demand" for her freedom on the basis of her sojourn in France. She asked that the court declare her free and award her wages from the institution of the suit. In answer, her owner alleged that he had never denied the plaintiff her freedom. She had continued to reside with him, rather, because she "is a drunken, worthless wretch, unwilling or unable to render any valuable services, or to support herself. . . . [A]ny services that she is willing or able to render are not worth her food, lodging and clothing." The owner of thirty slaves, Blineau claimed to support her "out of charity." A witness testified that Hélène told her that she had hired J. C. David to sue for her freedom, and that when David had approached her owner, Blineau stated that "she might go away for what she is worth—that he had no objection." Another witness testified that Hélène had told him that she "could not do without whiskey" and that he had seen her "quite drunk in a grog shop." Another witness, a white man, testified that Hélène had lived with him, and that he had seen marks of blows that her owner's wife had inflicted on her. Blineau admitted that he had advertised for her as a runaway slave in a local newspa-

17. Malotte, f.w.c., v. Hackett and Newby, No. 2712, First District Court of New Orleans, 5 March 1849.

per but denied that he or his wife had treated her cruelly. The judge of the First District Court must not have believed the testimony concerning Hélène's drunkenness, because he set her free and ordered the owner to pay the costs of the suit ($14.40). However, he denied her back wages.[18]

Another slave named Charlotte sued for her freedom in 1850, claiming that her owners had taken her to New York and Pennsylvania in 1833 and that she had remained in each state for two years. She stated, "Your petitioner became immediately free by putting her foot on free soil, with consent of her master." Upon her return to Louisiana, her master had sold her to J. S. Segur as a slave for life. Several quick sales followed, perhaps indicating that subsequent owners came to suspect that Charlotte no longer fit the classification of slave property. However, Charlotte and her attorney failed to secure or pay court costs, and the clerk of court stopped the case. There is nothing in the record to indicate that the case ever progressed to judgment.[19]

Continuing his dubious methods of soliciting business, in 1850 J. C. David convinced yet another slave to sue her master for freedom. In 1843, Eulalie had accompanied her owner's daughter and son-in-law to England, where she had remained for several months. In her petition for freedom, David alleged that she "became free instanter by putting her foot on the English soil." Eulalie alleged that her owner, Evariste Blanc, nonetheless continued to hold her as a slave. She asked the court to declare her free and award her back wages of $10 a month from the date of the lawsuit. Blanc admitted the facts in the petition but stated that he had purchased Eulalie, now sixty-eight years old and sickly, "out of kindness to her and [he] would have long since given her her freedom if it had not appeared to him cruel to do so as well as exposing himself to the risk of supporting her in her old age." Blanc testified that he had sent her to England, but that Eulalie "had soon become dissatisfied with the people of England where everybody is free but nobody cares for an old superannuated negro who speaks only creole French." Blanc had sent her back to Louisiana at her own request and had paid her passage home. He had sent her across Lake Pontchartrain to

18. Hélène, c.w., v. Blineau, No. 4126, First District Court of New Orleans, 11 January 1850; *Civil Code,* Art. 185, p. 29.

19. Charlotte, f.w.c., v. Lizardi and Segur, No. 4933, First District Court of New Orleans, 1 May 1851.

his brickyard to mind the slave children there, but "she was no better satisfied than she was in Liverpool," and he allowed her to return to New Orleans and hire herself out at a "mere trifle per month, not enough to pay her clothing and the medical attendance." Blanc further stated that he could not imagine who might have "put it into her head to be free for she is too simple & stupid to have conceived such a thing herself." He expressed the hope that her attorney would "take her for his fee and rid him of the burden of supporting her . . . that they might both profit by her travels in England." He concluded by declaring that he had no objection to the court declaring Eulalie free, but he asked the court not to award her back wages. The First District Court dispatched this case very rapidly, probably because Blanc did not mount a defense. J. C. David filed the lawsuit on Eulalie's behalf on April 16, 1850, and the court rendered judgment on April 19. The judge did grant wages from the date of the lawsuit, which came to $.90, to compensate the attorney for his services. The record does not indicate who paid the court costs of $13.70, but David realized no profit from soliciting Eulalie's business.[20]

Occasionally slaves feared that suing for their freedom might bring retaliation from their owners. Louisa's owners had brought her to France at the age of four, where she had remained for five years. In her petition the now sixteen-year-old girl alleged that her owners had "ill treated and abused her" following her claim for freedom. She stated that she feared being removed from the jurisdiction of the court to defeat her claim for freedom; accordingly, she asked the court through her curator to sequester her for her own protection. Being sequestered meant being confined in jail for safekeeping pending the outcome of a lawsuit. Louisa's owners agreed to free her if she dropped her demand for $360 in back wages. She agreed and the judge of the First District Court declared her free, denying her back wages. The judge did order her former owners to pay court costs.[21]

By the early 1850s, as the national crisis over slavery intensified, slaves who sued for their freedom on the basis of traveling to free soil began to have difficulty in gaining their freedom. In 1821, the twelve-year-old slave

20. Eulalie, f.w.c., v. Blanc, No. 4904, First District Court of New Orleans, 19 April 1850.

21. Louisa, *statu liber,* and Fonvalgne, curator, v. Giggo, No. 6020, First District Court of New Orleans, 22 March 1851. The *Civil Code* used the term *statu liber* to mean a slave who had acquired the right to be free at a future date. *Civil Code,* Art. 37, p. 8.

Liza had accompanied her owner, Hardy De Boisblanc, to Bordeaux to collect De Boisblanc's family and return to Louisiana. De Boisblanc never intended to reside in France and had stayed there for only two or three months. After the family returned to Louisiana, De Boisblanc gave Liza to his daughter at the time of her marriage to Dr. Puissant in 1830. Liza bore seven children before suing for her freedom twenty years later, in 1850; she petitioned the First District Court for their freedom also. In her petition she alleged that "she became free by putting her foot upon French soil." The trial court ruled against her on the basis that a brief sojourn did not confer freedom, and she and her attorney, J. C. David, appealed to the Supreme Court of Louisiana. That court cited the recent United States Supreme Court case, *Strader* v. *Graham,* which held that the laws of a free state could not confer freedom on a slave within the borders of a slave state. Finally the jurisprudence of the Louisiana Supreme Court had fallen in line with the United States Supreme Court.[22]

A brief stay in Ohio did not serve to make Sarah Haynes, alias Mielkie, free either. Haynes belonged to Edward C. Mielkie of Vicksburg, and she had nursed him through a serious illness. In return, in 1843 he had paid her passage to Cincinnati and had given her a written statement declaring that she had his permission to "pass unmolested" to Ohio or any free state. Haynes had remained in Cincinnati for a few days and then went to New Orleans, where she stayed except for a brief visit to Vicksburg in 1845. After Mielkie's death, the guardian of his minor daughter had Haynes seized as a slave, property of Mielkie's estate. The guardian claimed that Haynes had not become free by going to Cincinnati and that under Mississippi law she remained a slave. In 1851 the First District Court ruled against her on the basis that since an 1830 Louisiana law barred free people of color from entering the state, Haynes had come into the state illegally and thus had no rights in Louisiana, including the right to use the state's courts. Furthermore, the court held that the laws of the residence of her owner determined her status. As the Mississippi Supreme Court had decided that taking slaves to a free state, freeing them, and returning to Mississippi constituted a fraud on Mississippi law, her status remained that of a slave. Haynes appealed to the Louisiana Supreme Court, which affirmed the decision of the First Dis-

22. Liza, f.w.c., v. Puissant, No. 5632, First District Court of New Orleans, 21 December 1850; No. 2326, 7 La. Ann. 80 (1852). Also Strader v. Graham, 10 Howard (U.S.) 82 (1851).

trict Court. In 1851, the New Orleans police arrested her for remaining in the state in contravention of the 1830 law and for "keeping a house of assignation at No. 12 Carondelet street." Haynes might have subsequently returned to Mississippi, as no evidence exists to indicate that she ever stood trial for these offenses.[23]

The Third District Court heard another transportation case in which the owner's domicile constituted the main issue in deciding for the freedom of the slave. Lucy Brown, a slave born in the District of Columbia, had moved with her master in 1823 from Washington to New York, where he had taken up residence. He had remained in New York until 1825, when he had moved to Georgetown and then back to New York in 1829. Lucy Brown had remained in his service during the years that he resided in New York. Somehow she came to New Orleans as the slave of an army officer, who sold her. She sued for her freedom in 1851 on the basis of her former owner's residence in New York, and also on a New York statute that held that a slave brought to New York could not be held as a slave after nine months in the state. The Third District Court ruled that she had arrived in the Louisiana as a free person and accordingly declared her free. Her alleged owner appealed the case to the Louisiana Supreme Court, which affirmed the judgement of the trial court.[24]

Another slave woman, Ajoie, perhaps influenced by hearing of so many other cases of this nature, or being solicited as a client by her attorney, J. C. David, sued her master for her freedom on the basis of having lived in France for fourteen months in 1822, despite the fact that her owner, Bernard de Marigny, had long ceased claiming her as his slave. Marigny, who came from a wealthy creole family, had lost most of his fortune from a life of dissipation and extravagance. His journey to France had been a desperate attempt to collect on a debt that the king of France, Louis Philippe, had owed his father. The king had received him cordially but was deaf to his pleas for reimbursement. Bitterly disappointed, Marigny had returned to New Orleans with Ajoie. In her petition, Ajoie alleged that she had returned

23. Haynes, alias Mielkie, f.w.c., v. Forno, Hutchinson, and Hill, curator, No. 7091, First District Court of New Orleans, 26 December 1851; No. 2850, 8 La. Ann. 35 (1853). Also "An Act to Prevent Free Persons of Color from Entering This State," Act of March 16, 1830, *Louisiana Acts, 1830*, pp. 90–4; *New Orleans Daily Picayune*, 16 August 1851.

24. Brown, f.w.c., v. Smith and Taylor, No. 2761, 8 La. Ann. 59 (1853).

to New Orleans in 1823 "with the understanding that she was free & could not be returned to slavery on her arrival in New Orleans otherwise she would have remained in France." Still, because of "her devotion & love for her former master," she had continued to work as a dining room servant, for which he paid her wages of $6 a month. Marigny had never required her children—all born subsequent to her travel to France—to serve him, except on an irregular basis, and he had paid them for their services on those occasions. Her petition further stated that since 1823 she always had enjoyed her freedom and had acted as a free person of color with the knowledge of Marigny. David alleged that this "constituted an acquired prescription of more than 10 years." Under Louisiana law, an owner who allowed slaves to live as free for ten years lost the right to recover possession of them as slaves. In 1843, thirteen years prior to the institution of the lawsuit, Marigny had made a notarized declaration stating that he acknowledged the freedom of Ajoie and her children. However, Ajoie claimed in her petition that Marigny now threatened to reduce her and her children to slavery. In her petition she demanded that he come into court, declare her free, and pay the court costs. Marigny failed to appear in court to respond to the lawsuit, and the judge declared him in default, in effect confirming Ajoie's freedom. No evidence existed to prove that Marigny ever actually threatened to repossess Ajoie. Indeed, Marigny's actions in allowing her and her children to live as free for thirty-three years, paying wages for their services, does not suggest that he would have tried to take possession of them as slaves.[25]

In 1857 Marcellus Paine sued for his freedom and that of his five children on the basis of a shipwreck of the slave ship *Creole* that had landed him and his wife in Nassau in 1834. He claimed his freedom on the grounds of emancipation by the British government, which he claimed had compensated his former owner, John Waddel, of Wilmington, North Carolina. Waddel had promised to protect him and restore his liberty, but when Paine voluntarily returned to North Carolina, Waddel had sold him, his wife, and his children at auction to William M. Lambeth of New Orleans. Paine said that Lambeth knew the circumstances of his stay in Nassau, but Lambeth denied that being in Nassau would have freed Paine because the shipwreck

25. Ajoie, f.w.c., v. Marigny, No. 10,443, Fourth District Court of New Orleans, 1 December 1856; Dumas Malone, ed., *Dictionary of American Biography*, 20 vols. (New York: Charles Scribner's Sons, 1933), 12:282–3; *Civil Code*, Art. 3510, p. 532.

occurred well before the Webster-Ashburton Treaty of 1842, in which British officials agreed not to interfere with ships cast upon their shores because of accident, storm, or violence. Lambeth alleged that in 1834, the year of the shipwreck, slaves did not acquire freedom when an accident drove them into territory where slavery did not exist. He also denied that the British government had compensated Waddel for Paine and the children. Paine's wife had died before he filed the suit for freedom. The clerk of the Fifth District Court checked the State Department's records to see if Paine's and his wife's name appeared on the cargo manifest. It is clear that the British government had paid for thirteen of the twenty-two slaves who remained in Nassau. Although the clerk did find their names listed, he could not ascertain whether Paine and his wife numbered among the thirteen slaves. Since the court had no hard evidence that the British government had specifically paid for Paine and his wife, it ruled against Paine, and he and his children remained enslaved.[26]

The slave Ann, alias Anna, turned to J. C. David to sue to confirm her freedom in 1848, but the court did not render a final decision until 1857. Justin Durel and his wife had taken Ann to France in 1832. She had remained there for several months and then had returned to New Orleans. In 1838, she had given birth to a child. Durel stated in his response to the suit that he had never treated Ann or her child as slaves. He claimed she had voluntarily stayed with him after her return from France, and "they are free and have been always free to leave the house of this respondent and to enjoy their freedom." Ann, he claimed, had no right of action against him. Since Durel did not contest the lawsuit, it did not proceed. In 1857, Ann must have desired confirmation of her status, or perhaps her attorney persuaded

26. Paine, f.m.c., v. Lambeth, No. 2884, Fifth District Court of New Orleans, 28 February 1857. One of the provisions of the Webster-Ashburton Treaty involved the controversy over the slave ship *Creole*. In 1841 the slaves aboard the *Creole* revolted against their captors, and the ship landed on British territory in Bermuda. Since the British had abolished slavery in their empire, British officials on the island declared the slaves free. Southerners wanted compensatory payments for them. Eventually, the British agreed that in the future the British government would instruct colonial governors to avoid "official interference" with ships "driven by storm, accident, or violence" upon British territory. Finally in 1853 an Anglo-American claims commission awarded $110,330 to the owners of the former slaves on the grounds that the ship had not violated any law and that the British officials had violated international law by boarding a ship of another nation with armed force. See Robert V. Remini, *Daniel Webster: The Man and His Times* (New York: W. W. Norton, 1997), 558-9.

her of the need of such a confirmation. The judge of the Second District Court declared Ann and her child free people on March 10, 1857.[27]

The last case of this nature heard by the district courts also confirmed the freedom of a woman who had lived as free after being taken to a free state and freed by her owner, George A. Botts, a New Orleans slave trader. In 1839 Botts had taken his then sixteen-year-old slave mistress, Ann Maria Barclay, to Ohio for the specific purpose of freeing her. After her return to New Orleans, she had continued to live with Botts as a free woman of color. After his death in 1855, his executor seized Barclay's property, including real estate and a piano, claiming that Barclay still held slave status and, as such, could own nothing. She hired one of the most prominent attorneys in New Orleans, Christian Roselius, to sue to prove her freedom. She won in the trial court, and Barclay's executor appealed to the Supreme Court of Louisiana. The Supreme Court affirmed the judgment of the lower court, although it recognized that the general policy of the state forbade manumission "by assaults from without upon an institution throughly interwoven with our interior lives." However, it recognized that in 1830 the law recognized manumissions such as Barclay's, and that since she had attained the status of a free person, no law existed in Louisiana to reenslave her.[28]

This remarkable string of freedom suits demonstrates that judges of the New Orleans courts often ruled in favor of slaves seeking their freedom on the basis that sojourns on free soil had made them free, despite decades-old precedents of the United States Supreme Court to the contrary. Not until after the *Strader* v. *Graham* decision did the Louisiana Supreme Court fall in line with national precedents. In a society strongly supportive of slavery, these cases show that district court and Supreme Court judges ruled surprisingly often in favor of freedom until a heightened sense of crisis over the issue of slavery and a proslavery United State Supreme Court rendered

27. Ann, alias Anna, v. Durel, No. 1281, Second District Court of New Orleans, 5 March 1857.

28. Barclay, f.w.c., v. Sewell, Curator, No. 4622, 12 La. Ann. 262 (1857). Christian Roselius, a German immigrant, arrived in New Orleans in 1819 at the age of sixteen. After serving as a printer's apprentice, he developed an interest in Louisiana law. In 1828, he applied for admission to the Louisiana bar and became one of its most distinguished members. He also served as attorney general of Louisiana and dean of the law school at the University of Louisiana (now Tulane University). Glenn R. Conrad, ed., *Dictionary of Louisiana Biography*, 2 vols. (Lafayette: Center for Louisiana Studies, 1988) 2:696.

strong decisions to the contrary. Furthermore, slave plaintiffs had an attorney to represent them, so some attorneys did not disdain this sort of business. One in particular, J. C. David, actually solicited slave clients. What we know about him suggests that he desperately needed business, any business. No evidence exists that he had altruistic reasons for representing so many slaves in freedom suits, while proof abounds of his struggle to stay afloat financially.

2

"VOLEUR DE NEGRES"

The Strange Career of Jean Charles David

S laves chose one attorney for nineteen of the twenty-seven lawsuits for freedom based on transportation to a free state or country: Jean Charles David. David's career opens a window on the underside of antebellum lawyering. He emerges as the quintessential sleazy and often pathetically inept attorney. Why did slaves, who needed skilled representation to win their freedom in a legal climate dedicated to maintaining slavery, turn to him rather than to someone more ethical and competent? One reason might have been that David developed a reputation for success in freedom suits. Although his ethics left much to be desired, he did win a number of cases. Never mind that some of his cases proved almost laughably easy to win because the owner did not contest the suit; slaves saw his success. He seems to have charged little in fees, perhaps much less than more reputable attorneys. And more prominent attorneys doubtless preferred to represent slaveowners defending suits for freedom, propertied persons who could pay their fees. In short, slaves would have had many reasons to chose David. Before the national crisis over slavery induced Louisiana legislators and judges to fall in line with other slave states' laws on the liberating effect of free soil, Louisiana law and jurisprudence subverted this aspect of slavery, a subversion that even an inept and unprincipled attorney could exploit.

Born in France in 1810, David came to New Orleans sometime during the 1830s. The city directory lists him as a "teacher of French" in 1838, an occupation probably little in demand in French-speaking New Orleans. He became an attorney and applied for acceptance as a member of the bar, gaining admission on January 20, 1840. His string of victories in freedom lawsuits might well have marked the high point in his legal and personal life, even though he solicited some of the cases in a somewhat questionable manner. The rest of his personal and professional life reveals a deterioration in his personal relations, looming insolvency, professional incompetence, and a considerable amount of violence.[1]

Serving as an attorney for slaves put David at the bottom of New Orleans's professional and social ladder. One can readily imagine white New Orleanians' hostile reactions to David's espousal of slaves' suits for freedom—suits that if successful would usually mean a significant financial loss. David's actions increased the anxieties of the city's slaveholders about the security of their human property. Freedom suits forced them to confront their fear of loss of what most considered legal property at the hands of a tricky and mercenary attorney. By representing slaves, David made it impossible for prospective clients of wealth and social standing to trust him with their legal affairs. Small wonder that he lived deeply in debt for most of his career.

Sometime in the 1830s, David married a widow, Catherine Jacques Rideau. Rideau had four sons by her first husband, a house on Goodchildren Street, and eight slaves; the marriage seemed to be advantageous, at least at first. But the type of law he practiced ensured that the rest of his career would be blighted socially, financially, and professionally. In many instances, David manufactured his cases and solicited his slave clients. In 1847, he sued to become the tutor (guardian) of a young slave in order to have him freed. Apparently David solicited the boy's business; case records indicate that François Paillaset gave his "consent" to the lawsuit. David claimed that the slave boy's mother had purchased her son in order to free him but had died before she could take the steps to free him under the law. Other more prominent attorneys occasionally accepted slaves suing for their freedom as clients, but just as often they served as attorneys for those fighting freedom suits. For example, the well-respected attorney Christian Roselius represented a slave suing for her freedom in *Miller* v. *Belmonti* (1845) and a slaveholder fighting a suit for freedom in *Morrison* v. *White* (1861). Roselius fought both of these cases to the Louisiana Supreme Court and won. David, because of his reputation as an attorney for slaves, never represented slave-

---

1. U.S. Census, 1850; *Gibson's Guide and Directory of the State of Louisiana and the City of New Orleans* (New Orleans: J. Gibson, 1838), 53; Supreme Court of Louisiana, *Minute Book*, 6:59 (1840).

holders fighting suits for freedom. His solicitation of slave clients gave New Orleans slaveholders the unsavory impression that he took advantage of legal loopholes for his own pecuniary gain. In doing so, he allowed slaves to use his professional knowledge to gain their freedom.[2]

Even in the beginning of David's marriage to Catherine Jacques, signs of financial strain appeared. She might have had financial problems; it appears that shortly after their wedding David paid some of her debts. In any event, Catherine was not the only one with money problems. Whether because he mostly represented slaves, who by law could not possess anything, or whether he managed his money poorly, David soon fell into financial trouble. In 1850, his wife sued him for separation of property to protect the house and slaves that she owned from her first marriage from David's creditors. After her death in 1852, three of her sons sold their interest in her estate to the eldest son, ironically named Prosper Rideau, who himself sank deeply into debt. For several years, David and his son-in-law refused to expose Catherine's will to probate, lest creditors seize all of the assets. In the interim, the two men quarreled over who should administer the succession. The dispute probably arose because Louisiana law provided a fee for the administrator. David also claimed a fee from the succession for the education of his stepson. Rideau alleged that the boy could neither speak nor write English or French correctly, and that David had educated him poorly, if at all; therefore David should collect no fee. In 1857, creditors finally forced the sale of Catherine David's assets, including the slaves, at auction. Only the elderly slave Adele did not receive a bid high enough to justify a sale. The sheriff disposed of her at a separate sale at a later date. She subsequently committed suicide by drowning herself in the Carondelet Canal.[3]

2. David, praying to be appointed tutor *ad hoc* of François Paillaset, *statu liber,* No. 977, First District Court of New Orleans, 14 May 1847. For other solicitation cases, see Charlotte, c.w., v. Cazelar, No. 1078, Third District Court of New Orleans, 14 March 1849; Hélène, c.w., v. Blineau, No. 4126, First District Court of New Orleans, 11 January 1850; Eulalie, f.w.c., v. Blanc, No. 4904, First District Court of New Orleans, 19 April 1850; Miller v. Belmonti, No. 5623, 11 Rob. 339 (1845); Morrison, f.w.c., v. White, 16 La. Ann. 100 (1861). Roselius served as lead attorney in one of the lengthiest and most lucrative law cases of the antebellum period, the succession of John McDonogh. Succession of McDonogh, No. 2416, 7 La. Ann. 472 (1852). Conrad, ed., *Dictionary of Louisiana Biography,* 2:696.

3. Jacques, wife of David, v. David, No. 5398, First District Court of New Orleans, 21 October 1851; Rideau v. His Creditors, No. 3980, Fourth District Court of New Orleans, 19 November 1850; Succession of Jacques, widow of Rideau, wife of David, No. 11,427, Second

Whether because of an inadequate education or simply a want of attention to detail, David proved to be an incompetent attorney. When most attorneys appealed cases to the Supreme Court of Louisiana, they had identical briefs printed as small pamphlets for each justice's consideration. David hand-copied his briefs, probably because he could not afford to have them printed. Unfortunately, he also copied them so carelessly that the wording differed from brief to brief.[4]

In 1851, David sued to gain possession of a slave child whom he claimed remained illegally in the possession of the child's mother's former owner. The judge of the Third District Court rendered a judgment of non-suit against David's client, stating, "This case has been tried so injustly [ineptly] and there is such a *want of precision* and uncertainty in the evidence that the court is unable to come to a satisfactory conclusion." The following year the First District Court dismissed a freedom suit brought by David for the slave Angelina because he sued her owners in a New Orleans court when they actually they had legal domicile in Pointe Coupée Parish. In 1855, David sued to recover $262.95 for repairs performed by a client. In this case, he sued the wrong person—not the owner of the property.[5]

In 1857, David represented a free woman of color, Julia Arbuckle, who had been sold into slavery in New Orleans. After Arbuckle had successfully sued for her freedom before the Fifth District Court (represented by another attorney), she was not freed; the persons who had held her as a slave "kept [her] secretly and flogged her as a slave." She hired David to represent her in a suit for damages of $400. It was to prove a costly mistake. In open

District Court of New Orleans, 28 September 1860; David v. Rideau, No. 11,319, Second District Court of New Orleans, 10 March 1857; Dufour, Durand & Co. v. Rideau, No. 10,956, Second District Court of New Orleans, 7 December 1857, and No. 5611, unreported Louisiana Supreme Court case (1858); Stemphear v. Rideau, No. 11,895, Third District Court of New Orleans, 1856–1859; *New Orleans Daily Picayune*, 3 July, 18 June 1857. The Louisiana *Civil Code* set the administrator's fee at 2.5 percent of the net value of the succession (estate) after payment of the debts of the succession. As the debts of Catherine Jacques David's succession exceeded its assets, no money would have remained for the administrator's fee. *Civil Code*, Art. 1062, p. 160.

4. For example, see Arbuckle, f.w.c., v. Bouny and Talbot, No. 1632, 5 La. Ann. 699 (1850).

5. Denies, f.m.c., v. Nichols and Doré, No. 3845, Third District Court of New Orleans, 8 May 1852; Angelina, c.w., v. Parlange, No. 7144, First District Court of New Orleans, 7 January 1852; Camille, f.w.c., v. Rimassa, No. 10,475, Fifth District Court of New Orleans, 19 February 1856.

court David admitted that he believed that her purchaser had bought her in good faith. Acting in good faith automatically canceled an action for damages. This tactical blunder almost cost Arbuckle any hope of recovery. The judge of the Fifth District Court ruled in favor of the purchaser and dismissed Arbuckle's suit for damages. David appealed to the Louisiana Supreme Court, which decided to overlook David's error. It reprimanded him for a petition which, although "very inartificially drawn, is not without a cause of action" before remanding the case to the trial court with instructions to consider the issue of damages. The case dragged on for years. Finally, Arbuckle hired a new attorney and succeeded in getting a judgment for $240 in damages in 1865.[6]

On some occasions, David's conduct resulted in accusations of criminal acts. In 1854, Daniel C. Osbourne charged that David had furnished his slave, James Madison, with false free papers. David claimed to have proof in his office that Madison, born a free person of color, had been kidnapped as a child of seven years and sold to Osbourne as a slave. Madison asserted that he earned $150 in wages per year, and David sued Osbourne for Madison's freedom, back wages, and court costs. Regrettably, the record of this case has vanished, but a brief newspaper account indicates that David failed to prove Madison's freedom. The First District Court convicted David of giving false free papers to a slave, but the jury recommended him to the mercy of the court. The papers, found on Madison's person when his master recovered him after a few days' absence, read: "I certify that James Madison is a freeman of color & that I have in my possession the prove [sic] of his freedom—so he may work where he pleases, 20th October 1854, Conde Street No. 29—J. C. David, Atty." David, who served as his own defense attorney, successfully petitioned for a new trial. Two years elapsed before it took place, during which time David continued to practice law. For his second trial, David hired one of the most skilled and prominent criminal defense attorneys of the New Orleans bar, Alexander P. Field. Field argued the unconstitutionality of the act under which the court had convicted David. He also argued that David had believed in Madison's freedom. Finally, Field rued the fact that although John Graves, a free man of color, would testify to Madison's freedom, Graves had inconveniently disappeared.

6. Arbuckle, f.w.c., v. Bouny and Talbot, No. 2523, Fifth District Court of New Orleans, 4 June 1849. "Inartificially" is an old word meaning not characterized by art or skill.

Although convicted at the second trial, David apparently never served time in prison. In January 1857, he made a motion for a new trial and signed a bond that he would not leave the jurisdiction of the court.[7]

Less than a year later David found himself in court again, this time defending himself against a charge brought by a free woman of color, Sophia Parker. Parker accused David of inflicting "several violent blows" on her shoulder and hand with no provocation on November 30, 1856. After a hearing before a recorder's court, the case proceeded to the First District Court on a charge of assault and battery. David attempted to mount a defense, stating that Parker had insulted and abused him, but the court dismissed the charge. A number of witness testified both for and against David. He entered a plea of not guilty on November 13, 1857, and the prosecutor dropped the case with a *nolle prosequi* on November 26. But as a local newspaper reported, David "having been indiscreet enough to call one of Sophy's [Sophia's] witnesses a liar" in open court, the judge sentenced him to twenty-four hours in jail for contempt of court. As he climbed into the "Red Maria," the wagon that hauled prisoners from the court to parish prison, his officemate and fellow attorney, Constantine Rolland, ridiculed him. The newspaper reported that David "answered with a good deal of pungent pleasantry, considering the circumstances of the case." Rolland had little room to make fun of David. Three different clients had accused Rolland of embezzlement; he came before one particular city recorder so often that the official had commented that "he was tired of seeing him appear on so many kindred charges, and would have to deny him the privilege of bail if he came much oftener." One of these embezzlement charges gained Rolland a conviction and two years' imprisonment at hard labor in the penitentiary. During the same month as the trial for embezzlement, the First

7. State v. David, No. 13,188, First District Court of New Orleans, 26 November 1857; *New Orleans Daily Picayune*, 29 September, 1, 21 November 1857. A. P. Field came to Louisiana from Illinois, where he had served as attorney general. Field opened a law office in New Orleans and became one of the leading criminal defense attorneys in the city. He became attorney general of Louisiana after the Civil War and died in 1876. Conrad, ed., *Dictionary of Louisiana Biography,* 1:301. An article about his death appeared in the *New Orleans Times-Democrat,* 22 August 1876. *New Orleans Daily Picayune,* 3, 5, September 1857; 27 May, 1, 3, 6, 26 June 1858; 26 January, 3 February 1859; 15 January 1861. Ira Berlin states that in every southern city persons who he termed "Negro agents," usually struggling attorneys, often held the freedom papers for many blacks arrested and charged as runaways. Berlin, *Slaves without Masters,* 263.

District Court convicted him of "aiding and abetting a slave in his attempt to run away," for which he also received a sentence of two years at hard labor. Shortly after his release in 1861, the First District Court convicted him of assault and battery. Apparently David was so sleazy that Rolland—no saint himself—was about the only person willing to share an office with him.[8]

In 1859, a client accused David of embezzling $10.50 from her, as well as "breach of trust and swindling." Aurore Silvestre Noel, a free woman of color, had hired David to sue George Frank in a court of the Justice of the Peace. David had won, and Frank had paid him $9 to give to Noel. She alleged that she had given David $2.50 to pay court costs, which had actually amounted to $1.50, and that David had pocketed the difference. She also claimed that she had promised David a $2 fee for his services. Although the Orleans Parish Grand Jury indicted David, the prosecutor dropped the case with a *nolle prosequi* before trial because of the insignificant sum involved. David pocketed the money, including the fee.[9]

At times David became a victim of violence because of his professional life. On December 8, 1850, ten days after he sued for the freedom of the slave Liza in *Liza v. Puissant,* David and Liza's owner, Dr. Puissant, met by chance on the Elysian Fields streetcar. Puissant, overcome by rage, threatened to kill him for his efforts to free Liza. Calling David a "voleur de negres" (a stealer of Negroes), Puissant warned that he "should be armed and should kill your petitioner with pleasure." The next month, Puissant whacked David on the shoulder in the meat market "without any provoca-

8. State v. David, No. 14,304, First District Court of New Orleans, 18 January 1860; *New Orleans Daily Picayune,* 18, 23 December 1859, 19 January 1860. A *nolle prosequi* in a criminal case meant that the prosecutor declined to pursue the case further, usually for lack of evidence or witnesses willing to come forth. Black, ed., *Black's Law Dictionary,* 818. The city of New Orleans sold the police department's paddy wagons, the "Red Maria" and the "Black Maria," in 1855 to pay back salaries to public school teachers. The purchaser acquired them at half the original cost and then informed the police department that he would agree to hire out the wagons for police use. See Dennis C. Rousey, *Policing the Southern City: New Orleans, 1805–1889* (Baton Rouge: Louisiana State University Press, 1996), 72. In 1852, someone stole over $1,000 worth of law books from David's office. *New Orleans Daily Crescent,* 6 August 1852; *New Orleans Daily Picayune,* 5 August 1852. David and Rolland charged each other with trespass, but nothing came of the charges. *New Orleans Daily Picayune,* 12, 17, 26, August 1858.

9. State v. David, No. 14,304, First District Court of New Orleans, 18 January 1860.

tion." David brought charges against Puissant for assault and battery. The recorder sent the case to the First District Court, but it never proceeded to trial. Perhaps the court considered the rights of the "eccentric lawyer David" (as a local newspaper termed him) less important than those of a wealthy, respectable member of the creole community.[10]

David had two altercations—one verbal, one physical—with another member of the bar, H. R. Grandmont, over a case in litigation. In March 1850, both attorneys faced charges of violating Article 486 of the Louisiana *Code of Practice,* which stated, "Advocates must plead their causes with propriety and decency; they must not indulge in personal remarks against the parties, nor lose sight of the respect due to the court, to the witnesses, and to the jury; they should neither interrupt the one who speaks, not indulge in idle digressions having no bearing on the case." Both attorneys received a $20 fine and had to pay court costs.[11]

Just a year later David and Grandmont received a summons to appear before the judge of the Second District Court "to answer for a contempt of court within the precinct of the Court Room and resorting to personal violence." In that episode, Grandmont had whacked David over the head with his cane. In response, David had drawn a knife and attempted to stab Grandmont when the clerk of the court had stepped between them. David accidentally had cut the clerk's hand severely. As Grandmont had begun the altercation, the judge sentenced him to eight hours in jail, a fine of $10, and court costs. The judge lectured David about the practice of carrying a concealed weapon. David responded that he only carried the knife in self-defense, as "his life had been repeatedly threatened." The judge said that "it was necessary to make an example," and sentenced David to five hours in jail, a fine of $10, and court costs. New Orleans courts usually set the fine for carrying a concealed weapon at $20.[12]

10. State v. Puissant, No. 6005, First District Court of New Orleans, 27 February 1851; *New Orleans Daily Picayune,* 12 August 1858.

11. Minute Book, Second District Court of New Orleans, 9 March 1850; Fuqua, ed., *Code of Practice,* Art. 486, pp. 234–5.

12. Minute Book, Second District Court of New Orleans, 10, 11 March 1851; *New Orleans Bee,* 11, 12 March, 24 April 1851. *New Orleans Daily Picayune,* 24 April 1851. Many people carried concealed weapons in New Orleans in the 1850s. In 1856 a judge of the First District Court, John B. Robertson, came to trial for carrying a concealed weapon. He tried to use self-defense as a justification, but the prosecutor insisted that justification did not exist under the law for this offense. Although witnesses testified that Robertson had indeed carried

Such violence occurred with some regularity in the courts building. Local newspapers reported several acts of violence between attorneys in the courts between 1845 and 1853. The *New Orleans Bee* reported a courtroom incident in 1845 in which two attorneys shouted epithets at each other. The judge reminded the attorneys that they should treat each other as gentlemen. One of the participants replied that as for being gentlemen, "it is one of the legal fictions not always borne out in practice." An 1849 "match of fisticuffs" between two members of the bar resulted in a $50 fine and twenty-four hours in jail for both brawlers. Acting Recorder Fabre fined an attorney $10 for striking another attorney in the face and calling him a liar. His report noted that the offending attorney drew a large roll of bills out of his pocket and paid the fine "with apparent satisfaction." The judge of the Third District Court fined an attorney $100 and sentenced him to twenty-four hours in prison for throwing a glass tumbler at another attorney in court. In an even more dramatic episode, a lawyer raised his cane to strike a fellow attorney when the intended victim drew a pistol from his pocket, which accidentally went off, the "bullet entering on the instep and going quite through [his own] foot." The case between the two attorneys involved a dispute over 2,600 barrels of sand.[13]

Several times during the 1850s, David became involved in violent acts as either victim or perpetrator. Neither court records nor newspaper accounts give much information about the causes of these altercations. A few months after the row with Grandmont, a policeman accused David of assault and battery and having a "dirk" (knife) in his possession. Apparently the policeman had interfered when David had pulled a knife from his

---

a concealed weapon, the jury obviously thought him justified and found him not guilty, despite overwhelming evidence to the contrary. *New Orleans Daily Picayune,* 30 November 1856. In a grand jury report, jurors attributed the rapid rise in the number of homicides in the city to the practice of carrying concealed weapons. The grand jury further stated that in their opinion the usual fine of $20 did not deter individuals from carrying concealed weapons. *New Orleans Daily Picayune,* 12 November 1851. A local newspaper commented that the law against carrying concealed weapons "is . . . violated every day by nine-tenths of the male population of this State, very few of the magistrates, public functionaries, &c., being excepted." *New Orleans Daily Picayune,* 28 November 1861.

13. Quoted in Ariela Gross, *Double Character: Slavery and Mastery in the Antebellum Southern Courtroom* (Princeton: Princeton University Press, 2000), 35; *New Orleans Daily Picayune,* 22 November 1849, 30 May 1851; *New Orleans Bee,* 30 May 1851; *New Orleans Daily Picayune,* 6 March 1852, 18, 23 July 1853.

pocket and attempted to stab another man, a German named Gustave Trémé. When the officer had stepped between the two men, David had assaulted and struck him. Brought before the recorder, David accused Trémé of stealing from him and of having "violently assaulted and struck the complainant [David] in front of his own office." This case never proceeded to trial. One year later, Henry Hurd accused David of wounding him in the face and on the shoulder with a sword. The recorder charged David with assault with a dangerous weapon and wounding with intent to kill. Although the recorder sent the case to the First District Court for trial, no record of a trial transcript exists except a description of the original incident.[14]

In 1853, a man attempted "to cut Mr. David with a knife" at the steamboat landing. Three years later David had another man arrested for "having knocked him down on Chartres street, beaten him, tore his coat off, and caused his nose to bleed profusely." David was himself accused of having assaulted and struck a clerk in a store on Chartres Street. Contemporary newspaper reports do not indicate what sparked these violent acts.[15]

The next incident reported by a local newspaper, although equally perplexing, reveals something about David's extremely difficult financial position, as well as his character. In 1859, the First District Court convicted David of assaulting and beating a very small boy outside the courts building. At first David paid the $50 fine but refused to pay the court costs. He later withdrew the fine, and the sheriff threw him in jail. David appeared before the court and swore that he had no property, movable or immovable, only a few uncollectible debts owed him, and that he could not pay the "costs, fine, or anything else." The court ordered his release, as the newspaper reported, "to his expectant and welcoming friends in the city." Four days later, the sheriff arrested him again, this time on a charge of larceny and trespass. No record of any subsequent prosecution exists.[16]

David last appears in the New Orleans city directory in 1866. He is not listed in the 1870 U.S. census, nor is his name among New Orleans death certificates or on the lists of people buried in New Orleans cemeteries. His succession never underwent probate in a New Orleans court, but as he most

14. *New Orleans Bee*, 24 September 1851; State v. David, No. 8160, First District Court of New Orleans, 18 September 1852; *New Orleans Daily Picayune*, 18 September 1852.

15. *New Orleans Daily Picayune*, 11 December 1853, 25 May 1856; State v. David, No. 8160, First District Court of New Orleans, 18 September 1852.

16. *New Orleans Daily Picayune*, 6, 10 August 1859.

likely died penniless and had no heirs, no reason existed for probate. Perhaps he left the city to seek a livelihood elsewhere, or perhaps he lies in a pauper's grave somewhere in the city. Why he undertook so many slave manumission cases—whether motivated by money or an uneasiness with the institution of slavery, or because he was such a bad and corrupt lawyer that the business of slaves was about the only business he could get—we will probably never know.

3

CONTRACTING FOR FREEDOM
AND SELF-PURCHASE

Article 174 of the Louisiana *Civil Code* allowed slaves to contract for their freedom: "The slave is incapable of making any contract, except those which relate to his own emancipation." Self-purchase refuted the slave society's claim that bondage benefitted slaves because of their supposed inability to care for themselves. Obviously slaves who had the determination and means to purchase themselves gave the lie to this proslavery argument. Instances in which slaves successfully contracted for their freedom with their owners did not come before the New Orleans courts. It cannot be determined how often these manumissions occurred, but strong evidence exists that a large number of New Orleans slaves made a prolonged and determined effort to purchase their freedom. Self-purchase cases only appeared in the district courts of New Orleans when something went wrong in the transaction; slaves then used the courts to complete the contract. Although one historian has stated that self-purchase cases did not appear before Louisiana's district courts because self-purchase proved "out of the question," this historian worked mainly in the courts of rural Rapides Parish. Slavery in New Orleans constituted a very different institution than in rural areas; for one thing, slaves had more opportunities to work for wages in their spare time.[1]

Several factors influenced whether slaves could successfully purchase themselves. The owner had to approve of the purchase, or at least not oppose it, because slaves had no way to force a sale, even if they obtained a sum of money equal to their value. Also, the owner had to be willing to allow

1. *Civil Code,* Art. 174, p. 27; Morris, *Southern Slavery and the Law,* 384–5.

the slave to work overtime for wages. Financial self-interest motivated some owners to allow self-purchase. Permitting slaves to work for their freedom proved the best way to get the maximum amount of labor from them. Generally, slaves working without hope of freedom tended to utilize passive resistance, working as little as possible. Most of the slaves who purchased themselves lived in cities; the outlook for freedom on a plantation remained dim, if not hopeless. Most slaves purchasing themselves had some skills to sell. Often a slave had a marriage-like arrangement with a free partner, and both worked to buy the freedom of the enslaved partner. If the slave anticipated resistance to self-purchase, he or she could give the purchase money to a third party, who would purchase and take steps to free him or her. Probably the largest single manumission by self-purchase in Louisiana occurred in 1842, when eighty slaves of the wealthy merchant John McDonogh paid in full the agreed-upon amount for their freedom. They had earned the money by performing extra work for McDonogh and others. In 1859 a second community of forty-two slaves sailed for Liberia, freed by a stipulation in McDonogh's will that they could work to buy their freedom after his death. Whatever prompted McDonogh to allow his slaves to purchase themselves—some have suggested he thought it would motivate them to work as hard as possible—he still believed that blacks were an inferior race who ideally belonged in Africa.[2]

Theoretically, all of these self-purchase agreements should have been put in writing. The *Black Code* (the body of laws governing slaves) classified slaves as real estate, and the rules for the transfer of real property in Louisiana required a notarial act, signed by a notary public, properly witnessed, and registered in the conveyance office. However, most self-purchases came before the courts as informal agreements between owner and slave. This, of

2. Sumner Eliot Matison, "Manumission by Purchase," *Journal of Negro History* 33 (April 1948): 154–67; *New Orleans Daily Picayune*, 28 April 1859; Schafer, *Slavery, the Civil Law, and the Supreme Court of Louisiana*, 210–1; Conrad, ed., *Dictionary of Louisiana Biography*, 1:533–4. One historian has noted that slaves hoping to purchase themselves might have worked harder to gain a good reputation on which to build a life of freedom. He also has shown that, like McDonogh, slaveholders in Baltimore who allowed their slaves to purchase themselves often purchased additional slaves after manumitting others. T. Stephen Whitman, *The Price of Freedom: Slavery and Manumission in Baltimore and Early National Maryland* (Lexington: University Press of Kentucky, 1997), 115. On third-party manumissions, see Bogger, *Free Blacks in Norfolk*, 14–5; David Rankin, "The Forgotten People: Free People of Color in New Orleans, 1850–1870" (Ph.D. diss., Johns Hopkins University, 1976), 66.

course, put the slave at a serious disadvantage. The owner could pocket the money and never free the slave, or allege that the slave had never paid the purchase price. Without a written contract, slaves seeking freedom by claiming to have purchased themselves often found themselves without recourse in law.[3]

The Third District Court heard the first of these cases in 1847. Marie Duhulcod, alias Myrthé, sued the administrator of the succession of Frederick Charles, a free man of color, for her freedom. Duhulcod claimed that Charles had purchased her for $1,200 in 1840. A notary had passed the act of sale in proper form. This document contained the provision that as soon as Duhulcod paid two promissory notes of $600, Charles would take the necessary steps to free her. The act of sale specifically stated, "It was *agreed* and *expressly stipulated as a condition without which the sale would not have taken place* [italics in original], and that her purchaser would free her and her child following payment of the notes." By law, Charles could not have freed Duhulcod without also freeing her child. According to Article 196 of the *Civil Code,* "The child born of a woman after she has acquired the right of being free at a future time follows the condition of its mother, and becomes free at the time of her enfranchisement, even if the mother should die before that time." In freeing the mother, the child automatically became free.

In her petition, Duhulcod asserted that she paid the notes personally and "by her friends who assisted her on that occasion." After giving Charles the money, she asked him for her freedom and he told her that "she was free and could act as she pleased." However, witnesses testified that she had not paid $130 of her price. Charles had died in debt, and his widow had secured a judgment to sell Duhulcod as a slave. On the eve of the judicial sale, she had begged for a respite, and her sister, a free woman of color, had managed to come up with the needed amount. Charles's widow still refused to manumit her because Duhulcod and her child constituted the only property of the succession, a "common pledge of the creditors." Article 190 of the *Civil Code* expressly forbade freeing slaves in fraud of creditors. A witness for the plaintiff testified that Duhulcod, a seamstress, had not paid her

---

3. "An Act Prescribing the Rules and Conduct to Be Observed with Respect to Negroes and Other Slaves of This Territory," Act of June 7, 1806, *Orleans Territory Acts, 1806,* Sec. 10, p. 154 (hereafter cited as *Black Code*); *Civil Code,* Art. 461, p. 68.

wages over to Charles, which was evidence that he had not considered her a slave. Three years after Charles had purchased Duhulcod, she had asked his permission to marry a free man of color, Auguste Goban. Charles had told her to marry Goban, that he "was a good man and she was free." This was further evidence that Charles had considered her to be free, as Louisiana law prohibited slaves from marrying free people of any color, and marriages between slaves had no civil effects. Duhulcod won her suit; the judge of the Third District Court ordered the widow to free Duhulcod and her child and to pay court costs.[4]

A case similar to Duhulcod's arose later the same year. José Otis sold his slave Zabelle to his daughter, Eulalie Otis, on the express condition that Zabelle could at any time purchase her freedom for $400 and that her three children would become free when she did. On July 6, 1847, Zabelle attempted to give Otis the $400, but Otis refused to accept it. Zabelle then sued for her freedom in the Second District Court, where she was represented by J. C. David. David requested the court to order Otis to accept the $400 and pay Zabelle wages of $12 a month from the date of the institution of the suit. David himself took the witness stand at trial, testifying that he had approached Otis and asked whether she would accept the $400. David claimed that Otis had told him to deposit the money with a notary for safekeeping, which he had done. The court ordered Otis to free Zabelle and pay court costs. Otis died shortly afterwards, and the administrator of her succession accepted the $400 but refused to sign Zabelle's manumission papers. David returned to court to demand that the administrator sign the documents. He had to amend the petition for freedom to include Zabelle's newborn child as well as her three other children, whom he had neglected to include in the first petition. The court ordered the administrator to sign the papers, setting Zabelle and her four children free.[5]

Administrators of successions often were reluctant to free slaves, even when written proof existed that the owner wished it. Before he died, E. Crocker signed an agreement with his slave, Jean Baptiste, that he would be freed upon payment of $1,400. Yet the administrator of Crocker's succession

4. Duhulcod, alias Myrthé, f.w.c., v. Philippe, f.w.c., administrator of Charles, f.m.c., No. 447, Third District Court of New Orleans, 15 March 1848; *Civil Code,* Arts. 182, 190, 196, pp. 28–30.

5. Zabelle, f.w.c., v. Dolliole, administrator of Otis, No. 1201, Second District Court of New Orleans, 15 June 1848.

refused to honor the contract. In court, Jean Baptiste proved that he had paid some of his purchase price to Crocker and the remainder to the administrator after Crocker's death. The Fourth District Court ruled that Jean Baptiste had acquired the right to freedom and ordered the administrator to manumit him.[6]

Another slave child almost lost his chance for freedom when an administrator tried to thwart his mother's attempt to purchase him. The owner of the slave Gustave left a will stating that her slaves could choose their own master or mistress upon her death. Gustave, valued in the succession inventory at $400, chose Elizabeth L. Blanc, the daughter of the deceased, as his new owner. Blanc agreed to turn over Gustave to his mother, a free woman of color named Leocarde, when Leocarde paid Blanc $400 for him. Witnesses testified that Blanc knew that Leocarde planned to free her son. Leocarde said that she had paid Blanc the money for Gustave, but that shortly afterwards, Blanc's children had had her interdicted (a legal process designed to take over the affairs of persons not in possession of their faculties). Blanc's children refused to turn over Gustave to his mother. The Third District Court ordered Gustave delivered to Leocarde, who subsequently freed him.[7]

The following year the First District Court heard a case in which the former owner of four persons of color—Charity, Sarah Ann, and Sarah Ann's two daughters—had sold them, even though Sarah Ann and Charity had purchased their freedom years before. All four had lived as free for over ten years. Charity and Sarah Ann sued for their freedom and that of Sarah Ann's two daughters before the First District Court. At trial the former slave women testified that Noel Campbell had once owned them, but that in 1839 Sarah and Charity had given $600 to a free man of color, Thomas Atkins, to purchase them from Campbell. They affirmed that they had enjoyed their freedom without interruption since then, until Atkins, in need of money, sold Sarah Ann's daughters to Cornelius R. Payne, who placed the children in the slave yard of Elihu Cresswell, a prominent New Orleans slave dealer. One can only imagine the distress of the two young girls at

6. Jean Baptiste, praying for his freedom, v. Mix, administrator of Crocker, No. 3347, Fourth District Court of New Orleans, 27 April 1850.

7. Leocarde, f.w.c., v. Cammark, administrator of Blanc, No. 2889, Third District Court of New Orleans, 7 May 1850.

being placed in a slave pen, which were filthy and often overcrowded places that were filled with the stench of human beings forced to live in cramped quarters. Elihu Cresswell made a practice of hiring out his unsold slaves to realize the maximum profit from their labor. Although we cannot know whether Cresswell hired out Sarah Ann's daughters, the whole experience must have terrified the young girls. Sarah Ann's attorney asked the court to issue an injunction to prevent their sale pending the outcome of the suit.

Atkins stated that he had purchased Charity and Sarah Ann from Campbell, and he had a right to dispose of them as he pleased. Several witnesses said otherwise, testifying that the women had enjoyed their freedom since 1839 and that Sarah Ann had given birth to her daughters after she acquired her freedom; thus by law the daughters were also free. Others testified that Sarah Ann and Charity rented a house in the city and supported themselves as washerwomen. Sarah Ann had married a free man of color after she began living as free, another sign of her freedom. The judge of the First District Court ruled that although he was the nominal owner of Sarah Ann and Charity, Atkins "exercised no control or dominion over them but permitted them the full enjoyment of their liberty, although he resided in this city, frequently saw them, often conversed with them, treated them as free persons and not as his slaves, and even declared to different individuals that they were entitled to be free, and that he had no claim whatever over them." Judge John Larue went on to say that Payne could hold no title to Sarah Ann and Charity by virtue of sale from Atkins, since Atkins "could convey no better title than he possessed." Several witnesses testified that Charity "had paid him [Atkins] every cent of the purchase money."

In his ruling, Judge Larue affirmed the freedom of Charity and Sarah Ann on the basis of *Civil Code* Article 3510, which held that if owners allowed their slaves to live as free for ten years or more, the slaves acquired their liberty through prescription. Living free for over ten years with the knowledge of their nominal owner, Larue ruled, made an act of manumission unnecessary; they already possessed their freedom. After Larue handed down his decision, Sarah Ann and Charity's attorney, J. A. Nautre, sued Valsin Bonne, a free man of color, the husband of Sarah Ann and the father of her children, for $500, his legal fees in the case. Charity had died shortly before Larue's judgment, and Nautre caused Sarah Ann and her daughters to be sequestered until Bonne paid his legal fees. No further record exists in this suit, making it impossible to know whether Sarah Ann and her daughters regained their liberty or how long they remained in jail. Incarceration in an antebellum jail in New Orleans meant being confined to an unhealthy, vermin-infested, overcrowded, damp, and unheated cell.[8]

In 1851, Emilie Webber, a free woman of color, came into court to fight for possession of her daughter, Mary Jane. On July 5, 1846, Webber had purchased herself and her daughter with savings amassed by her own industry and through the "assistance of friends." On April 19, 1851, her former owner, Thomas W. Howard, a white "married man with minor children," went before a notary public and acknowledged Mary Jane as his child. He then petitioned successfully to be appointed tutor of the child and to take possession of her. Webber sued to recover her child, claiming that she feared Howard would take Mary Jane out of the state or cause her injury. She petitioned the Fourth District Court to grant an injunction against Howard's possession of the child until the outcome of her suit. In awarding her the injunction the judge ordered Howard "to refrain from molesting the plaintiff or in any way interfering with her in the possession, control, superintendence and guardianship of her minor child, Mary Jane Webber." Indignant, Howard responded that he had no intention of taking Mary Jane out of the state and that he only wanted to provide his daughter with an education in order that she not fall into prostitution. He alleged that he had appealed in vain to her mother to have her educated. He further complained that Emilie Webber "kept her in association only with negroes . . . instructing her in nothing except fear and aversion" toward her father. He described Webber as "wholly unfit [to raise Mary Jane] by reason of her character and propensities and especially by her entire insensibility of the advantages which might be conferred on said minor." The record does not indicate the

8. Sarah Ann, f.w.c., and Charity, f.w.c., et al., v. Atkins, f.m.c., No. 6468, First District Court of New Orleans, 6 August 1851; Payne v. Cresswell, No. 6532, First District Court of New Orleans, 6 August 1852; *New Orleans Daily Picayune*, 9 July, 7 August, 1851; *Civil Code*, Arts. 182, 196, pp. 28, 30; Walter Johnson, *Soul by Soul: Life inside the Antebellum Slave Market* (Cambridge, Mass.: Harvard University Press, 1999), 4, 168; Conrad, ed., *Dictionary of Louisiana Biography*, 1:201. In his will, Elihu Cresswell freed the slaves that he owned at the time of his death and provided funds to have them sent to a free state. Succession of Cresswell, No. 3521, unreported Louisiana Supreme Court case (1853); Nautre v. Bonne, f.m.c., No. 7191, First District Court of New Orleans, 22 April 1852. For descriptions of prison conditions, see the *New Orleans Daily Picayune*, 4 January 1860, and Logan, f.w.c., v. Hickman, No. 9470, Third District Court of New Orleans, 20 February 1857, and No. 5736, 14 La. Ann. 300; *New Orleans Daily Picayune*, 17 April 1857.

disposition of this case, meaning that one of the parties yielded and did not pursue the matter in court. One can only imagine the embarrassment of Howard's white wife at having such a matter exposed in open court.[9]

Records of the recorders's courts have not survived, but local newspapers regularly reported on their activities. Although usually brief, the newspaper accounts afford other glimpses of slaves attempting to purchase their freedom. In 1853 Louisa Morin appeared before Recorder Joseph Genois and made an affidavit that her slave Maria had deposited $300 with Benjamin Savanet, a free man of color and a cook on a steamboat, to pay for her freedom. Morin alleged that Savanet had made plans to sail with his ship without giving her the money. Recorder Genois issued a warrant for Savanet's arrest. We cannot know what happened to Maria, as the newspaper did not follow up on the story. In 1855 a newspaper reported the suicide of a slave. Samson Richardson, slave of Alexander McKeever, slit his throat with a razor "while in a fit of temporary insanity" (according to the *New Orleans Daily Picayune*) because the $1,200 he had saved to buy his freedom had somehow disappeared. The paper reported, "Deceased could read and write, and had written a good deal about $1,200 which he had entrusted to somebody to purchase him." His owner had decided to sell him and had advertised him for sale, precipitating the suicide.[10]

Samson Richardson's plight was not unique; slaves who entrusted their self-purchase money to others were sometimes defrauded. An unusual article in the *Daily Picayune* reported that the New Orleans police arrested a

9. Webber, f.w.c., v. Howard, No. 4682, Fourth District Court of New Orleans, 7 November 1851. According to the *Civil Code,* fathers could go before a notary and acknowledge an illegitimate child. This made the child what the code termed a "natural child," but not a legitimate child capable of inheriting as an equal with other legitimate children. Children of color had two additional limitations: they could not have legitimate status if fathered by a white man and they could not attempt to prove paternity except to a man of color. Also, children of any color born of adulterous relationships could never have legitimate status. *Civil Code,* Arts. 221–6, pp. 33–4. Another case in which the possession of the daughter of a freed slave went to court also involved the white father claiming that the girl's mother took poor care of her. Delphine, f.w.c., for *habeas corpus* of her daughter, v. Davenport, No. 4973, Fourth District Court of New Orleans, 28 January 1852. J. C. David served as the attorney for Delphine.

10. *New Orleans Daily Picayune,* 3 June 1853, 4 February 1855. On the same day another report of a suicide appeared in which Marcelin, slave of Mr. Pralon, killed himself by throwing himself off the balcony of the parish prison. Marcelin had previously attempted to slit his throat because his owner had threatened to sell him. Ibid., 4 February 1855.

"fine looking woman, about twenty-four years of age" for robbing a slave named Washington, a livery stable keeper in Mobile, of $680, which the slave had saved to purchase his freedom. The day after she had arrived in New Orleans from Mobile, news of the theft had followed her, and the police had arrested her in one of the larger boarding houses in the city. She immediately acknowledged the theft and returned the money. The slave's owner did not wish to prosecute her, stating that he came to New Orleans only to recover the slave's money. The *Picayune* commented, "It is said that she belonged to quite a respectable family in Mobile and was on the point of departure for Texas when arrested."[11]

Sometimes owners of slaves reneged on their promises of slaves' self-purchase, even when they had signed written agreements to that effect. In 1854, Henry Stream signed a document affirming that he would free his slave, Sally Dowd, alias Sarah, upon payment of $400. In the written statement he admitted that she had given him the money in a series of payments, and he had promised to free her within three months from the day he signed the document. By 1856 he had still not manumitted her, and she sued for her liberty in the Fifth District Court. Stream alleged that Dowd had never paid him any money, although he had signed a paper stating the contrary. Judge Donatin Augustine ruled in favor of Dowd's freedom and ordered Stream to pay court costs. He also denied Stream's request for a new trial.[12]

Lack of written proof denied another slave her freedom in 1856. Ester Bracey claimed her freedom from her owner, Louis Lombard, stating that she had paid $650 for her freedom in 1850. She alleged that her owner had committed the transaction to paper, but that he had altered the documents after signing them. She claimed that Lombard had promised to deliver her freedom papers but had reneged on his promise. Lombard had Bracey jailed pending the outcome of the suit, and Bracey testified that she feared he would sell her. Lombard denied that Bracey had ever paid him $650; he said he could sell her for $1,200. Bracey had no concrete proof that Lombard had promised to free her or that she had paid him $650. The judge of the

11. Ibid., 11 April 1855.
12. Dowd, f.w.c., v. Stream, No. 9921, Fifth District Court of New Orleans, 6 May 1856. A newspaper article noted that Auguste Barrand had agreed to manumit a "little quadroon" for $200, but he refused either to return the money or free the child. One of the city's recorders dismissed the charges against Barrand for lack of evidence. *New Orleans Daily Picayune*, 8 July 1856.

Fifth District Court dismissed the suit on the grounds that Bracey had failed to produce enough evidence to make her case.[13]

The slave Elizabeth claimed that her mistress had purchased her with the intention of setting her free but had died before the manumission took place. She further charged that her original act of sale stipulated that her deceased owner's daughter, Madame Pellandini, was obligated to free her upon payment of $400. Elizabeth had paid; but instead of setting her free, Pellandini had threatened to sell her. Elizabeth claimed to have receipts proving that she had paid her new owner the agreed-upon amount, and she offered into evidence thirty-seven receipts totaling over $400. Pellandini countered that Elizabeth had hired herself out—that is, worked for someone other than her owner for wages—and had turned over her earnings of $12 each month to Pellandini. According to Pellandini, "it was clearly understood that the receipts were for hire, not any account of any price of emancipation." Pellandini subsequently sold Elizabeth, who sued for her freedom. In response to the suit, Pellandini asserted that the "whole proceeding is contrary to the present policy of the public laws of the State." This was an exaggeration, since the act prohibiting all manumissions did not go into effect until March 6, 1857, four months after Pellandini's statement. Judge Augustin of the Fifth District Court dismissed Elizabeth's suit for lack of proof of payment and for an omission in the suit itself. Elizabeth's petition did not include a statement attesting to her good behavior for the previous four years, which Judge Augustin ruled was "fatal" to her suit. He also ordered her to pay court costs. The record of this case makes it difficult to assess the validity of Elizabeth's claim; we cannot know whether her payments to Pellandini consisted merely of wages or were cash installments toward her freedom. The records of the district court do not show further legal proceedings on this matter. The Act of March 6, 1857, followed the dismissal of this suit by only two months, making further action useless.[14]

In 1856, a woman who claimed to be free sued to prevent being sold as a slave. Elizabeth Claude declared that she had bought herself and her two children, Clothilde and Adolphe, from Étienne Claude for $500 eleven

13. Bracy, f.w.c., v. Lombard, No. 10,968, Fifth District Court of New Orleans, 5 May 1856.

14. Elizabeth, *statu liber*, v. Pellandini, No. 11,321, Fifth District Court of New Orleans, 9 January 1857; *Civil Code*, Art. 185, p. 29; "An Act to Prohibit the Emancipation of Slaves," Act of March 6, 1857, *Louisiana Acts, 1857*, p. 55.

years before she came into court to prove her freedom. She alleged that even prior to her manumission, she had lived free with the knowledge of her owner for four years before her self-purchase. She introduced into evidence a receipt for $250 and said she had paid the remainder but did not have a receipt for the balance. Étienne Claude had left New Orleans for France in 1856, whereupon his agent had seized her and had both her and her children jailed as slaves, stating that she owed another $350 or $400 for her freedom. The agent threatened to sell her and her children as slaves unless she paid what he claimed she owed. Elizabeth Claude characterized his threats as a "malicious attempt to force your petitioner to pay money which she does not owe."

Philomen Boutté, who had owned Elizabeth Claude before her sale to Étienne Claude, testified that in 1850 Étienne Claude, the owner of a looking-glass factory, had asked him to sell her and the children to him, "telling me at the time that the children were his." Boutté asked for $1,200 for the slaves, and Claude went away, saying he could not pay such a high price. He returned a few days later and offered Boutté $1,000, stating that "he would buy the slave Elisa for her freedom and that her children were also his children." At this time, Boutté testified, Elizabeth Claude gave him $250 to give to Étienne Claude. He did so and received a receipt. Testimony proved that Elizabeth Claude received some or all of the money from sympathetic whites. The trial record stated, "There was a subscription got up by the Planters in the neighborhood with a view to aid the Plff [Elizabeth Claude] in purchasing her freedom. She was a woman of good behavior." A witness testified that he knew Elizabeth Claude had purchased her freedom in 1850 for $500. He stated that he had negotiated the sum for her and had even contributed $50. However, he also testified that Étienne Claude told him that the $500 purchase price did not include the $250 she had paid him before 1850.

The judge of the Fifth District Court rendered a judgment of non-suit, ruling that Elizabeth had failed to provide enough evidence to prove her case. Her attorneys appealed to the Supreme Court of Louisiana. Étienne Claude's agent filed a motion to dismiss the appeal, stating that the judgment of the district court had denied Elizabeth's claim to freedom, and that as a slave she had no capacity to stand in court, no legal cause of action, and no right of appeal. Elizabeth Claude's attorney argued that under the *Civil Code,* slaves could contract for their freedom and maintain an action for their liberty. The defense responded that the Act of March 6, 1857, prohibited all manumissions. This lawsuit began in 1856, went to the Louisiana Supreme Court in 1858 and was not conclusively resolved until 1859. The last page of the Supreme Court record of the case contains an agreement signed by the attorneys on both sides to discontinue the case, with Elizabeth Claude paying the court costs. Nothing indicates what caused the attorneys to settle the case. Perhaps Elizabeth Claude somehow found the money to satisfy the agent. Perhaps they reached an agreement in which she would work for some specified period for wages to make up the purchase price. In any event, the fact that the court ordered her to pay court costs indicates a settlement unfavorable to her.[15]

This case raises larger questions. Why did Étienne Claude not free Elizabeth Claude before departing for France, or take her and his children with him to Europe? Was the agent acting on instructions from Claude or on his own? Nothing in the case record or in the local newspapers fully explains this case.

The last case heard by the New Orleans district courts concerning a disputed self-purchase, *Roberts* v. *Simmons and Co.*, occurred on the eve of the Civil War. The petitioner, John Roberts, claimed that since January 1, 1859, he had lived in "full enjoyment of his liberty." He had formerly belonged to Henry Swasey, who had sold him to Edward Jacobs in 1857 for $1,150 with the express condition that upon payment by Roberts to Jacobs of the purchase price, Jacobs would set Roberts free on January 1, 1859. After receiving the purchase price on the agreed-upon date, Jacobs relinquished all control of Roberts, setting him free. In his petition Roberts stated that he had "all of his life [been] honest and faithful, always behaved respectfully to white people." Roberts stated that after Jacobs freed him, an agent of Simmons and Company, a New York commercial firm, threatened to treat him as a slave and put him in a slave yard for sale. In his petition to the Third District Court, Roberts said that he feared "being carried out of Louisiana, and out of the jurisdiction of the court." Roberts asked the court to declare him free and not the property of Simmons and Company. The

15. Claude, f.w.c., v. Lombard, agent of Claude, No. 11,344, Fifth District Court of New Orleans, 12 June 1858; No. 5909, unreported Supreme Court case, 1859. *Civil Code*, Arts. 174, 177, pp. 27, 28; "An Act to Prohibit the Emancipation of Slaves," Act of March 6, 1857, *Louisiana Acts, 1857*, p. 55.

agent for Simmons and Company claimed Roberts as a slave for life and insisted that as such, he had no right to initiate or prosecute the action. Simmons and Company based their claim on a writ of *fi. fa.*, a creditor's action to seize property in order to collect a debt. In this case, Simmons and Company claimed that as Jacobs's creditors, they could stop him from freeing Roberts; the *Civil Code* prohibited manumitting slaves in fraud of creditors, and Roberts was a substantial asset that could pay Jacobs's debt. However, the 1860 judgment of the Third District Court declared Roberts free and ordered Simmons and Company "forever enjoined from asserting any rights over him." Although the court record provides no explicit explanation for the ruling, Jacobs incurred the debt after Roberts contracted for freedom; it seems that the judge did not allow the debt to affect the judgment. Simmons and Company did not appeal the case to the Louisiana Supreme Court. They may have won such a appeal, either on the grounds of the debt or the provisions of the Act of March 6, 1857, which predated the contract for freedom.[16]

Although Louisiana law prohibited manumissions after 1857, Royal A. Porter freed his slave, Virginia Talbot, and her two children, William and Douglas, six months before the Civil War began. Records in the New Orleans Conveyance Office show that Porter liberated the three slaves upon payment from Talbot of $1,000. In the act freeing her, Porter divested himself of "absolutely all rights of ownership on them." He gave them their freedom "as far as the law allows" and empowered Thomas Curry as their "protector." He ordered Curry to register Talbot and her sons in the mayor's office book for registering free people of color or else to remove them to another state and manumit them there. The conveyance records describe Talbot and her sons as *statu liberi* (slaves who had acquired the right to freedom).[17]

---

16. Roberts, f.m.c., v. Simmons & Co., No. 14,215, Third District Court of New Orleans, 22 December 1860; *Civil Code,* Art. 190, p. 29; "An Act to Prohibit the Emancipation of Slaves," p. 55. E. Filleul served as attorney for Roberts and also represented Étienne Claude in the previous case, more evidence that attorneys served clients on both sides of freedom suits. A writ of *fi. fa.*, an abbreviation for *fieri facias*, was a "writ directed to the sheriff of the parish where the property of the debtor is situated, and orders him to seize the property, real and personal, rights and credits of the debtor, and the sell them, to satisfy the judgment obtained against him." *Code of Practice*, Art. 642, p. 267.

17. Conveyance Office Records, 21 September 1860, 82:417–8.

Although the *Civil Code* guaranteed slaves the right to purchase themselves, bondservants sometimes had to resort to the courts to enforce such
contracts. A greedy owner could simply pocket the money paid and deny
that the slave had ever remitted the purchase price. Slaveowners could deny
the very existence of a contract for self-purchase. Slaves who could not provide concrete proof of self-purchase, such as contracts or receipts for payments to the owner, found themselves without recourse or remedy from the
courts. But a number of slaves found ingenious ways to prove that they had
purchased themselves, using the courts and the law to win their freedom.

4

FREEING SLAVES BY WILL

The Louisiana *Civil Code* made it legal to free slaves not only during the lifetime of the owner, but "by a disposition made in prospect of death," or by last will and testament. Leaving slaves their freedom by will happened frequently in New Orleans, although no figures exist to specify how often. Most of these transactions went smoothly, as long as the succession's debts did not exceed its assets after freeing the slave property and the designated slaves did not deprive legitimate heirs of their rightful inheritance. On some occasions, however, executors and/or heirs of the deceased disregarded the stated wishes of testators. Liberating slaves by will meant the loss of valuable property, often a large portion of the deceased's assets. Sometimes a dead man's legitimate white wife and children, driven by hostility, blocked the freeing of his slave mistress and children. When heirs or executors attempted to thwart the wishes of the deceased, slaves often appealed to the courts to force compliance with the terms of the will. This in itself is not surprising. What is surprising is how often they won, given their precarious position under Louisiana law. Most of these lawsuits occurred during the 1850s, a decade that saw increased abolitionist agitation and the founding of the antislavery Republican Party. Given the national backdrop, slaves suing for the freedom promised them by their owners' wills proved extraordinarily successful.[1]

In some instances, heirs and/or executors could make handsome profits

---

1. *Civil Code,* Art. 190, p. 29; Judith K. Schafer, "'Open and Notorious Concubinage': The Emancipation of Slave Mistresses by Will and the Supreme Court of Louisiana," *Louisiana History* 28 (spring 1987): 165–82.

by disregarding the wishes of the deceased and keeping slaves freed by will in bondage for long periods of time. In his will, Antoine General left his slave Louis his freedom when he reached the age of twenty-one. In the meantime, General entrusted Louis to his executor, David Cousins. He also instructed Cousins to have Louis taught a trade. Louis remained in the control of Cousins until the age of twenty-eight, at which time he petitioned the court for appointment of a curator to sue for his freedom. The court appointed a notary, Hugh Pedescleaux, as Louis's curator, and he sued for Louis's freedom before the First District Court. Pedescleaux claimed that although Louis was under the age of thirty (the required age for manumission), he deserved his freedom for "meritorious service"; moreover, Pedescleaux argued, Louis was entitled to $2,500 in back wages from age twenty-one to age twenty-eight and for unspecified "ill treatment." He further asserted that Louis had always behaved respectfully to white people. Cousins objected, alleging that Louis did not merit freedom because he had run away several times, was disobedient, and acted "generally disrespectfully toward white persons of this State." Cousins asked the court to deny the manumission. The judge of the First District Court dismissed Cousins with costs of $167.65 and ordered Pedescleaux to take steps to free Louis. Pedescleaux then petitioned the Louisiana legislature to pass an act exempting Louis from the age requirement for freedom. The legislature did so on March 16, 1848. This case went to the Louisiana Supreme Court on the issue of whether Louis needed a curator in order to sue for his freedom. The Supreme Court ruled that he did not: "No appointment of a curator was necessary to enable the plaintiff to maintain an action for his liberty. The *statu liber* (a slave who has acquired the right to freedom at a specific time) is authorized to appear in court unaided, for that purpose." This lawsuit dragged on, with Cousins's widow (Cousins had died near the time of judgment in the lawsuit) also claiming Louis as her slave. Finally, in 1850, Louis enjoyed his freedom unmolested.[2]

2. Louis, *statu liber,* praying to be emancipated, v. Pedescleaux and Cousins, No. 1453, First District Court of New Orleans, 30 May 1848; *Civil Code,* Art. 185, p. 29; "An Act Dispensing the *Statu Liber,* Louis, a Mulatto Man Aged about Twenty-Eight Years, with the Time Prescribed by Law for the Emancipation of Slaves," Act of March 16, 1848, *Louisiana Acts, 1848,* p. 104; *Ex Parte* Louis, 3 La. Ann. 467 (1848). The Second District Court denied the petition of Hannah, a free woman of color, for appointment as curator of her slave daughter, Clementine. Witnesses testified that Hannah lived on Basin Street in a part of town inhabited by prostitutes and that she had a "bad reputation" as "notoriously lewd and abandoned." A

Valcour Bacas, a free man of color, also resisted freeing a slave because he profited from collecting the slave's wages. In 1837, Desirée Hudson, a free woman of color, died, leaving a will that instructed her executor, Bacas, to free her slave, Louis. Bacas did not immediately assume his duties as executor of Hudson's succession. He paid no debts, distributed no legacies, and did not free Louis. Instead he hired Louis out at $15 a month and kept his wages. Hudson's legitimate daughter sued on behalf of Louis for his freedom. She expressed her willingness to surrender her claim to any possible inheritance from Hudson's estate in exchange for Louis's freedom, and she petitioned the court for Louis's back wages and $500 in damages. The daughter and Louis turned to J. C. David to represent them in court. The record of this case ends with the judge of the First District Court ordering Bacas to have an inventory made of the property of the deceased. One assumes that Bacas ultimately found himself forced to free Louis, although he probably never paid damages, even though by that time Louis had remained in slavery an extra twelve years. How the luckless David received a retainer, or whether he did, remains in doubt.[3]

In 1831 Dominique Petit, a free man of color, died, leaving a will in which he instructed his executor to free his slave woman, Marie, and her four sons, Ovide, Theodule, Honoré (alias Auguste), and Quiquite, for "their good and meritorious services." At the time of his death, Petit had debts of approximately $1,000, and he instructed his executor to hire out Marie and her sons until 1836; he intended their wages to pay off his debts. He also named Marie as his universal legatee, who would inherit everything after satisfying the debts of the succession. The executor hired Marie and her sons to E. A. Thompson for five years for $1,000. In 1848 Marie's sons still remained in Thompson's possession and in slavery; Marie had died sometime between 1836 and 1848. Marie's brother-in-law, Doresmon Crocker, a free man of color, petitioned the Second District Court to appoint him curator of the four slaves. He sued for their freedom, stating that they "were natives of Louisiana, always well behaved, respectful to white people, and

witness testified that she had just come out of the workhouse, a place of punishment for lesser crimes, where she had served a one-month sentence for "vagrancy," a code word for prostitution. Another witness alleged that Hannah "drinks from morning to night." Succession of Chappell, No. 7274, Second District Court of New Orleans, filed 10 April 1854.

3. Marcus, f.w.c., on behalf of Louis, c.m., v. Bacas, f.m.c., No. 1882, First District Court of New Orleans, 6 January 1849.

able to support themselves." He asked for $5,000 in back wages for their services from 1836 to 1848. Crocker also alleged that one Sebastian Hiriart had "taken and carried away Theodule out of the jurisdiction of the court by force and violence despite the order of the court," and that Hiriart "asserts the right of a master over him." A witness testified that Hiriart had taken Theodule on board the steamboat *Natchez* to his plantation in Baton Rouge just after Crocker had filed suit for the four slaves' freedom. Crocker asked the court to find Hiriart in contempt of court. Petit's executor replied that Petit could not name Marie as his universal legatee because she had died before gaining her freedom. Therefore, he claimed, her sons could not inherit anything. The record of this case ends here. One of the parties obviously decided not to pursue the matter. Probably Thompson simply released Ovide, Honoré, and Quiquite. Thompson and the executor might have paid nothing for the slaves' services between 1836 and 1848, but the three would doubtless have been satisfied just to gain their liberty. Theodule's fate remains murky.[4]

On occasion the executor of a will granting freedom to slaves simply neglected to take the legal steps to manumit them. Victor Navarre died in 1841, leaving a will instructing his executor to free his slave Caroline "for her good services." Navarre had been deeply in debt shortly before his death, but he had satisfied his creditors before he died. At that time, his succession contained nothing but Caroline, and his executor did not submit the will for probate. As a result, no one freed her. In 1850, J. C. David appeared before the First District Court and asked for the appointment of his client, Louis Amédé Fauvre, as executor of Navarre's succession for the purpose of freeing Caroline. The court did so and accepted the filing of Navarre's will for probate. Although the case record ends here, Fauvre probably freed Caroline without incident.[5]

An Alabama slave won his freedom in the Fourth District Court only to lose his case on appeal. Francis Gay, a resident of Mobile, Alabama, made a will in 1850 leaving his slave, Albert Young, to his white friend Stephen

4. Crocker, f.m.c., v. Benoist, f.m.c., and Thompson, No. 1304, Second District Court of New Orleans, 30 October 1848.

5. Succession of Navarre, No. 4847, First District Court of New Orleans, 5 April 1850. For a case in which debts of a succession prevented the manumission by will of two slaves, Zabeth and Edward, see Aicard, opposing emancipation, No. 5192, First District Court of New Orleans, 17 June 1850.

Charpentier. Gay instructed Charpentier, a barber in Mobile, to take Young to a free state where he could "remain free and emancipated forever." Gay left Charpentier $100 to facilitate taking Young out of Alabama. Instead, in 1851 Charpentier sold Young for $700 to the New Orleans slave dealers McRae, Coffman & Co. To justify his actions, Charpentier wrote a letter saying that Young had proved so difficult to control following Gay's death that he "could do nothing with him." Charpentier claimed that Mobile authorities had arrested Young for gambling, and Charpentier had refused Young's request to get him out of jail, saying that he should be "whipped out." In a statement that is difficult to believe, Charpentier alleged that he had offered to take Young to a free state but that Young had turned him down, and that he had disposed of Young in New Orleans "at his own request." Charpentier stated that he had apprenticed with Gay as a barber for three years and that Gay "esteemed him as his Son and gave me full controle of his property."

After Young's sale to the slave dealers, a remarkable series of sales followed. James White bought Young from McRae, Coffman & Co. in 1852 (price undisclosed); White sold Young to Mary E. H. McClean in 1852 (price unknown), who sold him to William Hughes in 1853 for $1,000. The act of sale from McClean to Hughes described Young as "yellow," twenty-three years old, and a "slave for life." Hughes sold Young to J. C. Egan at the end of 1853 for $300 in cash and fifteen shares of Port Gibson and Grand Gulf Railroad stock alleged to be worth $1,500. In 1854, Young sued Egan in the Fourth District Court for his freedom and for $500 for illegal detention. Egan's attorneys argued that Alabama law prohibited the manumission of slaves by will because the "greater part of the wealth of Alabama consists in her agricultural products. Liberate her slaves, and you sap the foundations of her prosperity." The Second District Court of New Orleans declared Young free, and Egan appealed to the Louisiana Supreme Court.

Justice Alexander Buchanan wrote the decision of the Supreme Court. He ruled that although Alabama law prohibited freeing slaves by will, no law prevented an owner from leaving a slave to another person to take out of the state to free. However, Buchanan reasoned, the will could not force that person to take the slave to a free state. Charpentier could thus do as he pleased with Young. He could hold him as a slave for life in Alabama, sell him to someone else in or out of Alabama, or take him to a free state and manumit him. In reversing the decision of the trial court, Buchanan wrote,

"The policy of Alabama . . . is to prevent the multiplication of the class of free persons of color, by restricting the power of emancipation. The testator . . . did not contemplate that the plaintiff should have his freedom in Alabama, or in any other slaveholding State. It does not seem to be carrying out the intentions of the will, to set the plaintiff free in Louisiana." The case demonstrates the corrupting influence of greed. Concern for his wallet quieted Charpentier's conscience; he chose to pocket the $100 from Gay and the price of Young rather than carry out his friend's wishes.[6]

Free people of color not infrequently became involved in nasty squabbles over slaves freed and left an inheritance by will. John Taylor, a free man of color, lived in New Orleans for several years with his female slave, by whom he had several children. In 1845 he freed her and her children and acknowledged the children as his own. In 1847 he made a will instituting his children as his universal legatees. He died in 1852. In 1857 Mary Jane Taylor, a free woman of color, filed suit in the Fifth District Court, claiming John Taylor's inheritance for her daughter, Medora, on the grounds of her marriage to John Taylor in 1843 in Indiana. As a result of this marriage, Mary Jane asserted, Medora was John Taylor's only lawful heir. The former slave children contested the validity of the marriage and denied the legitimacy and the identity of Medora. The records of this case have vanished, but the newspaper account reported that the jury, "after a few moments consideration," rendered a verdict in favor of Mary Jane Taylor and Medora. The writer noted with considerable satisfaction, "This will place the legitimate heir of John Taylor in possession of a handsome property, which has heretofore been held by his illegitimate children by virtue of the will made in their favor."[7]

Sometimes a person planning to free a slave died before doing so, and the slave fell into the succession as property. In 1852 a free woman of color sold the slave Nancy Walker to Stephen Jarvis, who obligated himself in the act of sale to free her (with permission to remain in the state) as soon as he

6. Young, f.m.c., v. Egan, No. 7462, Fourth District Court of New Orleans, 12 March 1855; No. 4075, 10 La. Ann. 415 (1855). The Fourth District Court refused to let a Mississippi slave use a Louisiana court to sue for her freedom and the Louisiana Supreme Court affirmed the decision. Brown, f.w.c., v. Raby, No. 7850, Fourth District Court of New Orleans, 14 May 1858; No. 5797, 14 La. Ann. 41 (1859).

7. *New Orleans Daily Picayune*, 24 May 1857; *Civil Code*, Arts. 220–1, p. 33. Christian Roselius served as attorney for the former slave children.

could do so. The record noted that Walker, present at the act of sale, "accepts this Act of Freedom with Gratitude." At that time, however, Louisiana law prohibited freed slaves from remaining in the state, and Nancy Walker remained a *statu liber.* In 1855, the same year that Jarvis died, this law was changed. Jarvis's executor refused to free Walker, and she sued for her freedom. In her petition, she alleged that she had always been of good conduct and sober habits. A native of Virginia, she had resided in Louisiana for nineteen years. She asked to be allowed to stay in Louisiana because "every consideration of affection binds her to this State." The jury of the First District Court granted her freedom with permission to remain in the state.[8]

Court records often reveal free people of color denying manumission to slaves freed in wills, especially if the person blocking the manumission stood to gain by keeping the slave in bondage. In 1841 Marie Joseph Castin, a free woman of color, died, leaving a will instructing her husband, Henri Castin, to free her slave boy, Réné Castin, as soon as possible or practicable after her death. She also left the three-year-old boy one-fourth of a piece of property, while designating her husband as her universal legatee. No evidence appears in the record to prove a blood relationship between Marie Joseph Castin, Henri Castin, and Réné Castin, despite the common surname, although the boy was probably the child of Henri by a slave. Henri Castin took no steps to free the child, no doubt because of his tender age. Perhaps Henri Castin also wanted to enjoy the use of the property that his wife had designated for Réné.

In 1856, Réné Castin sued for his freedom. In his petition, he alleged that he practiced "sober and industrious habits, [was] respectful of white people, not guilty of any crimes, and of good reputation." He earned $10 a month with board, and he could "earn an honest life." Réné Castin said he had asked Henri Castin to free him, but Henri had instead had him jailed. The slave further alleged that he feared that Henri Castin would "ill-treat" him or send him out of the jurisdiction of the court. He asked the court to order Henri Castin to take the necessary steps to free him. But Henri refused to appear in court. His attorney filed a letter denying responsibility for his client's nonappearance and saying that he had told Castin to get another

8. Walker, f.w.c., v. Succession of Jarvis, No. 9424, Second District Court of New Orleans, 13 February 1856; "An Act Governing the Emancipation of Slaves in This State," 214–5; "An Act Relative to Slaves and Free Colored People," 387–8.

attorney. Finally Castin answered the lawsuit, stating that Réné Castin had exhibited "disgraceful conduct and refused to obey him" and thus had no right to be free. Furthermore, Henri Castin alleged, he had sent Réné to a shoemaker to learn the trade, and the shoemaker had sent him wages for awhile but had then refused to pay. When Henri Castin had asked that the shoemaker return the slave, Réné Castin had refused to comply; he therefore had had Réné jailed. The record shows no judgment in this case, but it does reveal a seizure for $22 for court costs against Henri Castin on June 1, 1857. By this date the legislature had forbidden all manumissions in Louisiana. The judge of the Second District Court may have designated Réné Castin as a *statu liber*. Or he may have ruled against Réné because he had not attained the age of thirty. In that case, Henri Castin would have continued to enjoy the use of Réné's inheritance and labor until 1864, when the state constitution emancipated Louisiana's slaves.[9]

Executors of wills sometimes tried to thwart the deceased's wishes for unknown reasons. Jean Doubéde died in 1855, leaving a will in which he freed Mary Ann Johns and her three children. Instead of freeing them, the executor, B. Abadie, had them appraised and listed as slaves in the inventory of the deceased's property. Mary Ann Johns claimed her freedom not only on the basis of the will, but on the grounds that she had lived as free for more than ten years with the knowledge of Doubéde and had therefore acquired her freedom by prescription. She called a number of witnesses who testified that Doubéde had treated her as free and had told others that he had fathered her children. One witness testified that he thought Johns and her children "to be white persons" and so did the community. Citing Article 3510 of the *Civil Code,* the judge of the Fifth District Court declared Johns and her children free by prescription.[10]

9. Castin, *statu liber,* v. Castin, f.m.c., No. 10,503, Second District Court of New Orleans, 1 June 1857; *Civil Code,* Arts. 185, 193, pp. 29–30; "An Act to Prohibit the Emancipation of Slaves," p. 55; *Report of the Secretary of State of Louisiana* (Baton Rouge: News, 1902); Constitution of 1864, Tit. I, p.117.

10. Johns, f.w.c., v. Abadie, executor of Doubéde, No. 10,420, Fifth District Court of New Orleans, 13 March 1856; *Civil Code,* Art. 3510, p. 532; *New Orleans Daily Picayune,* 14 March 1856. In 1856, five slaves claimed their freedom on the basis of prescription. Two of them, Sarah (described as an "old woman with a wooden leg") and her daughter, successfully proved that they had lived free for over twenty years. The other three, however, failed to prove freedom by prescription. Ridell v. Lockwood, No. 10,781, Second District Court of New Orleans, 17 October 1856; listed as unreported Supreme Court case No. 4840, 13 La. Ann. xiii (1857).

Purposeful procrastination cost one young slave her freedom until the emancipation of all Louisiana's slaves. Aimé Gillet made a will in 1839 in which he freed his then-six-year-old slave Delphine, the daughter of his slave Mimi. He died in 1847, and his widow refused to free Delphine. In court, witnesses testified that Delphine had a good character, that she treated white persons respectfully, that she had never committed a crime, and that no one had complained about her. Furthermore, Gillet had had other slaves "chastized," but never Delphine. Another witness said that Delphine had become pregnant at a very young age, "so much so that it was the subject of great scandal. The fact of her accompanying her mistress, and going to church with her, aggravated the scandal." Another testified that Delphine had stayed at her house for a few days because she feared that Mrs. Gillet would beat her. Witnesses denied that Gillet had asked a Catholic priest to celebrate a "spiritual marriage between him and Delphine." All of this testimony suggests that Gillet had fathered Delphine's child, which may explain Gillet's wife's refusal to free her.

Detailed testimony in this case gives us a glimpse of the lax enforcement of the strict rules that were supposed to make slaves behave respectfully to whites. One man testified that Delphine liked to frequent a certain apothecary shop, where customers knew her well. "We were in the habit of joking with her at Deloche's [the drugstore] and she told me that if I did not cease she would slap me and she did touch me in the face. I complained of this the next day and she was chastized by her owner." Apparently the witness told Gillet that if he did not whip Delphine, he would report the incident to the recorder. Then he said, "I was in the habit of joking with her. She was not mad when she touched me. She was laughing." The druggist became

---

The following year a question arose in a recorder's court as to whether slaves allowed to live free for more than ten years with their owners' knowledge acquired their freedom outright or just gained the right to take the legal steps to freedom. The woman of color involved had been accused of scratching and assaulting a white man. The issue involved whether she should stand trial as a slave or as a free woman of color. The recorder thought that slaves acquired their freedom outright, but Alexander P. Field, one of the most prominent members of the New Orleans bar, contended that "under such circumstances the freedom of the negro is only inchoate, and though good against the master, the *status* of the party is not so changed as to entitle him or her to all the privileges of a free person of color, nor, indeed, can he or she be so entitled until a suit is instituted in the premises, and the freedom of the party is decided by a court of law." The court agreed with Field and tried the woman as a slave. *New Orleans Daily Picayune,* 9 July 1857.

concerned enough with the level of teasing that "I had to tell them not to take my apothecary shop for a brothel. . . . I did say to Mr. Gillet that he had a slave who was very familiar and pretty bold. . . . The young men who frequented my store at the time were not in the habit of teasing the girls who came there, except Delphine."

In 1854, Delphine sued for her freedom before the Second District Court. She claimed to have repeatedly asked the widow Gillet to free her, but all her pleas had fallen on deaf ears. Gillet admitted the bequest of freedom to Delphine but stated that she had not attained the age of thirty required for manumission. Gillet also declared that she could not positively affirm that Delphine had behaved well for four years before suing for her freedom. Delphine petitioned the trial court for a jury, which rendered a verdict that she had acquired the right to freedom and instructed the widow Gillet to institute proceedings for manumission. The widow appealed to the Louisiana Supreme Court on the grounds that Delphine had not proved that she had behaved well for four years prior to her suit for freedom. The Supreme Court sent the case back to the trial court for a new trial in 1856, stating that "as it concerns the public that none but worthy persons should be admitted to the *status* of freemen, it is our duty to extract the proof" (italics in original).

The jury in the new trial rendered its verdict on February 18, 1857, declaring Delphine "entitled to her freedom as soon as practicable" and ordering the defendant to proceed to free her without delay. The widow Gillet once more appealed. By the time the case reached the Supreme Court of Louisiana, the state legislature had prohibited all manumissions in the state. The Supreme Court ruled that the decision of the trial court "was probably correct, at the date of its rendition. But at that time, there were lawful modes of enfranchising slaves within this State. . . . The laws respecting the manumission of slaves fluctuate with the legislative will. . . . If the law should be changed, her remedy might be revived." As the laws regarding manumission did not change, we can assume that Delphine remained a slave until 1864.[11]

11. Delphine, f.w.c., v. Gillet, No. 7192, Second District Court of New Orleans, 17 May 1855, 18 February 1857; No. 4249, 11 La. Ann. 424 (1856); No. 5154, 13 La. Ann. 248 (1858). For a case in which a slave's bad character (her master had forced her into prostitution) prevented her manumission, see Carmelite, f.w.c., v. Lacaze, No. 4595, Second District Court of New Orleans, 15 December 1851; No. 2506, 7 La. Ann. 629 (1852); Judith Kelleher Schafer,

A court decision rendered on the eve of the Civil War denied freedom to six slaves and an inheritance to three of the six. In 1860, Heloise Nicolaë, a free woman of color, died, leaving freedom to her six slaves. She had no direct heirs, and she made three of those slaves her universal legatees. Her niece, Theresa Duria, a free woman of color, claimed Nicolaë's will null and void; as a collateral heir, she claimed all of the property, including the slaves. Article 908 of the *Civil Code* held that when a person died without "ascending or descending heirs" (i.e., parents and children), collateral heirs (i.e., brothers and sisters) or their descendants would inherit the property of the deceased. The inventory of Nicolaë's property reveals that she died possessed of $3,308.50. The Second District Court ruled in Duria's favor in April 1861, just after the start of the Civil War. Fortunately the six slaves would not have long to wait for their freedom, but they presumably never regained the property willed to them.[12]

The final case involving manumission by will presents the spectacle of a woman of color attempting to pass off her son as the son and legitimate white heir of Lucien Lartigue. Liza Discon, a free woman of color, and her son, Alexandre André, became free in 1849. Discon claimed that her son had died in a steamboat accident: "it has always been her impression that he was blown up by the explosion on said boat." When Lucien Lartigue died, he left a will leaving everything to his sister, Alexandrine Lartigue. When the will came up for probate, one Neville Lartigue claimed to be the legitimate son of Lucien Lartigue; as such, he claimed preference over the deceased's sister for the inheritance. Alexandrine Lartigue responded that Neville could not be a legitimate heir of Lartigue because he was a man of color, and that he and Discon's son, Alexandre André, were the same person. Discon then denied that Neville/Alexandre was her son, claiming that Lucien Lartigue had entrusted Neville to her to raise but that "she never knew Neville to be a colored man." She testified that Neville had a "Gasconne woman" as his natural mother.

The judge of the Second District Court (where the will came under probate), personally testified that Liza Discon "had perjured herself with fraud-

---

Slavery, the Civil Law, and the Supreme Court of Louisiana, 238–9. Lacaze's legal wife divorced him for adultery with a woman of color. Saizer, wife of Jean Lacaze, v. Her Husband, No. 10,842, Fifth District Court of New Orleans, 24 March 1856.

12. Duria, f.w.c., v. Perez, f.m.c., executor of Nicolaë, No. 17,781, Second District Court of New Orleans, 13 April 1861.

ulent intention to defraud the heir of the deceased of the succession." He asked that the court deal with Discon according to law. Alexandrine's attorney warned Discon "not to persist in not telling the truth, that Neville was really her son and a man of color." On November 30, 1861, a First District Court jury convicted Discon of "manifest perjury" but recommended her to the clemency of the court. The judge sentenced her to five years in the state penitentiary at hard labor and a fine of $1,000. Was Alexandre André the illegitimate child of Lucien Lartigue? If so, he could not inherit from Lartigue as a son. The *Civil Code* prohibited children of color from proving paternity from a white father.[13]

One can only speculate about the motives of slaveowners who left wills freeing their slaves. Concern for their eternal destination might have prompted some of these acts; freeing one's slaves was certainly a charitable act. At the same time, many slaveholders did not want to do without the convenience, social standing, and financial security that owning slaves provided during their lifetime. These issues would not matter after death. Why did executors and heirs sometimes refuse to comply with the instructions of the deceased? Freeing a slave involved alienating a significant financial asset from the succession, and the deceased's heirs often proved unwilling to part with such valuable human property. In these cases greed proved stronger than following the wishes of the deceased. Slaves had no choice in those instances except to remain in bondage or find a remedy in court.

13. State v. Discon, f.w.c., No. 15,533, First District Court of New Orleans, 6 December 1861; *Civil Code,* Art. 226, p. 34.

5

MANUMISSION IN NEW ORLEANS, 1855–1857

L ouisiana legislators revised the *Black Code* in 1855 in a statute entitled, "An Act Relative to Slaves and Free Colored Persons." Although this statute reiterated most of the criminal stipulations of the preceding *Black Code*, it contained a sweeping revision of the requirements and procedures for the manumission of slaves. Legislators, weary of the continuous pressure from the public to make exceptions to the 1852 act ordering freed slaves to leave the state, turned responsibility for manumission over to the Louisiana district courts. Slaveholders wishing to free their slaves had to sue the state in those courts. The statute charged district attorneys with the duty "to represent the State, and to urge all legal objections, and to produce such proofs as may be in his power to defeat plaintiff's demand." For this service, district attorneys received $20 for each suit for a slave's freedom filed by the owner. Regardless of the outcome of the suit, the manumitting owner had to pay that fee and all court costs. Owners wishing to free slaves had to state the age, sex, and color of those to be freed. They also had to provide an authenticated act of sale and a certificate from the Registrar of Conveyances to prove clear title to the slave, plus a certificate from the Recorder of Mortgages that no mortgage clouded the title. Lawmakers required slaveholders to establish that the slaves they sought to free were "of good character and sober habits" by producing character witnesses as well as proof that the slaves in question had no criminal convictions. In addition, anyone seeking to free a slave had to advertise in a local newspaper (in accordance with the law of judicial sales) at least five times during the thirty days before filing suit in order to prove that no one opposed the intention to manumit. The notices appeared under the heading of judicial sales because freeing a slave represented a transfer of property from the owner to the slave. Before filing suit, the owner also had to post a bond of $1,000 as a pledge that the slave would not become a public charge if freed and allowed to remain in the state.[1]

Moreover, the 1855 act required a jury trial for all suits for the manumission of slaves, defining them as adversarial procedures against the state. Jurors would not only decide whether slaves should go free, but also whether they would remain in the state. Slaves freed but not permitted to remain in the state could not be considered free until they left, and they would become slaves once again if they ever returned.[2]

The 1855 act went into effect on April 28, and it had an immediate and dramatic effect in New Orleans. Lawmakers had not anticipated the number of suits for freedom that the act would engender. Despite the numerous prerequisites needed for filing a freedom suit, the first suits for freedom in the First Judicial District Court appeared on the docket book during the first week of July. Thereafter they continued at a steady rate in this court, and later in the Second, Fourth, and Fifth Judicial District Courts as well. One historian has argued mistakenly that the Act of 1855 "was never effective insofar as manumission by jury trial was concerned," underscoring the value of the New Orleans district court records, to which he did not have access.[3]

1. The *Black Code* is the name usually given to the 1806 act of the Louisiana Territorial Legislature that constituted the first slave code of American Louisiana. "An Act Prescribing the Rules and Conduct to Be Observed with Respect to Negroes and Other Slaves of This Territory," Act of June 7, 1806, *Louisiana Territorial Acts, 1806*, p. 150–90; "An Act Relative to Slaves and Free Colored Persons," Act of March 15, 1855, *Louisiana Acts, 1855*, Secs. 71–2, 74, pp. 387–8. An "Act of Sale" is a civil law term used to describe real estate transfers. As the *Black Code* and the *Civil Code* classified slaves as real estate, Louisiana law required all sales of slaves to follow the form for real estate sales, including that the act be notarized, witnessed, and registered in the conveyance office. *Black Code*, Sec. 10, p. 154; *Civil Code*, Art. 461, p. 72. See Schafer, *Slavery, the Civil Law, and the Supreme Court of Louisiana*, 185.

2. "An Act Relative to Slaves and Free Colored People," Secs. 73–4, pp. 387–8.

3. Sterkx, *The Free Negro in Antebellum Louisiana*, 147. The Supreme Court of Louisiana ordered the First District Court of New Orleans to cease hearing civil cases and confine itself to its criminal docket. The case that inspired this ruling involved a contested election for the office of district attorney for Orleans Parish. Although the case had nothing to do with the manumission cases in progress, the election may have been contested because the office of district attorney had suddenly become more lucrative. State v. Judge of the First District Court of New Orleans and Benjamin S. Tappan, No. 4440, 11 La. Ann. 187 (March 1856). District courts served as local trial courts in Louisiana, not appellate courts, as in other states.

The trial records generated by these freedom suits give historians an in-depth view of attitudes toward slavery and freedom in New Orleans in the 1850s. None of these cases appear in published court reports, since district courts did not publish reports of their decisions in the antebellum period. Only one of these suits failed because of an outstanding mortgage on the slave. The manumitting owner must have paid off the mortgage, because the court freed the slave in a retrial two months later. Since no suits for freedom in 1855 or 1856 ultimately failed, none reached the Supreme Court of Louisiana, in which case they would have appeared in that court's printed reports. The 1855–56 manumission cases constitute a whole new body of evidence about slavery. The sheer volume of these cases—159 individual suits to free 289 slaves in just over sixteen months—indicates that the suits would have continued, perhaps up to the beginning of the Civil War, had not the Louisiana Supreme Court and the state legislature intervened. These cases present compelling evidence of a pent-up desire of some New Orleanians to free slaves without forcing them to go to Liberia, as well as the determination of some slaves to stay in the state even if it meant remaining in slavery. Indeed, several of these cases specifically state that the slaves seeking freedom would rather remain as slaves in Louisiana than live free in Liberia. And in the only freedom suit in which the jury freed a slave but denied him permission to remain in the state, the plaintiff sued the state again and won both his freedom and permission to stay. In another case, the owner of the slave Marianne declared that she wanted Marianne freed "provided the jury grants her permission of remaining in the State of Louisiana after her manumission and not otherwise." Indeed, the standard wording of the judgments freeing the 289 slaves in these cases usually reads, "forever free from the bonds of slavery, and that she/he be entitled to all the rights and privileges of a free colored person and further that she/he be allowed to remain in the state."[4]

4. Tremoulet v. State, No. 10,094, Second District Court of New Orleans, 7 May 1856, 2 July 1856 (Gothon). Four cases have disappeared and their outcomes remain unknown: Robin, f.w.c., v. State, No. 10,796, First District Court of New Orleans (Hannah), filed 7 January 1856; Dewes, testamentary executor, v. State, No. 10,918 (Zabel and Clem), filed 31 January 1856, transferred to Sixth District Court of New Orleans, 14 May 1856; Askew v. State, No. 10,967, First District Court of New Orleans, filed 15 February 1856 (Hannah); Fabre v. State, No. 10,196, Second District Court of New Orleans, 24 June 1856 (Elizabeth Belsamine). The transcripts of manumission cases are not on microfilm, and they have lain untouched among the records of the main criminal court of New Orleans and three other district courts since 1856.

The district attorney for Orleans Parish, Benjamin S. Tappan, answered each petition for freedom with exactly the same phrase: "The State pleads a general denial and demands strict proof." No evidence exists in any of these suits that Tappan made any other effort to impede the process. The New Orleans District Attorney's office lacked adequate staff, and its employees were consistently overworked. The 1855 act also put Tappan in a odd position. Whether he did his job well and obstructed manumissions or whether he mounted only nominal opposition, he received the $20 fee for each slave—for each individual slave, not for each suit—whom an owner sought to manumit. Why did Tappan fail to fight these suits more vigorously? Perhaps those suing for the freedom of their slaves had assembled all the necessary documents and had followed all the various procedures, making a strong defense useless. Another compelling possibility is grounded in monetary considerations. The $20 fee per slave constituted quite a windfall for the district attorney, who made a regular salary of approximately $600 a year in a part-time position. If Tappan collected $20 for each of the slaves whose owners sued for their freedom in the district courts of New Orleans, as the docket books indicate, he would have made $5,780 in fees at a time when the salary of the chief justice of the Louisiana Supreme Court was $6,000 and that of the district court judges was $2,500.[5]

One must scan the docket and minute books page by page to find cases that the clerk recorded as "Smith v. State of Louisiana" rather than the usual form of criminal cases, "State of Louisiana v. Smith." Almost all of the actual manuscript trial transcripts have survived intact, usually tied up in the same red tape (now faded to brown) with which the clerk tied them when the cases ended more than 140 years ago. For slaves preferring to stay in Louisiana, see Adams, alias Napoleon, f.m.c., v. State of Louisiana, No. 10,770, 11,084, 28 March 1856 (Simon); Duvernay, f.w.c., v. State, No. 9824, Second District Court of New Orleans, 13 February 1856 (Marianne). See also Widow Clay v. State, No. 10,764, First District Court of New Orleans, 3 December 1855 (Justine). For an example of the wording of a standard judgment, see Prieur v. State, No. 10,508, First District Court of New Orleans, 3 December 1855 (Harriet Rollis). All dates in case citations are dates of the final judgment unless otherwise noted.

5. Benjamin S. Tappan was not of the same family as the well-known abolitionist Tappan brothers. Tappan, a native of Tennessee, lived in New Orleans with his wife, Jane, according to the 1860 U.S. Census. The abolitionist Benjamin Tappan, a native of Massachusetts, died in 1857. See Bertram Wyatt-Brown, *Lewis Tappan and the Evangelical War Against Slavery* (Cleveland: Case Western University Press, 1969). Benjamin S. Tappan participated in the Louisiana secession convention in January 1861. He voted for the ordinance of secession from the federal union. *Journal of the Proceedings of the Convention of the State of Louisiana, 1861* (New Orleans: J. O. Nixon, 1861), 4, 231, 233. On fees, see the *Journal of the House of Repre-*

Who were the jurors who seemed so unconcerned about increasing the population of free people of color? We know that those who served in the First District Court received $1 per day for their services. But jurors serving in the other district courts of New Orleans received $1.50 *per case*. Is it possible that jurors of the Second District Court, which heard the second highest number of freedom suits, often running through several of them in a day, felt motivated to rush through as many cases as possible in order to collect higher jurors' fees? The records kept by the clerks of the district courts of the city make an extensive analysis of jurors difficult. Clerks consistently entered jurors' names in the minute books by surname and first initial. Thus W. Thompson, juror, is virtually impossible to discern among the city directory's listings of Walter, William, and Warren Thompson. But of those whose names are unambiguous, all seem to have been working people, some skilled, some clerical, and others manual laborers. The 1850 and 1860 United States censuses indicate that accountants, traders, laborers, carpenters, and tailors served on manumission juries. Clerks of the district courts drew the names of jurors from the voting rolls. Louisiana law required American citizenship and one year's residency in the state to vote, so the men who served on juries were not brand-new immigrants. Why were they so willing to free the slaves who came before them?[6]

One explanation may lie in the changing demographics of New Orleans in the 1850s. Because of the waves of German and Irish immigration, the white population grew dramatically from 1850 to 1860, from 89,459 to 144,601. In contrast, the population of free persons of color, which had declined precipitously from 19,226 in 1840 to 9,905 in 1850, grew only slightly between 1850 and 1860. These two factors meant that while free people of color comprised 8 percent of the city's population in 1850 (down from 18 percent in 1840), they only made up 6 percent of the city's population in 1860, despite a rise in real numbers. Rural legislators' fears of a rapidly in-

sentatives, 1852, Report of the Auditor of Public Accounts, 10. As the Committee on Retrenchment recommended that district attorneys serve a larger jurisdiction with no raise in pay, Tappan's salary probably did not rise substantially by 1855. Constitution of 1852, Tit. III, Art. 63. On the ineffectiveness of the district attorney's office in prosecuting cases, see Rousey, *Policing the Southern City*, 85.

6. "An Act Relative to Juries in the Parish of Orleans," Act of March 15, 1855, *Louisiana Acts, 1855*, pp. 342–3; *Cohen's New Orleans Directory for 1855* (New Orleans: Office of the *Daily Delta*, 1855); U.S. Census, 1850, 1860.

creasing free black population failed to materialize in New Orleans. Indeed, while the statewide population of whites grew by about 200,000 and the slave population by just under 100,000, the statewide population of free people of color rose by just over 1,000. By 1850, furthermore, 49 percent of New Orleans's white population were foreign-born; in the Vieux Carré, supposedly the enclave of the French-speaking creoles, this number rose to 56 percent. Little wonder that white creoles felt more solidarity with the mostly French-speaking creoles of color than with the new immigrants.[7]

Perhaps even more important, a secure place existed in New Orleans society, both socially and economically, for those who gained their freedom. This made a crucial difference. The people of New Orleans, accustomed to association with free people of color, did not fear the increase of the free colored creole population as did those in the country parishes. Manumission throughout the South tended to occur much more often in the cities than in the countryside. One Virginian noted that cities "naturally became liberalized on the subject of emancipation before the interior agricultural communities." As the influx of thousands of Irish and German immigrants in New Orleans accelerated, creoles, black and white, felt besieged. The overwhelmingly French-speaking free creoles of color had much more in common with their white counterparts than they did with the newly arrived, often desperately poor, Irish and Germans. The free black community in New Orleans, as the *Daily Picayune* reported in 1859, "are a sober, industrious and moral class, far advanced in education and civilization, far from being antipathetic to whites." Free persons of color represented some of the most skilled masons, tailors, carpenters, tradesmen, and merchants in the city; they actually monopolized several trades, including plastering and ironworking. Unlike many of the country parishes, which had large slave populations and very small or nonexistent free black communities, New Orleans had a place in society for free people of color. A newly freed slave in an overwhelmingly agricultural parish such as Tensas, which in 1858 had 1,255 whites, 13,285 slaves, and 7 free blacks, would have had difficulty subsisting or merging with the free population that consisted principally of white planters, small farmers, and overseers. In New Orleans in 1850, free people

7. Joseph G. Tregle Jr., "Creoles and Americans," in *Creole New Orleans,* ed. Hirsch and Logsdon, 164–6; Wade, *Slavery in the Cities,* 326.

of color owned an average of $3,800 in real estate alone; by 1860, that average had risen to $4,500.[8]

Evidence in most trial transcripts indicates that slaves freed in New Orleans proved that they were able to support themselves, as the 1855 act required. In one case a witness testified, "He has been supporting his wife and family a long time, besides paying his mistress for his time." In another, "He has a wife and has always supported her." A character witness testified that the slave Agenon Martin worked "as a waiter in the large hotels of this city. . . . I have no doubt he is entitled to his freedom." The man who sold Martin to his present owner had wanted to free him but had not done so because Martin wanted to stay in the state. A Second District Court jury freed François Naba, who for more than two years had run a grocery store worth $200 to $300. Naba testified he had paid for two-thirds of the stock and that he sold between $300 and $400 in groceries each month. He said about himself, "I can calculate and write a little. I need to go to night school." This is remarkable testimony, as Louisiana law forbade slaves from owning any kind of property and prohibited teaching them to read. Naba had paid his master $900 for his freedom, but his master had refused to set him free. The court then allowed Naba to sue for his own freedom. In the Fifth District Court, a witness for the slave Eugene Aram Smith described him as a clerk worth $600 a year because "he can read and write."[9]

8. Quoted in Berlin, *Slaves without Masters*, 143; quoted in David Rankin, "The Impact of the Civil War on the Free Colored Community of New Orleans," *Perspectives in American History* 11 (1977–78): 382; *Report of the Secretary of State of the Census of the State of Louisiana* (Baton Rouge: J. M. Taylor, 1859), 7; U.S. Census, 1850, 1860. Average real estate holdings for Orleans Parish in 1850 and 1860 were calculated from figures given in Loren Schweninger, "Antebellum Free Persons of Color in Postbellum Louisiana," *Louisiana History* 30 (fall 1989): 362–3.

9. Widow Bouny v. State, No. 10,735, First District Court of New Orleans, 3 December 1855 (Gaston Delille); Stewart, f.w.c., v. State, No. 10,785, First District Court of New Orleans, 1 February 1856 (William); Gardère v. State, No. 10,957, First District Court of New Orleans, 20 February 1856 (Agenon Martin); Naba, f.m.c., v. Derbigny, f.m.c., and Naba, f.m.c., v. State, Nos. 9252, 9723, Second District Court of New Orleans, 7 November 1855, 13 February 1856 (François Naba); Cocks v. State, No. 11,130, Fifth District Court of New Orleans, 27 May 1856 (Eugene Aram Smith); "An Act to Punish the Crimes Therein Mentioned, and for Other Purposes" (prohibiting teaching slaves to read and write), Act of March 16, 1830, *Louisiana Acts, 1830*, p. 96; *Digest of 1808*, Tit. VI, Chap. III, Art. 17, p. 40; *Civil Code*, Arts. 174–5, p. 27.

Trial transcripts indicate that twenty-one slaves freed by district court juries had purchased themselves. Some slaveowners required that slaves purchasing themselves reimburse their owner for their value plus interest. A few slaveowners who freed their slaves did not require such payment but required them to pay court costs and attorney's fees, both of which could be quite expensive. Each slave freed incurred the $20 fee for the district attorney, the $12 jury tax, and assorted other court costs. Usually the court costs for freeing one slave ran to about $50, not including attorney's fees. The docket books did not ordinarily record attorneys' fees, but the record in one case indicates a charge of $50. In an era when a dollar a day was the standard pay for laborers in New Orleans, court costs and attorney's fees in excess of $100 could be a formidable obstacle to a newly freed person.[10]

As the 1855 act required slaves to have exhibited "good character and sober habits," many cases contain testimony to that effect. A First District Court jury heard one witness testify about the slave Harriet, "She was the favorite and confidential servant of my niece." Another testified, "She was treated in my family as a servant entrusted to more than the ordinary confidences." In a different case, First District Court jurors heard a witness testify that the slave Nicolle "is the pet of Mr. Verret's family." One character witness said that he believed the slave Maranthe "incapable of doing anything wrong." A witness who knew the slave Damas Bonsignac testified that Bonsignac's master "treated him more like a friend than a slave," going on to say that Bonsignac "voluntarily followed his master from St. Domingo. He can oversee a small sugar plantation. . . . He is remarkably honest and faithful." A witness told the jury of the slave Justine's care of her master, nursing him through a long illness with "remarkable devotedness and self-sacrifice." In his suit to free Lucille, Paul Luciani stated, "I am not a married man. My purpose in giving freedom to Lucille is for treating me so well when I was Sick with yellow fever and other sickness." The attorney for the

10. See, for example: Laribeau v. State, No. 10,681, First District Court of New Orleans, 3 December 1855 (Overton); Dunbar, f.w.c., v. State, No. 11,311, Fifth District Court of New Orleans, 25 August 1856 (Annah). The manumitting mistress charged 8 percent interest to John, who purchased himself as recorded in Lathrop v. State, No. 10,437, Second District Court of New Orleans, 3 July 1856 (John); John also had to pay court costs and fees. One slave had to pay the attorney's fees: Peieira v. State, No. 10,678, First District Court of New Orleans, 3 December 1855 (Zulmé). The $50 attorney's fee appears in the Naba case, above; Wade, *Slavery in the Cities*, 42.

slaves Louis and Titine, who was also Titine's godfather, described her as a "perfect subject," but another witness said that Louis had done "some little grifting stealing." Despite this damaging testimony, the jury voted to free both. Jurors of the Fifth District Court freed a slave who had run away—hardly evidence of good character—because they believed that she was already entitled to her freedom. In two cases, character witnesses attempted to reassure jurors that if freed, the slaves in question would not set a bad example for the creoles of color or slaves in the city. One testified that the slave Nancy Watkins "would give good example to the slave population"; another stated that if freed with permission to stay in the state, the slaves Zélime and Eugène "would not be a bother to the community."[11]

The jurors of the New Orleans district courts probably saw little difference between the seventy free persons of color who won their suits to free their slaves and the newly freed slaves themselves. If their owners were their relatives, their new status probably had little impact on their day-to-day lives. Except for the legal ramifications of possible sale for the debts of the owner, slaves owned by their family members lived as free. But not all slaves freed before the district court by free people of color in 1855 and 1856 were owned by relatives. In those cases, manumission resulted in a change of status as dramatic as that experienced by the freed slaves of whites.

Two cases demonstrate the strength of family ties among free creoles of color, the solidarity of the free black community, and the genuine concern of some whites for blacks' welfare. In the first, James Ross, the white executor of a deceased free man of color named Richard Green, sued for the freedom of Green's slave wife, Suzan, and their three children. Green, a barber, had left instructions in his will for Ross to free his wife and children as soon as it became legal for them to remain in the state. Green died after the 1852

11. McCulloch v. State, No. 10,663, First District Court of New Orleans, 3 December 1855 (Harriet); Schmitt v. State, No. 10,682, First District Court of New Orleans, 29 November 1855 (Damas Bonsignac); Verret v. State, No. 10,933, First District Court of New Orleans, 16 February 1856 (Nicolle); Widow Clay v. State, No. 10,764, First District Court of New Orleans, 3 December 1855 (Justine); Luciani v. State, No. 10,808, First District Court of New Orleans, 3 February 1856 (Lucille); Livaudais v. State, No. 10,772, First District Court of New Orleans, 20 February 1856 (Louis and Titine); Skipworth v. State, No. 11,133, Fifth District Court of New Orleans, 30 May 1856 (Hilsey or Elsay); Everard v. State, No. 11,068, Fourth District Court of New Orleans, 5 May 1856 (Nancy Watkins); Widow Abat v. State, No. 11,029, First District Court of New Orleans, 5 March 1856 (Zélime and Eugène).

act became law, and Ross held the succession open because he could not comply with the terms of the will. After the Act of 1855, Ross filed suit to free Suzan and her children. Ross and the attorney in the case, Frank Haynes, put up the $4,000 bond required by law to ensure that Suzan and her children would not become a public charge. Witnesses described Suzan as sober, industrious, and able to support herself as a nurse. Two physicians testified as to her character. The First District Court jury freed Suzan and her children with permission to remain in the state.[12]

The other case involves a slave mother's willingness to give up her daughter in order that she might gain her freedom. Eugène Ducatel gave his five-year-old slave, Marie Felicité, to Justine Boisblanc, a childless free woman of color, to raise with the express condition that Boisblanc free the girl as soon as possible. The child's mother—who belonged to Ducatel—gave up her child in order that Marie Felicité would be freed. A witness testified, "I do not believe there is a better woman in the State. Felicité is very well brought up by Justine." Another stated, "Felicité is a very good little girl. She waits at table." On March 3, 1856, a First District Court jury freed Felicité with permission to remain in the state.[13]

Despite their small numbers in the city's total population, free people of color made up nearly half of all those who freed their slaves in New Orleans under the Act of 1855. The trial records describe almost 60 percent of newly freed slaves as mulattoes, reflecting the demographics of the city; the overwhelming majority of free people of color were mulattoes. Females outnumbered males almost two to one in the total number of slaves freed, and three to one if only counting adult slaves. These lopsided figures reflect the population of slaves and free people of color in the city as a whole. Women of color made up 67 percent of the free black population and 66 percent of the slave population. And demonstrating the effect of the Act of 1852, which required manumitted slaves to depart the state for Liberia, the owners of at least one-fourth of the slaves freed in 1855 and 1856 had sold them after the passage of the 1852 act with the express condition that their manumis-

---

12. James Ross, testamentary executor of Green, f.m.c., v. State of Louisiana, No. 10,413, First District Court of New Orleans, 11 November 1855 (Suzan, Henry, Luda, Gardiner). The record does not indicate why Green did not emancipate Suzan and her children between the time he purchased her in 1837 and the passage of the 1852 act.

13. Boisblanc, f.w.c., v. State, No. 10,956, First District Court of New Orleans, 3 March 1856 (Marie Felicité, alias Evelina).

sion not take place until they could remain within the state. Remarkably, every slave freed by the New Orleans district courts in 1855 and 1856 received permission to remain in the state. This permission became so routine that the Fifth District Court had a printed form with blank spaces for the clerk to fill in the name of the manumitting owner and the name of the slave, but with the words "with permission to stay in the state" in print.[14]

Many trials held in the Second and Fifth District Courts seem to have been largely *pro forma*. When put into a national context, this is extraordinary. As proslavery fervor intensified, many southerners denounced manumission as harmful to slaves. A Tennessee legislator exclaimed, "The responsibilities of freedom are too great for them, hence the man that emancipates his slave entails upon him a curse." At a time when the political crisis over slavery was at its height and many people in the South considered manumission an act of outright sedition, juries in New Orleans methodically and speedily freed scores of slaves and allowed them to remain in Louisiana. In some instances the courts ran through several cases in rapid succession on the same day. For example, essentially the same jury in the Second District Court heard nine manumission cases on May 7, 1856, the same month in which the congressional debate over the civil war in Kansas became so heated that Congressman Preston Brooks of South Carolina caned Senator Charles Sumner of Massachusetts until he fell, bleeding and unconscious, to the floor of the United States Senate. During the summer of 1856, as the national crisis over slavery deepened, twelve jurors in New Orleans gave Independence Day a new meaning. Over the two days before July 4, 1856, one jury, led by foreman Charles Lafitte, freed forty-two slaves in twenty cases. In all of these trials, the clerk's notation in the minute book reads,

14. David C. Rankin, "The Tannenbaum Thesis Reconsidered: Slavery and Race Relations in Antebellum Louisiana," *Southern Studies* 18 (spring 1979): 21; Wade, *Slavery in the Cities,* 329–30. For cases of manumission with permission to remain in the state, see: Labiche v. State, No. 10,489, First District Court of New Orleans, 30 August 1855 (Marie Louise); Montreuil v. State, No. 9820, Second District Court of New Orleans, 2 December 1856 (Louise); Forstall, testamentary executor of Forstall, f.w.c., v. State, No. 9614, Fourth District Court of New Orleans, 24 January 1856 (Mary); Hagan v. State, No. 11,074, Fifth District Court of New Orleans, 23 May 1856 (slaves Lucy Ann Chateaur, her two children, Fredrika and Dolly, and William Loundes). John Hagan was a prominent slave trader who had slave pens in Charleston and New Orleans. Hagan had purchased these slaves for $50 on 19 January 1856 and promised to free them within three months. The form appears in Goines, f.m.c., v. State, No. 11,310, Fifth District Court of New Orleans, 18 August 1856 (Marthe).

"After hearing the evidence and argument of Counsel, the Jury received a charge from the Court, and *without leaving their seats,* rendered the following verdict, to wit; Verdict for the slave [name], with permission to remain in the state" (italics mine). In all, Second District Court juries decided twenty-seven cases freeing forty-two slaves "without leaving their seats." A Fifth District Court jury heard ten suits for freedom on August 18, 1856, and freed twenty-two slaves without retiring to deliberate. Seven trials that resulted in freedom for seventeen slaves had the petition filed, the testimony heard, the certificates presented, and the judgment rendered all on the same day, during which the jurors did not leave their seats to arrive at a verdict.[15]

In 1856 the Louisiana legislature considered a bill to change the state's manumission policy. The *Daily Picayune* expressed alarm at the growing population of free people of color, who were a "plague and a pest in the community." The editorial specifically criticized the Act of 1855 and the volume of manumissions that it had sparked in New Orleans. The writer argued that it had been a wise policy to require freed slaves to leave the state. Previously, emancipation was a special reward for a particularly meritorious slave. But now, he observed, the effect of the Act of 1855 "has been to renew, in an aggravated form, all the evils which the act of 1852 was designed to abolish. The number of emancipations has increased greatly. Almost every parish paper comes to us filled with notices of the intent to emancipate slaves, with intention to remain in the State; and our city courts are filled with the same sort of applications. Hundreds are thus made free and thrown upon the community—in most cases without any special merit." The editorialist pointed out that many of those freed went to New Orleans, swelling its "worthless population." The article ended by calling upon the legislature to forbid the manumission of slaves unless they left the state immediately after gaining their liberty.[16]

Two 1856 decisions of the Supreme Court of Louisiana affected the

15. Tennessee legislator quoted in Berlin, *Slaves without Masters,* 368; for court cases, see: Henry v. State, No. 10,152, Second District Court of New Orleans, 2 July 1856 (Eliza); Fox, f.m.c., v. State, No. 10,153, Second District Court of New Orleans, 2 July 1856 (Françoise, alias Peggy); Walker, f.m.c., v. State, No. 11,309, Fifth District Court of New Orleans, 18 August 1856 (Lucinda); Brewerton v. State, No. 11,314, Fifth District Court of New Orleans, 18 August 1856 (Delia).

16. *New Orleans Daily Picayune,* 8 March 1856.

manumission proceedings in the district courts of New Orleans. In April the Supreme Court decided *State* v. *Judge of the First District Court of New Orleans,* which ordered the First District Court to confine itself exclusively to its criminal docket. This decision did not quash the freedom suits already filed but not concluded in the First District Court, however; the clerk of court transferred all of the pending manumission cases to the other district courts. Four cases went to the Second District Court, six to the Fourth District, and six to the Fifth District. All of the reassigned cases ended in freedom for the slaves in question, with permission to remain in the state. Those who still wanted to free their slaves began to file freedom suits in other district courts. In all, 74 suits involving 127 slaves originated in the other district courts, all of which freed the slaves brought before them with permission to remain in the state.[17]

On December 8, 1856, the Supreme Court announced its judgment in *State* v. *Harrison,* an appeal of a conviction of a slave for murder. Although not a direct response to the flood of manumissions in the New Orleans district courts, the Supreme Court ruling declared the Act of 1855 unconstitutional. The court based its decision on the Louisiana constitution of 1852, which prohibited legislative acts from encompassing more than one object. In a remarkable defense of the status of free persons of color, Justice Alexander Buchanan explained that "in the eyes of the Louisiana law there is, with the exception of political rights, social privileges, and the obligations of jury and militia service, all the difference between a free man of color and a slave, that there is between a white man and a slave." Buchanan noted that the decision did not create any substantial void in Louisiana slavery laws, since most of the 1855 act simply reiterated preexisting statutes, "with the exception of sections 71, 72, and 74, which treat of the mode of proceeding for the emancipation of slaves."[18]

How did Buchanan's ruling affect emancipation suits already in prog-

17. State on relation of Fonte, praying for a writ of prohibition, v. The Judge of the First District Court of New Orleans and Benjamin S. Tappan, No. 4440, 11 La. Ann. 187 (1856).

18. State v. Harrison, No. 4464, 11 La. Ann. 722 (December 1856). The Constitution of 1852, Article 115, states, "Every law enacted by the Legislature shall embrace but one object, and that shall be expressed in the title." See Wayne M. Everard, "Louisiana's 'Whig' Constitution Revisited: The Constitution of 1852," in *In Search of Fundamental Law: Louisiana's Constitutions, 1812–1974,* ed. Edward F. Haas and Warren M. Billings (Lafayette: Center for Louisiana Studies, 1993), 37–51.

ress? Did it mean that the 289 slaves already freed would be compelled to return to slavery? In an editorial on December 10, the *Daily Picayune* recognized that the decision in *Harrison* was of the "greatest importance to the community," arguing, "In Consequence, the new process of emancipating slaves falls to the ground, is null, and with it all suits now in progress for the emancipation of slaves. How it will affect those already free, is more than we can at present determine." The docket books of the courts of the Second, Fourth, and Fifth Districts reveal that they ceased to process all freedom suits in progress on the day of the Supreme Court's decision. This left seventeen suits for the freedom of thirty-seven slaves in limbo, those wishing to free slaves in the future without recourse, and the status of those already freed unclear.[19]

Just after the Supreme Court's decision in *Harrison,* rumors of an interstate slave insurrection circulated in the lower South during the Christmas holidays. On the day after Christmas, the *Daily Picayune* published an article that reported the arrest and trial of the slave John in Assumption Parish for plotting to incite a rebellion among slaves. The jury found him guilty, and the judge sentenced him to two months in the parish jail, 350 lashes, and two years in irons. Although most southern newspapers suppressed news that might inspire slaves to revolt, the *Picayune* broke with this policy two days before Christmas by taking notice of rumors circulating about the South of unrest among slaves. It placed the blame for a possible slave revolt squarely on the Republican Party. Warning of the possibility of an imminent slave uprising, the newspaper published a front-page editorial instituting a campaign to encourage the legislature to pass stricter laws concerning slave discipline. As the editorial warned, "from the various quarters in many States, there are evidences of a very unsettled state of mind among the servile population—a vague impression among them that a critical change in

19. *New Orleans Daily Picayune,* 10 December 1856. In the same issue, the *Picayune* printed without comment, "STAMPEDE OF FREE NEGROES. The *Nashville Patriot* of the 2nd inst. says: The free negroes at Murfreesboro took a compulsory stampede from that place last week. Their depredations had become insufferable to the citizens, and their pernicious influence among the slave population made them a serious grievance. Self-preservation compelled the whites to stringent measures to get rid of them, and a general stampede was the consequence." For district court cases, see: Avegno, f.w.c., v. State, No. 11,106, Second District Court of New Orleans, filed 21 November 1856 (Therésa); Petron v. State, No. 13,337, Fifth District Court of New Orleans, filed 26 August 1856 (Josephine and four children).

their condition is at hand, to be effected by a powerful party in the United States [the Republican Party], which temporarily defeated at the polls, is ready to give them the help of arms and troops when they shall undertake to rise on their own account." The date of the uprising, the *Picayune* speculated, was to be Christmas Eve. Rumors of the same plot abounded in Kentucky, Arkansas, Tennessee, Mississippi, and Texas. The editorial predicted that when the legislature convened, the "whole subject of the Black Code will doubtless be taken up, with a view to adapting it more efficiently to the wants and developments of the times."[20]

The *Picayune* also wrote that a "return [is] called for, back to the strictest rigor of police law . . . for the maintenance and subordination among the blacks, and the keeping of them from the contaminating influences . . . at work for mischief. . . . We have in New Orleans a large amount of the class of population, most likely to be influenced by these evil counsels. . . . They form a facile medium of communication with the slaves."[21]

On January 2, 1857, in an article entitled, "The Negro Rumors," the *Picayune* admitted that the holidays had passed with no trouble from the black community. It now claimed, "There was never any fear of a concerted attempt to rise, or a general insubordination." Indeed, the *Picayune* bragged, New Orleans slaves "are, in general, contented, cheerful and happy, beyond the laboring classes of any other nation under the sun." However, the article warned, the weakness of slaves' minds demanded new and stricter laws to keep them from going astray: "It is the greatest mercy to the negro . . . to preserve him from contact with these adversaries, who would mislead him to his inevitable ruin; and the time has evidently come for putting the whole system of slave police and slave discipline into a new order. . . . A short and terrific doom should be made to fall, with certainty, on every man who . . . lends himself to the promotion of discontent and insubordination among the blacks, or wantonly disturbs the peace of Southern communities."[22]

The Louisiana legislature convened in regular session on January 19, 1857. In his address to a joint session of the House and Senate, Governor Robert C. Wickliffe indicated his increased hostility to free people of color

20. *New Orleans Daily Picayune*, 23, 26 December 1856; Judith Kelleher Schafer, "The Immediate Impact of Nat Turner's Insurrection in New Orleans," *Louisiana History* 21 (fall 1980): 361–76.

21. *New Orleans Daily Picayune*, 23 December 1856.

22. Ibid., 2 January 1857.

as well as slaves. He warned against increased immigration of free people of color from other states, and he urged passage of a law to remove all free blacks from the state because of their "pernicious effect on the slave population." On January 28, Senator Henry H. Hyams of Orleans Parish introduced a bill to prohibit all manumissions. Hyams stated that passage of the act would "destroy at one full swoop, the power which the law confers on courts and juries." The *Daily Picayune* expressed its delight that no strong opposition to the bill had surfaced since the "necessity for preventing the further accumulation of a worthless and dangerous free black population was recognized by all." Another *Picayune* article fulsomely proclaimed, "Already has the Senate stricken at the root of the great evils of the lax system under which the State has so long labored. . . . It [the proposed act banning all manumissions] does away with all of the tortuous forms which have resulted in creating so large and so worthless a free black population." Senator G. W. Munday of East Feliciana Parish asked for an amendment to the bill allowing slaves who reported insurrection plots to gain an exemption from the prohibition of manumission. Hyams responded that the only exception he would accept was saving the life of the master or the master's family. Munday noted that "it was but a few short months ago that a conspiracy existed among the servile population," and only the "timely information given by a faithful and devoted servant" had prevented its success.[23]

Senator M. Ryan of Rapides Parish agreed with Munday, stating that although he would place "every possible legal check in the way of indiscriminate emancipation," he favored making an exception for slaves who revealed insurrection plots. Furthermore, he blamed the New Orleans district courts for making Hyams and others believe that only a total prohibition of manumission could safeguard the state. He explained that while the courts and juries of Orleans Parish might be lax in official morality, this situation did not apply to his own parish. Ryan claimed that not one slave had gained freedom in the Rapides Parish district court—a telling fact that demonstrates what a huge gulf existed between rural and urban slavery. Ryan went on to complain that Hyams's act did not prohibit legislative manumission,

23. *Official Reports of the Senate of Louisiana: Session of 1857* (New Orleans: John Claiborne, 1857), 11; *Official Journal of the House of Representatives of the State of Louisiana: Session of 1857* (New Orleans: John Claiborne, 1857), 7; *New Orleans Daily Picayune*, 22, 30 January 1857.

which invited a return to a practice that he described with contempt: "a system of log-rolling will be introduced; these halls will be crowded with interested parties. . . . [T]he regular course of legislation will be impeded, and in short there will be a return to that state of things which might be witnessed here previous to the passage of the law of 1855—a state of things so harassing and annoying that the legislature, to escape from it, threw the power of emancipating into the hands of the courts."[24]

Ryan warned against adding an exception for slaves who performed meritorious services for their owners, asserting, "For the smallest service, on the part of a slave, rendered the State—even the preservation of a snag boat—some cunning attorney might claim that he was entitled to his freedom." The bill to prohibit all manumissions of slaves except those who informed on slave conspiracies passed the Senate on January 27. On the same day, Senator Henry W. St. Paul of Orleans Parish introduced a bill to allow slaveowners to file suits to reclaim as slaves any persons that the New Orleans courts had freed under the Act of 1855. He explained, "The judgment of the Supreme Court rendered some legislation necessary to settle the status of the slaves emancipated from the time of the passing of the act to the rendering of the judgment." The Senate sent St. Paul's act to the Judiciary Committee, over his strenuous objections. As he complained, "A pile of bills . . . had already been referred to that committee. There they seem to lie entombed, and whether they would break the cerements of their resting place before the day of general resurrection, was a question of which he entertained some doubt." The bill died in committee, and those freed under the terms of the Act of 1855 remained free. We have no record of the Judiciary Committee's failure to recommend the bill, but as Article 189 of the *Civil Code* held that an "emancipation, once perfected, is irrevocable," St. Paul's bill clearly would have been in conflict with the law.[25]

In 1857 the House of Representatives also considered a bill to prohibit slave manumission except in cases in which slaves saved the life of their master or their master's family or revealed a slave conspiracy. Representative Julien T. Hawkins of St. Martin Parish proposed an amendment requiring any slave freed for saving the life of his or her owner to leave the state rather

24. *Journal of the Senate, 1857,* 12.
25. Ibid., 12, 18. Snag boats were used to free Louisiana's bayous and rivers from snags. *Civil Code,* Art. 189, p. 29.

than increase the local population of free people of color. He avowed, "The emancipation of negroes is spreading and shedding its blighting influence, like the Upas tree, over Louisiana and the whole South. I hold, Sir, that the negro is not benefitted by emancipation . . . by turning him loose upon the world in his old age to subsist by his own exertions. I am in favor of putting a full stop to all emancipations." Representative Haynes objected to Hawkins's amendment, saying, "The master feels a sentiment of gratitude toward the slave who has rendered these acts of fidelity." Representative Thomas Jenkins Semmes of Orleans also disapproved of requiring freed slaves to depart for Africa, declaring, "I believe slavery to be the best condition for the African race. If the freedom of that race is a boon, then our slavery system must be a lie. Slaves do not regard freedom as a boon if they are to be sent away. They have a repugnance to wooly-headed government." Hawkins said that he would rather see the legislature flooded with petitions for manumissions rather than make exceptions to the prohibition against freeing slaves. In fact, he affirmed, he would drive all free people of color from the state—people he termed a "nuisance, and operating insidiously upon our slave population"—but for the protection given them in the Louisiana Purchase.[26]

Representative D. L. Beecher of Jefferson Parish suggested that the wholesale manumissions in the New Orleans district courts called for a total prohibition of manumission. He said, "Under the former law granting the courts the authority to emancipate, our courts were crowded, especially in the City, and hundreds upon hundreds of slaves were emancipated—1,500 are said to have been emancipated—notwithstanding the guard thrown around it and the heavy costs to be incurred." Beecher continued, "I was informed by a gentleman from New Orleans that a negro woman who had been sent from Virginia for poisoning her mistress was emancipated in New Orleans, and the District Attorney told me that, despite of [sic] everything, the juries would emancipate."[27]

The following day, Representative George C. Lawrason of Orleans amended the bill to prohibit all manumissions with no exceptions whatsoever. Hawkins spoke in favor of this amendment, citing the "blighting effects

26. *Journal of the House, 1857,* 81. The upas tree, a member of the mulberry family, is extremely poisonous.

27. Ibid., 81.

of emancipation . . . over the whole State." Representative E. Wooldridge of Orleans Parish asked his fellow legislators to address the problem of *statu liberi*, slaves who had acquired the right to be free but whose owners had not yet freed them. He spoke eloquently of a "faithful old shoeblack" in New Orleans who had saved the life of his master's child and who would find himself without recourse if the legislature prohibited all manumissions; he decried such an injustice "[h]ere in Louisiana, where we properly appreciate slavery, where we know how to treat our slaves, and where we understand the institution. We cannot pass a law to impair the validity of contracts. The Supreme Court has said that slaves can contract with their masters for freedom. I ask the lawyers of the House to consider this. This law impairs hundreds of contracts with slaves now *statu liber*. Hasty action on this subject . . . would furnish rich food for Northern abolitionists—would be trumpeted over the whole land." At the end of the day, the House voted 45 to 17 to pass the bill, stripped of all amendments. A joint House and Senate committee agreed on the House version of the bill, and on March 6, 1857, the possibility of legal manumission ended for Louisiana's approximately 300,000 slaves. Although the legislature could have passed a new manumission law that reiterated the provisions for slave manumission contained in the Act of 1855, the legislators' attitudes toward manumission had hardened. In no small part, the freeing of 289 slaves in New Orleans contributed to their determination to prohibit all manumissions.[28]

Even before the Act of 1857 passed, the *Daily Picayune* had published an editorial suggesting that legislators should prohibit manumission. Noting that the new laws had greatly increased the number of freed slaves with permission to remain in the state, the *Picayune* remarked, "Almost every parish paper which comes to us is filled with notices of the intention to emancipate slaves with the intention to remain in the State; and our city courts are filled with the same sort of application. Hundreds are thus made free and thrown on the community—in most cases without any special merit—and the State gets an increase of a worthless population—more than its share falls upon the city of New Orleans."[29]

In the 1858 term of the state legislature, lawmakers introduced five petitions for the manumission of slaves. The Judiciary Committee gave them all

28. Ibid., 83–4; "An Act to Prohibit the Emancipation of Slaves," 55.
29. *New Orleans Daily Picayune*, 20 March 1857.

an "adverse report" or "laid them on the table indefinitely." Henry St. Paul, chair of the Judiciary Committee, justified the committee's actions by explaining, "[We] must sternly adhere to the present wise policy of this and [the] preceding Legislature, in refusing to increase the number of free colored people residing in this State."[30]

Still, the 1857 law prohibiting manumission did not entirely stop owners wishing to free their slaves from doing so. Eight months before the Civil War began, Charles Gardner made a renunciation in favor of his slave Adele and her children. Renunciation is an old term meaning divesting oneself of a right, in this case a right of property; it is an affirmative act of divestiture. The Conveyance Office records show that Gardner renounced the right to hold Adele and her children as slaves and gave her permission to leave the state to satisfy Louisiana law. He also gave her leave to sue for her freedom in court when the law might permit such a suit. In a remarkable statement, Gardner promised to let Adele continue "under his protection" if she refused to leave the state.[31]

Even after 1857, manumission continued in practice and by a few private arrangements. Some owners who wished to free their slaves simply allowed them to live as free. But slaves whose owners permitted this quasi-freedom lived precarious lives. They not only faced seizure and sale in the event of their owner's death or debts, but their very freedom could be challenged at any time.

30. *Official Journal of the Senate of Louisiana: Session of 1858* (Baton Rouge: J. M. Taylor, 1858), 11, 19, 24, 58, 40, 88, 104. In the only reported vote to table a petition for manumission indefinitely, legislators voted 17–2 in favor.

31. Conveyance Office Records, 17 July 1860, 82:342; Black, ed., *Black's Law Dictionary*, 1021.

View of Jackson Square and St. Louis Cathedral in New Orleans. To right of the cathedral in this image is the Presbytere, which housed the district courts.
Special Collections, Howard-Tilton Memorial Library, Tulane University

Sale of estates, pictures, and slaves in the Rotunda, New Orleans.
The Historic New Orleans Collection, Acc. No. 1953.149

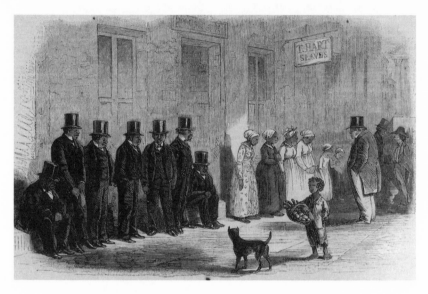

A New Orleans slave pen before an auction.
The Historic New Orleans Collection, Acc. No. 1958.43.24

Slaves cleaning a street in the faubourg Ste.-Marie, New Orleans.
Note the punishment collar on the slave woman near the fence.
The Historic New Orleans Collection, Acc. No. 1937.2.3

Slaves in transit.
Special Collections, Howard-Tilton Memorial Library, Tulane University

Checking slave passes at night.
Special Collections, Howard-Tilton Memorial Library, Tulane University

Laurent Millaudon, whose slave Milky sued for her freedom after she accompanied
Millaudon's wife to France. The First District Court of New Orleans upheld her claim.
Special Collections, Howard-Tilton Memorial Library, Tulane University

Bernard de Marigny, a scion of one of New Orleans's wealthiest families. His slave
Ajoie was declared free by the court after her return from France. Marigny did not
appear to contest her suit, and it is not clear that he wanted her to remain enslaved.
Special Collections, Howard-Tilton Memorial Library, Tulane University

Attorney Christian Roselius, who successfully represented both slaves and masters
before the New Orleans district courts and the Louisiana Supreme Court.
Special Collections, Howard-Tilton Memorial Library, Tulane University

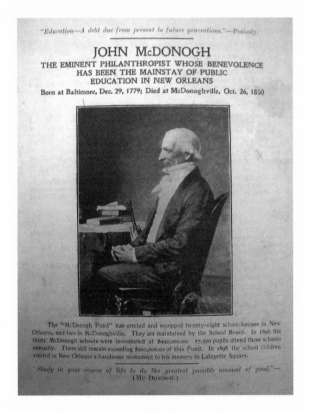

The immensely wealthy New Orleans philanthropist John McDonogh, who allowed
dozens of his slaves to buy or work for their freedom—although he
continued purchasing slaves himself.
Special Collections, Howard-Tilton Memorial Library, Tulane University

The Federal fleet in the Mississippi River at New Orleans in May 1862.
Special Collections, Howard-Tilton Memorial Library, Tulane University

Men of the First Louisiana Native Guards under the American flag at Fort
Macombe. The Native Guards, made up of free men of color, originally formed
in order to fight for the Confederacy. After Union capture of New Orleans,
they entered the service of the United States.
Special Collections, Howard-Tilton Memorial Library, Tulane University

6

THE STRUGGLE TO STAY FREE

The struggle to remain free often proved quite as challenging as the fight to become free. Whites often attempted to use the law to harass and even enslave free persons of color. In many instances the law failed to protect them. Even when they won, the district courts often assessed court costs on them, a kind of racial tax. Not wanting to take any chances of losing their freedom, most free persons of color whose freedom came into question felt the need to hire attorneys to represent them. Maintaining one's freedom thus could prove expensive as well as harrowing. The records of the district courts give clear evidence of the vulnerability of free people of color to legal harassment. Free people of color had to prove their freedom over and over again; they lived in the shadow of losing it, suddenly, permanently, and in a humiliating manner.

In 1850, New Orleans had 9,905 free people of color; ten years later, that number had risen to 10,939. Although free people of color had rights unknown to slaves, they still suffered a number of serious legal disabilities. For example, they could commit the crime of "insulting a white person." Section 40 of the *Black Code* warned that free persons of color "ought never insult or strike white people, nor presume to conceive themselves equal to the white; but on the contrary that they ought to yield to them on every occasion, and never speak or answer to them but with respect, under penalty of imprisonment according to the nature of the offense." The *Black Code* made this offense a crime unique to free persons of color, in a telling reminder that they should not equate freedom with equality. If white persons insulted each other, they could be charged with assault or even assault and battery, but never with "insulting a white person." The First District Court heard dozens of "insulting" cases between 1846 and 1862, and the recorders' courts heard even more. The usual penalty for conviction of "insulting" involved a week or so in parish prison or the workhouse and the payment of court costs. Often the prosecutor submitted a *nolle prosequi* (to stop the prosecution) in these cases because the complaining witness declined to proceed, but the free person of color usually had to pay court costs whether convicted or not. The payment functioned as a reminder that the free person of color had stepped out of his or her place and had to be penalized for it. The penalties for "insulting" did little to dissuade those who wished to insult white persons. In 1852 the *New Orleans Daily Picayune* published an editorial complaining, "This practice has become quite too common in almost all parts of the city. Negroes have been allowed so many liberties that in many cases they now take advantage of it and frequently vent their dirty abuse on white persons, that they imagine that they are helpless. Many of the cases which have come to our knowledge lately have been those where white ladies of respectability have been greatly abused at their residences, while the male portion of the family were [away] from home."[1]

The enforcement of "insulting" laws was a relatively mild form of racial harassment, but more sinister forms of harassment could endanger the very freedom of free people of color. They could be arrested and forced to prove their freedom at the whim of any policeman, recorder, or ordinary citizen, and they faced incarceration until they could prove their status to some official's satisfaction. Although they had the right to testify against whites in court, a right unknown in any other southern state except Delaware, simply

1. *Black Code*, Sec. 40, pp. 188–90; *New Orleans Daily Picayune*, 29 October 1852. For examples of "insulting" cases in the First District Court, see State v. Black, f.w.c., No. 1095, 11 June 1847. Julia Black, herself a prostitute, called a white woman a "Huzzey [*sic*] and old whore & a bitch." Maurice Charles, f.m.c., insulted two men in French and English in a ten-day period in 1847. He called one a *"fils de putain"* and an *"enfant de garce"* (a son of a whore and a child of a naughty woman) and another a "son of a bitch." State v. Charles, f.m.c., Nos. 1159, 1302, 28 June, 8 July 1847. The newspapers reported on recorders' courts' handling of insulting cases. In 1855, a local newspaper reported that "Mary Douglas, a free woman of color, whose impertinence to her white neighbors on Carondelet street has recently become utterly unbearable, was fined no less a sum than $25." *New Orleans Daily Picayune*, 13 September 1855. Under city ordinance, the penalty for a slave insulting a white person was twenty-five lashes. Henry J. Leovy, ed., *The Laws and General Ordinances of the City of New Orleans* (New Orleans: E. C. Wharton, 1857), No. 757, p. 259; Rankin, "The Forgotten People," 67; Wade, *Slavery in the Cities*, 326.

claiming free status did not satisfy city officials in the city at large. Since New Orleans paid a $10 reward for each runaway slave brought to the police jail, the law encouraged policemen to arrest blacks whose status they deemed questionable. With a salary of only $45 a month ($50 after 1855), many policeman sought to augment their income by arresting people of color in the hope that they might be runaway slaves.[2]

The ability to differentiate between free people of color and slaves proved extremely difficult in New Orleans. Slaves and free people of color who attempted to pass for white compounded the problem. For example, on one occasion the police imprisoned a dark-skinned man named Miguel Semmerio as a man of color. He remained in parish prison for several months until he proved that "he was a Mexican and not a negro." A man named George Miller claimed he had papers, which authorities "supposed to be illegal, representing him as a white man, while the impression in police circles is, that he is colored and a runaway." Police arrested John T. Tricky in 1862 for passing himself off as a white man. The *Daily Picayune* commented, "If all the persons, male and female who play the same trick on white persons in this city . . . were arrested, the jails would be far too small." In 1859 a woman turned herself in to the chief of police and said that she was free and white, but that she had been kidnapped and put in a slave pen for sale. Upon investigation, her owner appeared and presented an act of sale for $800, thereby fatally undermining her claims. A complaint filed in 1858 demonstrates the near impossibility of determining color or racial origin in New Orleans with any certainty:

> A complaint against an officer for giving a colored woman a jerk led to a lengthy investigation. Though colored in fact the woman proved not to be colored in law, as her father was a German and her mother an Indian woman, and an Indian's *status* is as pure in law as a white man's. The woman appeared to be darker than Indians usually are, hence the mistake of the officer was a very natural one. Moreover, she was seated on the door step of a house tenanted by lewd women when the officer ordered her in and jerked her because she refused to go. The Recorder

2. Robert C. Reinders, *End of an Era: New Orleans, 1850–60* (New Orleans: Pelican, 1964), 65; Rankin, "A Forgotten People," 55; Rousey, *Policing the Southern City,* 96; Berlin, *Slaves without Masters,* 328–9.

finally dismissed the case, on the ground that the officer had done no more than he considered his duty.[3] [italics in original]

Theoretically, gradations of color could help determine slave from free. Louisiana law presumed that light-skinned persons of African descent were free; dark-skinned "Negroes," as the law termed them, were presumed to be slaves. In equating blackness with slavery and lighter skin with freedom, the law reflected the real racial situation in southern Louisiana. In New Orleans, approximately 80 percent of the city's "Negroes" held slave status while the remaining 20 percent were free; conversely, more than 70 percent of light-skinned people of color were free. Slaves who ran away to New Orleans compounded the problem of distinguishing free from slave. Runaway slave ads often warned that slaves would attempt to flee to the city. In one ad for the runaway slave Amos, his Bayou Goula owner stated, "Having many acquaintances in New Orleans, he will probably go there as he has done when he ran away before." In 1859, the *Daily Picayune* noted that five Negroes—Victor, Lewis, Jeferan, Matthew, and Adde—surrendered themselves to the chief of police, claiming protection and asserting their freedom. They alleged that a Mr. Lake of St. John the Baptist Parish had illegally held them as slaves. Lake proved ownership, and the recorder put them on board the steamer *Music,* accompanied by a police officer, to return them to their owner. The reporter commented, "It seems that some pettifogger up the coast had made the slaves believe they were entitled to their freedom, but the court thought otherwise." In 1860 the *Picayune* reported the arrest and return of a slave who had managed to remain in New Orleans as a runaway for twelve years before being caught:

The other day an old negress was in the Mayor's office to give evidence in a case, representing herself as free. Chief McLelland asked her to see her papers, and she said she had lost them, but was well known here, and gave the name of a gentleman in the Third District who would vouch for her. The Chief of Police telegraphed immediately for the gentleman, who came up and testified that he had known the woman for many years, but never had any positive evidence of her freedom, as she always stated

3. *New Orleans Daily Picayune,* 1 March 1857, 25 January 1858, 25 January 1862, 13 October 1859, 28 August 1858. City ordinances prohibited lewd women from sitting outdoors on the sidewalk or steps of a brothel. Leovy, ed., *Laws and General Ordinances,* No. 1095, p. 379.

that she had lost her papers. Not satisfied, the Chief detained the negress and instituted an investigation, when it was discovered that she was a slave, belonging to one of our planters and had been runaway for twelve years. She will find it hard to return in bondage after so many years of freedom, but she cannot plead prescription.[4]

Sometimes a personal quarrel could escalate into a threat of loss of freedom for a free person of color. In 1846, Betsey Pope, a free woman of color, sued Barry Wright for $500 in damages and court costs. Pope alleged that Wright had entered her house one day and struck her with a piece of wood. The next day, she claimed, he had "cowhided her on the arms and shoulders . . . thereby inflicting serious injuries to your petitioner and besides wounding her feelings." In response, Wright claimed to have acted in self-defense and denied that Pope had free status or that she legally resided in Louisiana, saying "that all the laws upon the subject of persons of color do not recognize her as a citizen." Wright demanded that Pope prove her freedom. Fortunately for Pope, she possessed her freedom papers, an act of manumission from Louisville, Kentucky. She had also registered herself and her child in the registry of free colored persons, as required by a legislative act of 1830. The registry listed Pope, age forty-five, as a washerwoman born in Louisville. Faced with this thorough documentation of freedom, the First District Court ruled in Pope's favor and awarded her damages of $75 and costs of $28.55. However, she still had to pay her attorney's fees. This case demonstrates the obstacles faced by free people of color in preserving their freedom, circumstances that would not apply to whites.[5]

Even a dispute over a small amount of money could degenerate into a threatened loss of freedom. Victoire, a free woman of color, rented a house

4. Adele, f.w.c., v. Beauregard, 1 Mart. (O.S.) 183 (1810); State v. Cecil, 2 Mart. (O.S.) 208 (1812); John Blassingame, *Black New Orleans, 1860–1880* (Chicago: University of Chicago Press, 1973), 11; *New Orleans Daily Picayune,* 18, 24 May 1859, 23 June 1859, 8 September 1860. The slave Harriet declared in a recorder's court that she had been born free in Indiana but had recently been sold after the death of her master. Described as a "very bad subject," her owner tried to rescind the sale because he declared her "worthless." The court held the purchaser to the sale, and he took possession of Harriet. *New Orleans Daily Picayune,* 27 October 1854.

5. Pope, f.w.c., v. Wright, No. 256, First District Court of New Orleans, 6 February 1847; "An Act to Prevent Free Persons of Color from Entering This State and for Other Purposes," Act of March 16, 1830, *Louisiana Acts, 1830,* Sec. 12, p. 94.

from Jean Ferrand. When she moved out, Ferrand sued her for $15 in back rent and seized her personal possessions and clothing under a landlord's lien. Victoire claimed that she only owed him $10, and that he "pretended" that she owned him $5 more for not giving notice that she planned to vacate his property. Victoire asked the court to set aside the seizure, as Ferrand's actions were "arbitrary & malicious acts" designed to harass her. She asked for $275 in damages, including a $25 fee for her attorney. Ferrand countered by claiming that Victoire had no proof of freedom, and he denied allegations that he had acted maliciously. He demanded that she prove her freedom. The record of this case ends here, meaning that one of the parties did not chose to pursue the matter. Victoire might have paid the $15 rather than risk her freedom, or Ferrand might have been satisfied with having her property to sell for his back rent.[6]

Even free people of color who had enjoyed their freedom for many years could find themselves threatened with the loss of their liberty. In 1847 Apasie filed a writ of *habeas corpus* because a creditor of her former master had her seized for his debts and the sheriff had put her up for sale to satisfy the creditors. Her former owner, Paul Lestrade, had purchased Apasie as a slave in 1838 with the promise that he would free her as soon as possible. In 1842, he had taken her to Hamilton County, Ohio, and had her declared free. At this time, no law prohibited taking a slave to a free state, manumitting them, and returning with them to Louisiana. The creditor claimed that Apasie did not have free status, as she lived in "open concubinage with Lestrade." Louisiana law prohibited manumitting a slave in fraud of creditors or giving a concubine more than one-tenth of one's property. The creditor asserted that she had procured the act of freedom "by aid and assistance of evil-minded persons who conspired conjointly with him [Lestrade] to put up at the defiance of the laws of this State and to defraud and injure his creditors." The creditor also pointed out that the act of manumission in Ohio had occurred a full year after he had had a judgment against Lestrade. This case dragged on for a year, during which time Apasie remained in jail. Finally, in 1848, the judge of the Second District Court rendered a decision declaring her free, with the creditor paying the costs of suit.[7]

6. Victoire, f.w.c., v. Ferrand, No. 624, Second District Court of New Orleans, 25 March 1847.

7. Apasie, f.w.c., for *habeas corpus*, No. 849, Second District Court of New Orleans, 29 May 1848. Article 1468 of the *Civil Code* stipulated that those who lived together in open concubinage could not donate to each other immovable property (real estate) and were only allowed to give each other one-tenth of their movable property. *Civil Code*, Art. 1468, p. 223;

In an 1853 lawsuit, a free woman of color sued William M. Lambeth for holding her as a slave for eight years. In 1838, Tom Sloane, a free man of color, had purchased his daughter, Jacquette, from Bernard de Santos and had manumitted her. The act of manumission, recorded in the office of a notary public and dated July 23, 1840, stated that Jacquette had permission of the police jury to remain in the state and that she could "enjoy her freedom as if born free." The notary had recorded Jacquette's presence at the act of manumission and had stated that she "accepts [her freedom] with gratitude." However, in January 1840 Sloane had sold Jacquette for $900 to Lambeth, although Jacquette had no knowledge of the sale. In the act of sale, Lambeth had promised to free her as soon as possible. This case indicates some fraudulent dealings between Lambeth and Sloane. Apparently Sloane had purchased another slave, whose wages he had said could go toward that slave's freedom, but instead had gone to de Santos to purchase Jacquette. Lambeth's executor (who died during the proceedings) claimed that Lambeth had purchased Jacquette from Sloane to divest Sloane of her to cover some questionable dealings between them. According to Jacquette's petition, Lambeth had "violently seized" her and brought her to his plantation late in 1844. There he had "compelled [her] to work in the fields, under the power and control of the overseer." Jacquette claimed that the overseer had "whipped and chastised her as a slave." Lambeth held her as a slave until 1852, when he sent her to the widow Harris, "who forcibly holds her and subjects her to all duties and obligations of a slave, compelling her to account for her daily wages and punishing her and chastising her as a slave." She alleged to have suffered "damages to body and mind" of $3,000, and claimed a right to wages of $25 a month from 1844 to 1852. Furthermore, she alleged, she feared either Lambeth or Harris would remove her from the jurisdiction of the court and sell her as a slave. She requested sequestration for her own protection. After three months in jail, the First District Court declared Jacquette free but gave her no damages. The court ordered Lambeth and Harris, however, to pay costs of the suit.[8]

Art. 190, p. 29. For two other similar cases, see King, f.m.c., for *habeas corpus,* No. 2266, First District Court of New Orleans, 17 May 1848; Smith, f.m.c., for *habeas corpus,* No. 2279, First District Court of New Orleans, 19 August 1848. See also Schafer, "Open and Notorious Concubinage," 165–82.

8. Jacquette, f.w.c., v. Lambeth and Harris, No. 8644, First District Court of New Orleans, 28 June 1853. William M. Lambeth is the same individual who purchased Marcellus Paine after being shipwrecked on the *Creole.* See Chap. 1 n. 27.

In 1854 the *Daily Picayune* reported that police had arrested a woman named Pelagie Brown as a fugitive slave. She had lived as free in the city for twelve years and "was so nearly white that few could detect any traces of her African descent." After her arrest, a Mississippi man, Ursin Raby, claimed her as his runaway slave. She in turn claimed her freedom and said that she had never belonged to Raby; she "had a house well furnished, and was in the habit of letting out in rooms." The recorder had her sequestered in jail for safekeeping. Judge John Reynolds of the First District Court ruled that she belonged to Raby. The following day Brown petitioned the court to allow her to remain in New Orleans until her former master, Mr. Walker of Mobile, from whom she had gained her freedom, arrived to testify in her behalf. This case dragged on until 1859, when the Supreme Court of Louisiana ruled in favor of Raby. The court held that Brown ought not to "be permitted to have her rights judicially investigated in this State, but ought to resort to the courts of Mississippi, where her master resides." Furthermore, the justices observed, "It would be useless to remand the case, as under our present laws, no slave can be emancipated."[9]

Two other suits for freedom that went up to the Supreme Court of Louisiana on appeal lost on similar grounds. Louisa Marshall, a free woman of color, sued for her freedom in the Fourth District Court on the basis that the will of her former Kentucky master had stipulated that she become free at age thirty. The owner's nephew had sold her to a New Orleans slave trader after the owner's death. Held as a slave in New Orleans until she reached the age of thirty, she sued for her freedom in 1858. She went to Kentucky and obtained a court decree declaring her to be free. Her New Orleans owner testified that she had forfeited the right to freedom in Louisiana "by her misconduct and vicious habits, lewd and dissipated, she was unwilling to work and was constantly in the habit of running away from her owner." Nevertheless, the trial court ruled in her favor, stating that since the case involved a "question more of liberty than of property, the court is of the opinion that the Law should be construed in its most liberal terms and that all should be done to protect the applicant in such a case." Her

---

9. *New Orleans Daily Picayune*, 7, 8, September 1854; Brown, f.w.c., v. Raby, No. 5797, 14 La. Ann. 41 (1859). The Third District Court denied a Louisiana slave a claim for freedom because she sued her owner in New Orleans when he lived in Rapides Parish. *New Orleans Daily Picayune*, 17 April 1857; Logan, f.w.c., v. Hickman, No. 5736, 14 La. Ann. 300 (1859).

owner appealed to the Louisiana Supreme Court, which overturned the decision of the trial court on the basis of domicile. The decree of a Kentucky court, the justices argued, could not be binding in Louisiana.[10]

Simply walking down the street at night got William Johnson arrested and forced to prove his freedom. Lieutenant C. Petric of the Second Municipality Police arrested Johnson at eleven o'clock on the night of July 26, 1850, and had him confined in the watch house. Petric accused Johnson of being a slave out after curfew without a pass. City ordinances required slaves to be off the streets by 8:15 P.M. in winter and 9:15 P.M. in summer unless they could produce a pass written by their owner specifically giving them permission to be out. Johnson replied that he was free and therefore not bound by curfew laws. Johnson lost his suit for damages in the justice of the peace's court, and he appealed to the Third District Court, asking for $100 in damages and court costs. The judge of the Third District Court rendered a decision in his favor but awarded him only $1 in damages. In his decision the judge ruled, "Defendant has cited neither law nor ordinance to justify the arrest or detention of the plaintiff nor have my own researches enabled me to find any—there was however no malice found or was alleged against defendant. . . . [C]ounsel states that his client asked for nothing but a judgment which would carry costs." Of course, the $1 award would not have even covered court costs, much less the attorney's fees.[11]

Men of color were often forced to prove their freedom due to restrictions on interracial sexual relations. In 1855, police discovered a white woman, Eliza Morris, and Célestin Mollier, a free man of color, living together. The recorder sent Morris to the workhouse for six months and sent Mollier to prison to prove his freedom. The *Daily Picayune* commented, "He is black and anything but comely." Another 1855 news item began with the headline "Practical Amalgamation." The article reported the arrest of two "abandoned" women, living in "unlawful connection with a negro Wm. Jackson, who claims to be free but who is believed to be a runaway." The two women received sentences of thirty and fifty days in the workhouse, and

10. Marshall v. Watrigant, No. 5808, Fourth District Court of New Orleans, 20 December 1853; No. 5220, 13 La. Ann. 619 (1858). The court rendered a similar judgment in a case involving a Mississippi slave. Haynes, alias Mielkie, f.w.c., v. Forno, Hutchinson, and Hill, curator, No. 2850, 8 La. Ann. 35 (1853).

11. Johnson, f.m.c., v. Petric, No. 3158, Third District Court of New Orleans, 10 December 1850; Leovy, ed., *Laws and General Ordinances*, No. 766, p. 261.

the recorder sent Jackson to prison to prove his freedom. The newspapers described white women in these relationships as "abandoned" (a polite way to indicate a prostitute), "dirty shameless white women," or "worthless." One reporter wrote, "The vile habits of this beast of a woman are too disgusting to relate."[12]

Some actions against free people of color appear motivated by nothing more than a desire to harass. In 1854, David King, a free man of color, sued for a writ of *habeas corpus* to question his incarceration in the parish prison. In his petition, he alleged that he had lived in New Orleans for the past thirty years as free, and that he supported himself and his family. He claimed to be held without having been charged, and that no affidavit or witness had come forth to charge him with anything. The judge of the First District Court discharged King, but he still had to pay for the services of an attorney.[13]

At times, seizures of people of color amounted to much more than harassment; they were serious attempts to enslave or reenslave them. In 1841, Mathilda Matin Turnbull and her husband Walter freed their thirteen-year-old slave Marguerite Turnbull before the district court judge of Pointe Coupée Parish. Since Marguerite was described as a mulatto "having nearly straight hair," one wonders if Walter Turnbull could have been her father. In 1856, Marguerite Turnbull brought suit for her freedom and that of her two children, ages six and three, alleging that the Turnbull's five children had seized her and her children as slaves. Claiming that being held in slavery had "greatly injured her in peace, feelings and reputation," she asked for a declaration of her freedom and $5,000 in damages. The defendants alleged that they had never claimed her as a slave; they said that she had remained with them of her own free will and therefore did not need to bring the lawsuit. The judge of the Third District Court ruled that the defendants "be perpetually enjoined from disturbing said plaintiff and her children in

12. *New Orleans Daily Picayune*, 22 December 1855, 15 March 1856, 19 January 1855, 5 and 21 September, 17 February 1853. Martha Hodes's new book on sexual relations between white women and black men in the antebellum South excluded Louisiana because the presence of a large class of free people of color complicated the issue of sex across the color line. Martha Hodes, *White Women, Black Men: Illicit Sex in the Nineteenth-Century South* (New Haven, Conn.: Yale University Press, 1997), 12.

13. King, f.m.c., for *habeas corpus,* No. 9591, First District Court of New Orleans, 8 June 1854.

the enjoyment of her freedom." Although she received no damages, the court did order the defendants to pay court costs.[14]

In 1853, Ann Bonford, a free woman of color, sued for a writ of *habeas corpus* for herself and her two children, Debra, age five, and Frank, age three. Bonford claimed that even though her owner had freed her in 1851, his creditors had subsequently seized her and her children to pay his debts. After remaining in the parish prison for over two months, Bonford presented her manumission papers to the judge of the First District Court, who ruled in her favor.[15]

In a similar suit in 1859, Allen Taylor, a free man of color, sued the Orleans Parish sheriff, Edward T. Parker, for illegal imprisonment. The sheriff had seized Taylor to sell him in order to satisfy the debts of Taylor's former owner, Polly Reason, a free woman of color. Taylor proved that Reason had freed him in 1851 with permission to remain in the state. He petitioned the judge of the Second District Court to set him at liberty. He also asked for damages of $275, claiming that he had been forced to hire an attorney "and spend a good deal of money to prove his freedom." He alleged that he had showed Parker his freedom papers when the sheriff had first seized him, but that Parker had nonetheless "maliciously caused the arrest and imprisonment." Although the judge ordered Taylor immediately released and discharged from the sheriff's custody, he awarded no damages.[16]

In 1857, a free man of color, William Johnson, sued the captain of the police of the Fourth District for arresting him with no cause and holding him in jail overnight on two different occasions. He precipitated his first arrest by not carrying his free papers on his person and refusing to make a practice of carrying them. At the time of his arrest, Johnson claimed that he

14. Turnbull, f.w.c., v. Turnbull, No. 7953, Third District Court of New Orleans, 22 February 1856; *New Orleans Daily Picayune,* 10 January 1856.

15. Bonford, f.w.c., praying for a writ of *habeas corpus,* No. 8653, First District Court of New Orleans, 14 June 1853. Newspapers reported a number of *habeas corpus* actions by free people of color claiming they had been jailed as runaways. For example, John Stanley, who claimed to have been in enjoyment of his freedom since 1838, brought a writ of *habeas corpus* to obtain his release. *New Orleans Times Picayune,* 30 November 1855. See also Spear, f.w.c., v. Blanchard, keeper of the police jail, No. 11,451, Fourth District Court of New Orleans, 12 June 1857; State (Johnson, f.m.c., relator), praying for a writ of *habeas corpus,* No. 14,190, Third District Court of New Orleans, 9 December 1859.

16. State (relator Taylor, f.m.c.) v. Parker, Nos. 15,566, 15,626, Second District Court of New Orleans, 30 May, 23 November 1859.

was building a large brick building on Magazine Street, and that his arrest had caused a "great loss." Also, he alleged, he had suffered greatly in his "feelings and reputation." He asked for damages of $2,000. Johnson proved that he had been born free in New Orleans, and that he had registered himself as a free person of color according to law and thereby "had acquired the privilege of walking through the streets and highways of this city at all hours of the night." The arresting officer testified that he had been caught "in the company of slaves," and specifically with a black woman named Rebecca, a runaway slave. Rebecca's owner came for her the next day. Although he proved his freedom, Johnson lost his lawsuit against the police, and the court ordered him to pay court costs of $42.35.[17]

Each week the *Daily Picayune* reported instances in which the police arrested people of color as runaway slaves and jailed them until they could prove their freedom. For example, the paper reported in 1853 that "Gabriel Holmes, Green Smith, George Harris and Isaac Johnson, negroes, are in custody and will remain so until they can prove their freedom." Police sent Elizabeth Carpenter and her children, William and Ann, to prison in 1857, "the mother having no evidence of her freedom." The following year John Kirby, "representing himself as a freeman, but having no evidence of the fact, was sent to prison as a runaway, with permission to prove, if possible, his freedom." The newspaper used the initials "f.m.c." behind the names of some of those arrested, even though they went to jail to prove their status: "Mssrs. Célestin and Simon, f.m.c., were sent to jail this morning by Recorder Summers, and ordered to remain there until they could produce evidence of their being what they allege they are, free." In 1858, Rosa Gigot, "sporting a free woman of color, but having no evidence of her freedom, was arrested on Liberty street this morning, and committed till she can prove her freedom." Of course, some of those arrested might actually have been runaway slaves. But all free people of color were susceptible to arrest solely because a particular police officer did not know them and their appearance indicated some degree of African origin.[18]

17. Johnson, f.m.c., v. Steip and the City of New Orleans, No. 8523, Fifth District Court of New Orleans, 10 April 1857. In 1856, W. H. Nichols, f.m.c., was arrested for having beaten two policemen who, not knowing whether he was free or a slave, demanded his manumission papers or a pass from his owner. This type of incident happened routinely in New Orleans in the 1850s. *New Orleans Daily Picayune,* 26 June 1856.

18. *New Orleans Daily Picayune,* 7 June 1853, 6 November 1857, 9 April, 30 August, 20 September 1858; also 31 January, 26 March, 11 May 1859.

The *Daily Picayune* also reported dozens of cases in which free people of color committed minor crimes and suddenly found themselves having to prove their freedom. Whites committing the same offence would not escape punishment, but their freedom never came into question. For example, in 1860 the police arrested Charles Paul, a free man of color, for carrying concealed weapons. At his arraignment, a "new question arose as to his freedom. Paul had to go to Parish Prison and stay there until he can [sic] prove his right to the mystic letters—f.m.c." A police officer arrested several men of color in 1860 for "unlawful assemblage." They included "Billy, a free boy of color; Charity and Allen, slaves of Mr. Bibb; Victor, slave of Dr. Degrange; Jacob, slave of Mr. Piera, and Caleb, slave of Mr. McGarrity. This morning Recorder Emerson sent the slaves to the police jail, and remanded Billy to the Parish Prison to prove his freedom." A few months later, police arrested Harry, a free man of color, for carrying concealed weapons and sent him to the parish prison to prove his freedom. The newspaper editorialized, "We hope Harry will soon learn that it is much more safe to respect the laws of the State than to carry bowie knives to protect one's self against night prowlers." Even overindulging in alcohol was fraught with risk. Jean Baptiste, a free man of color, "got terribly drunk last night in Penn street, and was taken up by special officer Price, to whom he would give no evidence of his freedom, being too gloriously drunk at the time. He satisfied Recorder Emerson, however this morning, but went away quite dissatisfied, having had to pay $20 as a fair average of the damage done to the public peace during his jollification."[19]

Sometimes people of color languished in jail for months and even years before being released as free. In 1851 Charlotte Jones, a mulatto woman from Baton Rouge, remained in jail for three and a half months before she could prove her freedom. The *Daily Picayune* commented, "Jail Keepers are advised in such cases to make dillgent [sic] inquiries to ascertain the facts." In 1855, a free woman of color named Martha Ann Hicks spent ten months in the parish prison before she could prove her freedom. After doing so, "she was at once discharged. The case had been brought specially to the notice of the Recorder, by the District Attorney, or she might have still been kept in prison." In 1859 the Orleans Parish Grand Jury com-

19. Ibid., 8 January, 23 August, 5 December, 12 September 1860; Leovy, ed., *Laws and General Ordinances,* No. 753, p. 258.

mented, "Action is recommended in the case of negroes detained in the Police Jail, some since twelve months and upwards, as unable to prove their freedom." Perhaps the most outrageous instance of jailing free persons of color until they proved their status involved the case of Betsey Doubelval and Judy Wyereau, who police arrested for claiming to be free, but who had no evidence of their freedom. Their arrest had occurred on November 26, 1851. A newspaper article in 1859 commented that "no one being particularly interested in these women, they have remained in custody from the day of their commitment to the present time. They are both aged and of meek and peaceful demeanor. Efforts have lately been made to trace out their history, and it appears that the parties who knew the fact of their freedom, and who would have interested themselves for their protection, are all dead. The Recorder, leaning to the side of humanity, discharged them without entering into the question of their status. One of them immediately found a home, being taken as a servant in the family of a gentleman present." In a rush of proslavery sentiment, the *Daily Picayune* commented, "She seemed delighted to have one who would again stand to her in the relation of master and protector."[20]

At times the *Daily Picayune* enjoyed making fun of people of color, even free blacks incarcerated for long periods of time. In 1858 the newspaper reported the arrest of W. H. Going, described as the "colored gent who was the other day caught perambulating under a false white man's wig, [and who] was examined and sent to prison to await the proving of his freedom. The former *status* of Going, like the occupation of Othello, seems wholly 'gone.'" Five months later the paper reported that Going had finally managed to prove his freedom and the recorder had discharged him. Originally arrested for drunkenness and disturbing the peace, Going's real offense (at least in the eyes of the reporter) involved wearing a wig and associating with a Mexican man:

> During his night's incubations [*sic*] in the lock-up . . . his head covering, which was not natural, but artificial, got displaced, and a crop of kinky locks of very small dimensions, but patently insinuating Ethiopian origin, were seen peering from his proper scalp. Great was the excitement

20. *New Orleans Daily Picayune,* 29 March 1851, 13 December 1855, 5 January, 5 April, 5 January, 1859.

thereat, among the guardians of the purity of the city's status, and greater the consternation of the betrayed victim of the treacherous 'fire water.' The original charge against him was merged in that naturally arising from such a state of affairs, and he was locked up until he proved his freedom. This he did five months afterwards.[21]

Occasionally slaves claimed freedom to escape burdensome situations. Thomas Frisby, a slave dealer, claimed Caroline Hunt as his slave, but she surrendered herself to the "protection of the law, alleging that Frisby beat her with a stick." She also claimed not to be a slave, but a free woman. Frisby proved that she had had a series of owners in New Orleans, and the recorder surrendered her to her present claimant. The recorder also advised her that if she really considered herself free, she should sue for her liberty before one of the district courts. There is no record of a further lawsuit.[22]

For a person of color, even owning property could result in a challenge of one's freedom. In 1856 George A. Botts, a slave dealer, died. His mulatto mistress of seventeen years, Ann Marie Barclay, owned a piece of property, a piano, and some furniture, which she had paid for with her own money. The curator of Botts's succession, Edward Sewell, questioned whether Barclay had the capacity to own property on the grounds that she remained a slave. Witnesses testified that Barclay and Botts had lived together as husband and wife since her manumission at age fifteen. Sewell admitted that Botts had taken Barclay to Ohio in 1839 to free her. He nonetheless contended, "Emancipations decreed in the state of Ohio cannot have . . . any legal effect within this State." Barclay hired prominent attorney Christian Roselius to take her case. She won in the Second District Court, and Sewell appealed to the Louisiana Supreme Court. The high court upheld the decision of the lower court, stating that according to the Act of 1830, owners of Louisiana slaves could take their slaves to other states and free them. Barclay thus had a right to "call upon the Courts of the State to protect her in her rights." The court held that "by the law of Ohio, the *status* of the plaintiff was changed. She became free by the act of emancipation: that there was no law in force in 1839 in Louisiana entailing slavery upon her on re-

21. Ibid., 1 July, 26 November 1858.
22. Ibid., 21, 22 August 1857.

turning to this State, and no subsequent law can change that *status*" (italics in original).[23]

As in the case of *Barclay*, freed slaves could never count on being secure in their liberty, even after many years of freedom. Martha Jones, a free woman of color, seized Davis Jones, a free man of color (relationship, if any, unknown), as a runaway slave and had him locked up in the parish prison. Davis Jones proved that Priscilla Donaldson Borditch had freed him more than ten years prior to his imprisonment. He petitioned the court to protect him from being removed from the jurisdiction of the court and sold as a slave. Martha Jones never answered the petition, and the court declared Davis Jones free. But he still had to pay attorneys' fees and court costs. The Second District Court required William Wight, who claimed to have lived as free for over twenty years, to prove his freedom after the heirs of his former owners seized him as a slave. Wight asked to be released under a writ of *habeas corpus*. The judge ruled that since he had been arrested because he did not have freedom papers on his person and was therefore presumed to be a runaway, he would have to institute a suit for his freedom. The judge sent him back to jail "from whence he came."[24]

Four free people of color who had lived as free for many years found themselves forced to prove their freedom just before the Civil War. George Montigue, a free man of color, sued the sheriff of Orleans Parish for illegal detention in the city jail. He claimed to have committed no crime, but the recorder had sent him to jail anyway until he could prove his freedom. He claimed to have offered the sheriff proof of freedom, which the sheriff had refused to accept. The judge of the Fourth District Court did not find that Montigue had sufficient proof of his freedom, writing, "The proof offered does not overcome the presumption raised by his color. . . . Certainly if he be a free man of so long acquaintance . . . he could produce more than one witness, who seems to know very little that is direct and positive. And the

23. Barclay, f.w.c., v. Sewell, No. 8019, Second District Court of New Orleans, 25 March 1856; No. 4622, 12 La. Ann. 262 (1857); "An Act to Prevent Free Persons of Color from Entering This State, and for Other Purposes," Act of March 16, 1830, *Louisiana Acts, 1830*, Sec. 16, p. 94; *New Orleans Daily Picayune*, 29 April 1857.

24. Jones, f.m.c., v. Jones, f.w.c., No. 13,086, Fifth District Court of New Orleans, 23 April 1859; State v. Marigny, Sheriff, *habeas corpus* of Wight, No. 9393, Second District Court of New Orleans, 10 October 1855. See also *New Orleans Daily Picayune*, 8 January 1858.

representation made for him by counsel, that he was born free, does not sustain the affiant in regard to 'free papers.' If he is free, he can establish it by satisfactory proof which he has not yet accomplished."[25]

Also in 1860, Françoise, a free woman of color, and her son complained to the Third District Court that even though Françoise had been free for more than twenty years and her son, Arthur, had been born free, one Jean Pezant had recently begun to treat them as slaves. Françoise alleged that Pezant knew of their freedom and continued "putting impediments to their freedom." Because of his actions, which Françoise characterized as "malicious," she asked the court to award her damages of $250 and court costs. The court declared Françoise and Arthur free. Once more, however, the plaintiffs found themselves forced to forgo damages just to ensure their freedom. The record notes, "By consent of parties, plaintiff abandons damages in consideration of the confession of judgment in this case." Françoise and her son kept their freedom but had to pay their attorney and court costs.[26]

Two months later in the same court, Florianne, a free woman of color, sued for her freedom, stating that although she had lived as free for nearly twenty years, her former owners had recently had her arrested and imprisoned as a slave. She asked for the court to declare her free and award her $1,500 in damages. Her former owner replied that she had had Florianne seized because she had threatened to institute a suit for her freedom on the basis of prescription (having lived as free within the state for more than ten years with permission of the owner). Her former owner denied allowing her to live as free. The record of this case ends without resolution. We cannot know whether the former owner ceased to press her claim, or if Florianne failed to prove that her owner had allowed her to live as free.[27]

The last case of persons of color finding themselves forced to prove their freedom happened after the Civil War began. New Orleans police arrested Lucy Holmes, a free woman of color, and her five-year-old son in October 1861 as the slave of an "alien enemy." Holmes hired an attorney and sued

25. Montigue, f.m.c., v. E. J. Parker, sheriff, No. 13,992, Fourth District Court of New Orleans, 7 August 1860.

26. Françoise, f.w.c., v. Pezant, No. 15,013, Third District Court of New Orleans, 16 June 1860.

27. Florianne, f.w.c., v. Duplessis, f.w.c., No. 15,223, Third District Court of New Orleans, 17 November 1860.

for a writ of *habeas corpus*. The judge of the First District Court brought her into court, where she declared that she had been illegally detained; she lived as free and had done so for many years. Two free women of color testified as to her freedom for at least five years. So did her landlord and two merchants (one in furniture, one in carpets), who took the opportunity to claim that Holmes owed them $69.05 for merchandise received. The record of this case ends here. The fate of Lucy Holmes and her child cannot be determined.[28]

Although free people of color had far more extensive legal rights than slaves, they still had major legal disabilities. A constant susceptibility to having their freedom challenged arbitrarily, frequently, and in a humiliating manner proved one of the most onerous burdens of being free but not white. Any white person, not just the civil authorities, could and did force free blacks to prove their freedom. Those who could not do so faced the sudden and permanent loss of their liberty. Even more horrifyingly, unscrupulous whites could and did kidnap free people of color and sell them as slaves, sometimes far away from their homes. When this occurred, free people of color had little recourse except to institute a suit for their freedom. Those who had innocently purchased a kidnapped free person of color as a slave would be reluctant to lose the purchase price and lifelong labor of the "slave." How many of these crimes went undetected, we will never know.[29]

28. Holmes, f.w.c., for *habeas corpus,* No. 15,623, First District Court of New Orleans, 10 December 1861.

29. "An Act Relative to Slaves and Free Colored People," Sec. 31, 35, p. 382.

7

KIDNAPPING FREE PEOPLE OF COLOR

Kidnapping free people of color was a far more sinister and threatening form of harassment than simply accusing them of being slaves and forcing them to prove their freedom. Although Louisiana law prohibited kidnapping and mandated severe penalties for those who broke the law, not one criminal prosecution for kidnapping appears in the district court records between 1846 and 1862, although plenty of evidence of this crime appears in suits for freedom. Apparently, if the victims were black, race trumped the law. Even so, some kidnapped free persons of color used the courts in ingenious and persistent ways to successfully regain their freedom.

The only prosecution for kidnapping of a free person of color did not represent a true kidnapping in the legal definition of the crime. Elizabeth Carpenter, a free woman of color, indentured her free twelve-year-old daughter for $400 to Elizabeth McMichael of St. Helena Parish for six years. In the agreement, Carpenter expressed the hope that McMichael would teach her daughter to be a good house servant and fieldhand. McMichael transferred the daughter to William McMichael (relationship unknown), a New Orleans slave dealer, who sold her to Alexander Miller of Hinds County, Mississippi. The record does not make clear whether McMichael sold her for her remaining indenture or whether he represented her as a slave for life. Elizabeth Carpenter brought charges against McMichael and Miller for kidnapping, saying that the indenture could not be transferred to another party. An Orleans Parish jury found the two men guilty but recommended them to the mercy of the court. As a result, the sentence handed down consisted of only twelve months in the parish prison instead of the more usual sentence of several years in the state penitentiary at hard labor.

Mary's case received prosecution because her mother became aware of what had happened and pressed charges against the two men. Most free blacks kidnapped and brought into Louisiana would have had no advocate to advance prosecution for their kidnapping.[1]

Louisiana's slave system placed all free people of color at risk for being kidnapped and sold as slaves. At any moment their freedom could be snatched away, perhaps forever. If a slave dealer bought slaves in one state and then brought them to Louisiana for sale, he had to pay for the slaves themselves and for their transport to New Orleans. Then he had to sell the slaves at a profit. If a slave dealer kidnapped free people of color and sold them as slaves, he only had to pay for their transport to Louisiana, which vastly increased the profit margin. Unscrupulous traders thus saw kidnapping as an attractive way to improve their bottom line. As the price of slaves rose in the 1850s, the incidence of kidnapping increased. The increasingly shrill proslavery propaganda that described blacks as happier and better cared for in bondage than in freedom helped to mute the repulsion that many had for this crime and made it more difficult to apprehend and convict kidnappers.[2]

An 1819 Louisiana law specifically made it a felony to kidnap a free person of color. A person convicted of kidnapping a free person of color faced fourteen years in jail and a fine of $1,000. Louisiana law also outlawed stealing slaves or horses. These crimes carried a penalty of seven to fourteen years at hard labor in the state penitentiary (later changed to three to seven years). Severe sentences did not seem to deter kidnappers, probably because the authorities did not vigorously enforce the law. Free persons of color were well aware of the ever-present threat of abduction; they knew that, once enslaved, they would find it extremely difficult to regain their freedom. Their purchaser would almost certainly not listen to their claims of freedom and would silence them with the whip if they persisted. If they could prove their freedom, it would cost the buyer the purchase price, the lifelong value of the enslaved person's labor, and conceivably trigger a criminal prosecution for kidnapping. The number of people dragged into slavery in this manner will never be known. The evidence of the many incidences

1. State v. McMichael and Miller, No. 13,052, First District Court of New Orleans, 21 January 1858.

2. Berlin, *Slaves without Masters*, 160.

of kidnapping comes from those who claimed to have been abducted and who resorted to the courts to reclaim their freedom.[3]

An 1830 act of the Louisiana legislature designed to prevent free people of color from coming into Louisiana contained a provision prohibiting anyone from bringing a free person of color into the state as a slave. Violators of this provision faced a fine of $1,000 and were potentially liable to civil damages. The provision did not use the words "kidnap" or "abduct"; it seems to have been aimed at persons bringing free blacks into the state who would otherwise not have been allowed to come into Louisiana. An article in the *New Orleans Daily Picayune* contended that smuggling free persons of color into the state by passing them off as slaves constituted an act "intended for the vilest purposes." One historian has argued that out-of-state or illegally freed blacks bribed local whites to claim them as slaves. After pretending to be slaves for a time, they pressured their nominal owners to free them. Newspapers regularly reported false manumissions. One editor claimed that "free negroes born in free states [are] being admitted here, contrary to law (who were sent here for insidious purposes) and who by false testimony of ownership, obtain free papers from the courts with permission to remain in the state."[4]

In 1857, the attorney general of Louisiana reported to the legislature that many free blacks entered the state illegally with forged passes describing them as slaves, which allowed them to claim residency. Whites argued that this activity caused the New Orleans courts to free hundreds of slaves

3. "An Act for the Punishment of Crimes and Misdemeanors," Act of May 4, 1805, *Orleans Territory Acts,* Sec. 8, p. 418; "An Act to Amend the Several Acts Enacted for the Punishment of the Crimes and Misdemeanors, Committed by Free Persons, and for Other Purposes," Act of March 6, 1819, *Louisiana Acts, 1819,* Secs. 6, 7, p. 64; Levi Peirce et al., eds., *The Consolidation and Revision of the Statutes of the State of a General Nature* (New Orleans: Bee Office, 1852), 207; "An Act Relative to Slaves and Free Colored People," Act of March 15, 1855, *Louisiana Acts, 1855,* Sec. 35, p. 382; Carol Wilson, *Freedom at Risk,* 120; Berlin, *Slaves without Masters,* 160; Sterkx, *The Free Negro in Antebellum Louisiana,* 181. For cases in which people received convictions for stealing slaves, see State v. Ritchie, No. 1613, First District Court of New Orleans, 13 January 1848. Ritchie received a sentence of two years' hard labor in the state penitentiary. James Smith received a sentence of fifteen years' hard labor for stealing slaves and aiding them in running away. State v. Smith, No. 10,055, First District Court of New Orleans, 30 June 1855. For a case of horse stealing, see State v. Ettinger, No. 5161, First District Court of New Orleans, 27 July 1850.

4. *New Orleans Daily Picayune,* 24 October 1847.

each year. In one case, officials charged a free woman of color and a notorious prostitute, Phoebe Black, with swindling for passing off as her slave a
free woman of color, Sarah Lucas, who she then mortgaged to James Kathman. Lucas testified that she had lived in Louisville, Kentucky, until 1849,
when Black had enticed her away by promising her employment as a cham-
bermaid. She testified that Black had told her that in order to avoid the contravention laws, she would have to be recorded as Black's slave. Kathman
declined to prosecute, and the recorder dropped the charges against Black
when he discovered that Lucas had left the state.[5]

The most famous kidnapped free person of color who was brought to
Louisiana and sold as a slave, Solomon Northup, did not have to file suit for
his freedom. After laboring for twelve years on a Red River plantation, he
got word to an acquaintance in New York of his whereabouts. The acquaintance convinced the governor of New York to intervene to regain Northup's
freedom. Confronted with clear documentation, Northrup's Louisiana master released him, although grudgingly. Most abducted free people of color
did not find regaining their freedom that easy. And Northup had been held
as a slave for twelve long years.[6]

Under Louisiana law, those held as slaves had the right to contest their
enslavement. In 1847, Charles Morrison sued for his freedom in the Third
District Court. He alleged that he held free status on the basis of his birth
in the territory of Illinois in 1812. The Northwest Ordinance of 1787 prohibited slavery in areas that would later become the states of Illinois, Indiana, and Ohio. Morrison claimed his freedom on that basis and on the
grounds that the Illinois state constitution outlawed slavery. Nonetheless,
he alleged, his owner had sold him to Charles A. Townsend, who had sold
him to Isaac Stone, who had brought him to Louisiana. Stone then moved
to Cuba, leaving Morrison in the hands of his agent, William Thomkins, who
held him as a slave "unlawfully and by force and violence." Morrison en-
gaged the services of James Morrison of St. Claire County, Illinois, to repre-

    5. "An Act to Prevent Free People of Color from Entering This State," Act of March 16,
1830, *Louisiana Acts, 1830*, Sec. 8, p. 92; *New Orleans Daily Picayune*, 24 October 1847, 19, 26
October 1850; Richard Tansey, "Out-of-State Free Blacks in Late Antebellum New Orleans,"
Louisiana History 22 (fall 1981): 376; Sterkx, *The Free Negro in Antebellum Louisiana*, 112–3;
Berlin, *Slaves without Masters*, 263.

    6. Solomon Northup, *Twelve Years a Slave*, eds. Sue Eakin and Joseph Logsdon (Baton
Rouge: Louisiana State University Press, 1968).

sent him. Immediately the defense charged the Illinois attorney with being an abolitionist, which he denied. In fact, he stated that he "detested" abolitionists and that he had known Morrison all his life as a slave of his uncle's. When the attorney Morrison came to New Orleans, he told Charles Morrison that all slaves in Illinois had been freed by the Illinois court decision of *Jarrott v. Jarrott* (1845). Remarkably, the Illinois attorney took Charles Morrison to a New Orleans attorney to sue for his freedom. On July 1, 1848, the judge of the Third District Court of New Orleans declared Morrison free.[7]

In a similar case, Samuel Brown sued for his freedom on the grounds of his birth in Chillicothe, Ohio, in 1815. He later moved to St. Louis, where he agreed to become the paid servant of a Virginia man. While in Virginia, a slave trader named Sherman Johnson seized him and brought him to Louisiana for sale as a slave for life. Christian Roselius, Johnson's attorney, had Brown jailed as a flight risk. Johnson alleged that he had purchased Brown as slave for life from G. W. Afferson in Virginia. Brown countered that he had witnesses in Chillicothe and St. Louis who could substantiate his story and prove his freedom, and he asked the judge to send a commission to those cities to take statements from them. No evidence exists in the record to indicate that the court ever tried to contact the witnesses. The case dragged on for more than two years, during which Brown remained in prison. Finally, Roselius petitioned the court to cancel the writ of sequestration and dismiss Brown's suit for lack of evidence. In the last action in the case, the judge canceled the sequestration and released Brown to Johnson.[8]

In 1845, the slave Julia Arbuckle lived in Ray County, Missouri, with her master, Samuel Arbuckle. Arbuckle had thirty-eight slaves, twelve of whom he had freed before his death. In his will, he freed the other twenty-six, "each and every one of them absolutely and unconditionally manumitted and set free for ever." An acquaintance of Samuel Arbuckle testified that Arbuckle had told him that "nobody should enjoy the labor of his slaves after his death." Shortly after Arbuckle died, Julia Arbuckle found herself in the grip of a slave trader, William Talbot of New Orleans, who sold her to Victo-

---

7. *Civil Code*, Art. 177, p. 28; Morrison, f.m.c., v. Townsend and Thomkins, No. 509, Third District Court of New Orleans, 1 July 1848; Melvin Urofsky and Paul Finkelman, *A March of Liberty: A Constitutional History of the United States,* 2nd. ed. (New York: Oxford University Press, 2001), 339–40.

8. Brown, f.m.c., v. Johnson, No. 743, Third District Court of New Orleans, 8 June 1849.

rine Bouny. She told Bouny that she was free at the time of sale, but Bouny did nothing to ascertain her status and showed no inclination to release her. Instead, she put Arbuckle to work in her bakery and on the streets as a bread seller. Arbuckle hired an attorney to sue for her freedom, and she won her case in the Fifth District Court. After the decision, Talbot and Bouny appealed to the Louisiana Supreme Court, and they illegally held Arbuckle in slavery pending the outcome. The Supreme Court ruled in Arbuckle's favor the following year, affirming her freedom.

When the judge rendered the decision of the Fifth District Court, Talbot and Bouny's sons removed Julia from the parish prison where she had been sequestered and took her to a house, where for a time she remained a virtual prisoner while Talbot beat her as a slave. Upon her release she hired J. C. David to sue Bouny and Talbot for damages of $400 for cruel treatment and loss of wages as a "good bread seller." David's incompetence, as we have seen earlier, initially lost Arbuckle's case in the Fifth District Court; on appeal, the Louisiana Supreme Court ordered a new trial, which dragged on for years. Talbot fled the city, his occupation destroyed in May 1864, after the emancipation of Louisiana's slaves. With a new attorney, Arbuckle won a favorable judgment and damages of $240 with interest from the date of the suit shortly after the Civil War ended. Bouny appealed to the newly reconstructed Supreme Court of Louisiana on November 6, 1865, but no record exists to show that the court ever considered the appeal.[9]

Although witnesses at the new trial testified that Arbuckle had "industrious habits" and that she worked on steamboats as a cook and a washerwoman, newspapers and district court records provide clear evidence that she had become one of the Crescent City's most notorious "lewd and abandoned women." In 1857 she faced a charge of assault and battery on a white person. Apparently this incident stemmed from a fight between some of her "ladies" and the "girls" of a neighboring house of ill-fame owned by William McElroy, who himself had been convicted of keeping a brothel and about whom the *Daily Picayune* reported that he "has a colored family." The alleged victim claimed that Arbuckle had pushed her against a wall and injured her, "using foul and obscene language toward [her] in the public

9. Arbuckle, f.w.c., v. Bouny and Talbot, No. 1570, Fifth District Court of New Orleans, 11 October 1848; No. 1380, unreported Louisiana Supreme Court case (1849); No. 2523, Fifth District Court of New Orleans, 4 June 1849, 22 July 1865; No. 1632, 5 La. Ann. 699 (1850).

streets." Arbuckle pleaded not guilty in May 1857, and the district attorney disposed of the case with a *nolle prosequi* the following month because the alleged victim refused to continue with the case. A few months later the *Picayune* commented, "The reputation of Julia is anything but good." In late 1860 a First District Court jury found Arbuckle guilty of "keeping a disorderly house and a house of prostitution." On December 6, the judge sentenced her to three months in parish prison and court costs. In 1862, police arrested Arbuckle for assault and battery on the charge that she "wantonly, unprovokedly, maliciously threw a handful of salt" into the face and eyes of a five-month-old baby. There is no disposition of this case, which ended on May 9, 1862. By that time the Federal forces had taken control of New Orleans, and the courts had closed.[10]

In 1850 a man whose kidnapping rivaled Solomon Northup's both in length and complexity sued for his freedom in the Fourth District Court. William Houston claimed to be a British citizen, a native of Liverpool, and a free man. He said he was born in Gibraltar, the birthplace of his father, and that his mother had kept a sailors' boarding house near Queen's Dock in Liverpool. He had left Liverpool in 1840 as a steward on a ship commanded by a man named Davis. Upon arriving in New Orleans, Houston had left Davis's ship because he planned to travel to Savannah. While walking about New Orleans a man had approached him and promised to help him get him to Savannah. He had accompanied the man upriver in a steamboat. When the boat arrived in St. Martinsville, however, the man had ordered Houston to work as a cook and thereafter had held him as a slave for five years. Houston alleged that the man had destroyed his freedom papers. Then a series of sales had followed. His abductor had sold him to one Burton, a New Orleans bartender, who held him for two months before selling him to George Lynch, who owned a dry goods store in the city. Lynch held him two years, after which he had hired him out to one Captain Willis, who had taken him to Malamoroo, where he had been wounded in the Mexican War battles of Monterey and Buena Vista. After the war, Willis had returned Houston to Lynch in New Orleans, and Lynch had sold him to a Mr. Rich-

10. State v. Arbuckle, f.w.c., No. 12,767, First District Court of New Orleans, 2 June 1857; *New Orleans Daily Picayune,* 25 September, 5 November 1857; State v. Arbuckle, f.w.c., No. 14,740, First District Court of New Orleans, 6 December 1860; State v. Arbuckle, f.w.c., No. 15,815, First District Court of New Orleans, 9 May 1862.

ardson, who held him as a slave for one year. But somehow Richardson heard that the title to Houston had what the law termed a "cloud" upon it, and he refused to pay Lynch the purchase price. Lynch then put Houston in prison for "safekeeping" and sold him at a sheriff's sale in the St. Louis Hotel to a Mr. Howard, who possessed him at the time of suit in 1850. After his release, Houston went to the British consul and told his long story of bondage. Although the consul wrote down the facts and promised to help Houston, he then had him seized, confined to the workhouse, and sold at another sheriff's sale in 1851 for $405 to J. F. Lapice. On November 29, 1851, the judge of the Fourth District Court declared Houston free, but Lapice agreed to drop opposition only if Houston signed an agreement demanding no damages, and if he paid court costs. Houston had also to pay his attorney's fees. Still, after eleven years, he finally regained his freedom.[11]

The following year, the Third District Court heard the case of a free woman of color and her two children who found themselves held in slavery in New Orleans. Elijah Mix of Georgetown had freed the woman, Lucy Brown, at the age of fourteen in 1823. He subsequently had moved to New York with Brown, whose free parents had apprenticed her to Mix as a "waiting maid." She had lived in New York for three years, after which, in a series of conveyances, she somehow became described in a transaction as a "slave for life," her freedom papers lost or mislaid. She had two children following her manumission in 1823. In her suit for freedom, she asked for release from slavery for her and her children and damages of $250 for the year preceding the suit, $20 per month in wages, and $250 damages for her children. The jury returned a verdict in her favor with wages of $5 a month from the date of the institution of the suit. As the judge ruled, "She had acquired a right of freedom of which no power could divest her." Even her return to a slave state could not reenslave her.[12]

In 1853 another free person of color, Richard Lester, sued for his freedom after having been kidnapped and brought to New Orleans for sale as a slave. Lester alleged that he had lived in San Fernando, Mexico, as a free man with his wife and children on his cattle ranch. He had often served as an interpreter in Eagle Pass, Texas. In 1853 three men had kidnapped him

11. Houston, f.m.c., v. Lapice, No. 3729, Fourth District Court of New Orleans, 29 November 1851.

12. Brown, f.w.c., v. Smith, No. 3555, Third District Court of New Orleans, 13 May 1852.

in Eagle Pass and had brought him to San Antonio for sale as a slave. Fortunately, acquaintances in that city had recognized him as a free man, and he had instituted legal proceedings in a San Antonio court that confirmed his liberty. Finding himself without sufficient funds to return to Mexico, he had worked in San Antonio for a few weeks. During this time, a "pretended friend," George Martin, enticed him out of town, where he found himself surrounded by a group of men who seized him, put him in chains, and sent him to New Orleans. Upon his arrival, J. Preau claimed him as his slave. Lester filed suit for his freedom, alleging that Martin and Preau had conspired to reduce him to slavery and planned to sell him as a slave. For time lost, bodily harm, and mental suffering, he asked for damages of $10,000. He also asked the court to sequester him to prevent Preau from selling him. The case dragged on and Lester remained in jail. He died of typhoid fever in prison in 1854 before the case ever came to trial. The jailer listed his fees as 25 cents per day for 146 days, a turnkey fee of $1, and thirty medical visits at $22.50, a total of $60. It is perhaps some small justice that Preau had to pay the fees.[13]

The same year, sixteen people who had been allowed to live as free for many years found themselves forcibly taken to New Orleans from Pointe Coupée Parish and placed in a slave pen for sale. The case began as a *habeas corpus* action in the First District Court. Judge John Larue ruled that the writ of *habeas corpus* did not apply to their case, but he reserved the right of the petitioners to sue for their freedom. Eulalie, the mother and grandmother of the kidnapped sixteen persons of color, alleged that her former owner, Simon Porche, had allowed her to live as free with a free man of color, a half-brother of Mrs. Porche, for forty-five years until 1852. Then, despite her elderly husband's feeble resistance, "certain armed persons" had taken her and her children and grandchildren from their homes in the night and had brought them to New Orleans for sale. The defendants contended that Eulalie and the others had never gained their freedom and therefore remained slaves. Eulalie won in the trial court, and the defendants appealed to the Louisiana Supreme Court. The court affirmed the judgment of the lower court on the basis that a woman who had enjoyed her freedom for forty-five years with her owner's knowledge could not be reduced to the

13. Lester, f.m.c., v. Preau, No. 7129, Fourth District Court of New Orleans, filed 19 December 1853.

status of a slave. The high court cited *Civil Code* Article 3510, which held that slaves allowed to live as free with the consent of their owners for more than ten years could not have their status returned to slavery: "If a master is denied a right of action to recover possession, after suffering his slave to enjoy his liberty for a certain length of time, there is no principle on which a resort to violence, in order to reduce him again to slavery, could be justi-fied or tolerated by any one." The defendants once more appealed to the Supreme Court. This time the court seemed to understand the real cause of the seizure, apparently the greed of the heirs of Porche, who, although not named in the suit, stood to benefit the most from the sale of the sixteen as slaves. As Justice Buchanan commented, "Their bill of sale gives no origin to the vendor's title. . . . These are circumstances calculated to inspire a suspicion that the true parties in interest are keeping out of sight. And if so, the reason may be easily imagined." Buchanan's ruling confirmed the free-dom of Eulalie and her descendants.[14]

The coming of the Civil War prevented the resolution of another kidnap-ping, the case of *Logan v. Hickman,* which began as a petition for freedom by Mary Ann Logan. Logan claimed that her master had freed her as a child of six years in Richmond, Virginia. She had lived with her aunt in Toronto for fourteen years; then she had moved to New York, where someone had kidnapped her, reduced her to slavery, and sold her to a slave trader in New Orleans. Peter Hickman had purchased her, but before he could take her to his plantation in Rapides Parish, she sued him for her freedom in the Third District Court. Hickman had her sequestered for safekeeping. The case dragged on, with Logan remaining in prison. Her health declined as a result of her incarceration, and her attending physician chillingly testified about the grim prison conditions in the city. The crowded cell had no bed; Logan had only a blanket. According to her doctor, she developed an inflammation of the stomach and a fever that he considered serious. After more than a year in confinement, she successfully petitioned the court to allow her to leave the prison to recuperate. The judge of the Third District Court re-leased her because "above all [there is] the question of humanity." He also ruled in favor of her suit for freedom. Hickman appealed to the Supreme

<hr />

14. Eulalie, f.w.c., v. Long and Mabry, No. 8668, First District Court of New Orleans, 26 May 1853; No. 3227, 9 La. Ann. 9 (1854); No. 3979, 11 La. Ann. 463 (1856). *Civil Code,* Art. 3510, p. 532.

Court of Louisiana. The Supreme Court reversed the decision of the trial court on the basis that the law required the institution of the suit in the parish of the owner's domicile, Rapides Parish. The high court dismissed the suit "without prejudice to the plaintiff's right of action at the domicile of the defendant." No record exists of further action in this case.[15]

Members of another large family who had lived for many years as free found themselves in the hands of a slave trader, who advertised to sell them in the *New Orleans Bee* on January 15, 1859. Euphrémie and her seven children, seized by her sister-in-law when her husband died, sued for her freedom and $5,000 in damages in the Third District Court. The defendants, both free women of color, Juliette Maran and her sister, J. B. Jordan, alias Noble, also had seized a free woman of color named Andrinette and her seven children and had offered them to a New Orleans auctioneer for sale. Both Andrinette and Euphrémie asked the court for an injunction to prevent their sale until a court could resolve the issue of their freedom. Maran and Noble claimed that all the persons seized as slaves had belonged to their brother, Charles Maran, who had died in 1851. A. P. Field, one of the most gifted members of the New Orleans bar, represented Maran and Noble; Euphrémie and Andrinette also had skilled counsel. As the *Daily Picayune* noted, "several members of the bar have volunteered for the plaintiffs," rare evidence of *pro bono* work by the early New Orleans bar. Two prominent law firms represented the plaintiffs, Dufour & Tran and Budd & Lambert, making this a trial by legal superstars. Field warned the trial court judge of the dangers of "letting loose in our midst . . . persons of color." He also reminded the judge of the "dreadful events which have lately taken place at Harper's Ferry." Infuriated, the judge told Field that his court constituted a "Court of Law and not a Court of Expediency." The judge also reminded Field of the gallant service provided by the free people of color at the Battle of New Orleans. He declared Euphrémie and Andrinette and their children free, and the defendants appealed. The beginning of the Civil War and the closing of the courts in 1862 delayed the decision in this case. In 1865, a newly reconstituted Supreme Court declared them free, a moot point by that time.[16]

15. Logan, f.w.c., v. Hickman and Robertson, No. 9470, Third District Court of New Orleans, 2 March 1857; No. 5736, 14 La. Ann. 300 (1859).

16. Euphrémie, f.w.c., v. Maran and Jordan, alias Noble, No. 13,231, Third District Court of New Orleans, 24 December 1859; Andrinette, f.w.c., v. Maran and Jordan, alias Noble, No.

In 1859, Andy Foster sued for his freedom before the Third District Court. He claimed that his mother's owner had freed her before his birth in Clark County, Kentucky; therefore, he had never held slave status. He further claimed that his white father had taken him to Ohio to educate him. Sometime after his father's death, kidnappers had seized him in St. Louis, Missouri, and had brought him to New Orleans for sale as a slave for life. William Mish had purchased him. The trial court dismissed his lawsuit, holding that Foster could not sue for his freedom because of the 1857 Louisiana law that prohibited all manumissions. Foster appealed to the state's Supreme Court. In a strong decision, the court reversed the decision of the Fourth District Court and declared Foster free. As Justice Thomas Land wrote in the decision of the court,

> It is a grave error to suppose, that free persons of color, who have been wrongfully and illegally deprived of their freedom, and sold into slavery in this State, have no right of action in our courts for the recovery of their liberty. If no right of action in such cases existed, then free negroes might be kidnapped in any part of the Union, and sold into slavery in this state, with impunity—a species of slave-trade, which our Legislature never intended to legalize by the Act of 1857, prohibiting emancipation.[17]

In 1860 the Third District Court heard the case of *Bass and Johnson* v. *Chase*. Peter Bass and his wife, Dolly Johnson, sued for their freedom, claiming that Dr. O. G. Chase had kidnapped them in Illinois and intended to bring them with him to Texas, where he planned to settle. Peter Bass, born of a free woman in Carroll County, Tennessee, had obtained papers from the clerk of the county court there describing him as a twenty-one-year-old "yellow" man. The clerk wrote, "He is free where ever he may go." Dolly Johnson, described as "cross-eyed with a scar under her chin and strongly built," had free papers certified by the clerk that stated that her master, Thomas Johnson, had freed her in his will. A white man named Green Lee Bumpass, also of Tennessee, testified that he knew Johnson and

13,266, First District Court of New Orleans, 24 December 1859; Nos. 6740, 6741, unreported Louisiana Supreme Court case (1865); *New Orleans Bee,* 15 January 1859.

17. Foster, f.m.c., v. Mish, No. 12,249, Fourth District Court of New Orleans, 21 February 1858; No. 6344, 15 La. Ann. 199 (1860).

Bass as free people of color. An attorney named Thomas Jefferson Earhart represented Bass and Johnson. In his petition, Earhart, who by this time had represented a number of slaves and free persons of color before the New Orleans courts, asked the judge to restore their liberty and award them damages of $1,000. At trial, the chief of police produced a handbill giving notice of their kidnapping in Illinois and warning planters not to purchase them, as "they are really free people." The judge rendered a decision in their favor. No record exists to indicate any damages awarded to Johnson and Bass, nor any subsequent prosecution of Chase for kidnapping.[18]

In October 1861, two brothers, Thomas and James Scales, concocted a unusual justification for kidnapping a free man of color named Isaac in Commerce, Missouri, and bringing him to New Orleans for sale as a slave. The Scales brothers, who were accompanied to court by their father and another brother, admitted that they had organized a company of twenty-five men to go with them to the northern border states "to steal all the bombs they could secure, get every possible information, and report to the Southern generals; [they] thought it would be a good and profitable joke to kidnap that dark skinned abolitionist and bring him to the city to sell as a slave." They claimed that General Gideon Pillow had commissioned them to perform those tasks (but not the kidnapping), and they produced written and signed authorization from Pillow. They further alleged that Isaac had served as one of the best agents of the underground railroad in Missouri. The *Daily Picayune* commented, "The Mayor did not seem to like that air of Scales just arrived from Commerce. The negro may be a slave after all, or granting that he is a free negro, he may be a spy brought to our plantations to corrupt other negroes." The mayor of New Orleans, John T. Monroe, sent the case to the grand jury. Isaac named a few respectable men in New Orleans who would testify as to the soundness of his principles. He firmly denied being an abolitionist. The *Picayune* editorialized, "At any rate it would be queer policy, let honesty alone, to steal free negroes who are Abolitionists and bring them among the slaves of our plantations; they would soon infect the whole black population of the State." No record of prosecution of the Scales brothers exists, nor does any evidence of what happened to Isaac.[19]

18. Bass and Johnson, f.p.c., v. Chase, No. 14,642, Third District Court of New Orleans, 4 May 1860; *New Orleans Daily Picayune*, 25, 26 October 1861.

19. *New Orleans Daily Picayune*, 25, 26 October 1861.

The fact that just one criminal prosecution for the kidnapping of free people of color appears in the records of the district courts, despite so much evidence of kidnapping in the same records, suggests that laws against kidnapping went unenforced because the victims were black. Free people of color in the North and the South always lived in fear of being abducted and sold as slaves for life. Except in unusual circumstances, such as Solomon Northup's discovery of a white man willing to help him, the courts remained a kidnapped person's only recourse. The logistics and cost of hiring an attorney and instituting a suit for freedom must have been daunting. Securing sufficient proof of freedom, especially if the kidnappers had destroyed it, could be a formidable obstacle in an age of slow communication and poor record keeping. Whites willing to help blacks, especially in the South, risked the enmity of their slaveholding neighbors. This proved especially true as national tensions over the issue of slavery increased and hostility to free blacks grew. Many southerners began to blame free people of color for problems with slavery, and many came to regard them as a nuisance at best and a menace at worst. Almost all of the southern states, including Louisiana, tried to keep free people of color from entering their borders; some, including Louisiana, launched a systematic campaign to drive away those already in the state.

8

BEING IN THE STATE
IN CONTRAVENTION OF THE LAW

From the beginning of the American possession of Louisiana, government officials worried about the steady increase of the population of free people of color in the territory. New Orleans, especially, proved to be a magnet for free blacks from other states, who found there a large community of their peers and opportunities to support themselves working in construction, on the levees, as waiters, barbers, domestics, or even as prostitutes. High wages and the attraction of a more relaxed racial climate than any other southern city lured free people of color to New Orleans from all over the United States. Although their labor filled a real need in the growing city, and although white men contributed to the growth of this population by illicit sexual relationships with free women of color, many viewed the growing population of people of color with alarm. Whites feared that the presence of autonomous, self-supporting free people of color might provide a "bad" example to the city's slaves, giving them hope of freedom and certainly proving false the notion that black people could not take care of themselves. Whites also believed, and not without reason, that free blacks might help slaves to run away, hide fugitive slaves, and incite and lead slaves into insurrection.[1]

In 1807, the year after the territorial legislature passed a comprehensive *Black Code*, lawmakers passed a harsh act to prevent free people of color from moving into Louisiana. This act set a fine of $20 per week for a free person of color who entered and remained in the state illegally for more than two weeks. If the person did not pay the fine and leave Louisiana im-

---

1. Berlin, *Slaves without Masters*, 108–34; Tansey, "Out-of-State Free Blacks," 376.

mediately after detection, the act authorized the parish judge to jail the offender and sell him or her for a term sufficient to pay the fine and court costs. If no purchaser was found, the free person of color was to be employed at public works for the number of days he or she had remained in the state illegally. In 1809, a large influx of refugees, originally from St. Domingue, came to Louisiana from Cuba as refugees, including whites, free people of color, and slaves. Overnight the population of free blacks in the state grew to 3,102, a number that included 1,297 children, 1,377 women, and 428 men. Although the territorial governor, William C. C. Claiborne, complained, "We have at this time a much greater proportion of that kind of population than comports with our interest," humanitarian motives prompted the people of New Orleans to accept the refugees. The presence of so many women and children and the low number of men no doubt helped to win over those who might otherwise have wanted to keep them out. Still, Claiborne wanted the Act of 1807 enforced on the refugee men of color. Although the mayor of New Orleans fumed that the law did not give him sufficient authority to enforce the act, he also pointed out that the new arrivals behaved irreproachably. Not one had given cause for arrest or court action. It seems that the Act of 1807 served as a method to control free men of color by threatening them with fines and expulsion, not by actually expelling them.[2]

To the increasing alarm of state legislators, the free black community in New Orleans had grown to 8,041 by 1830. In April of that year, Louisiana lawmakers passed an new act to prevent further immigration of free people of color into the state. For the first time, this act included provisions to eject some blacks already there. The act required any free person of color who had come into the state since 1825 to depart within sixty days. Refusal to comply increased the risk of prosecution. If convicted, a person could be sentenced to one year of imprisonment at hard labor, after which he or she had to leave Louisiana within thirty days. Failure to do so resulted in imprisonment for life at hard labor. The act did allow the departing person to have one year to dispose of any property or slaves on which he or she had paid

2. "An Act to Prevent the Immigration of Free Negroes and Mulattoes into the Territory of Orleans," Act of April 14, 1807, *Louisiana Territorial Acts, 1807*, pp. 180–2; Paul Lachance, "The 1809 Immigration of Saint-Domingue Refugees to New Orleans: Reception, Integration, and Impact," *Louisiana History* 29 (spring 1988): 109–41.

state taxes in the preceding year. If a person left the state under orders, any return would result in prosecution and possible condemnation to a life of hard labor. "Being in the state in contravention of the law," or simply "contravention," was the name given to this offense.[3]

The Act of 1830 forbade free people of color who voluntarily left the United States from returning to Louisiana and required newly freed slaves to leave the state within one month of manumission. Failure to comply meant that the manumitting owner had to forfeit a bond of $1,000. However, slaves whose owners took them to a free state and manumitted them there would not be subject to deportation if they returned. The act further required all free black sailors who came to Louisiana to leave the state when their ship departed or else leave the state within thirty days.[4]

The act contained strong warnings for whites and free people of color concerning their dealings with each other. It warned white persons against "using any language, with intent to disturb the peace or security . . . in relation of the slaves of the people of this state, or to diminish that respect which is commanded to free people of color for the whites . . . or to destroy that line of distinction which the law has established between the several classes of the community." Whites convicted of these very general actions incurred a minimum fine of $300, on up to a $1,000 fine and a jail term of six months to three years; free blacks convicted of similar offenses received a $1,000 fine and imprisonment at hard labor from three to five years, after which they faced banishment from the state for life. Another legislative act, passed the same day, forbade teaching slaves to read or write.[5]

To assist officials in differentiating between legal resident free persons of color and those who were newly arrived and illegal, the 1830 act required free persons of color who had arrived in the state before 1825 to register themselves in the mayor's office, stating name, place of birth, color, gender, occupation, and date of arrival or proof of birth in New Orleans. Registration cost fifty cents; failure to register could merit a fine of $50 and one month in jail.[6]

3. "An Act to Prevent Free Persons of Color from Entering This State, and for Other Purposes," Act of March 16, 1830, *Louisiana Acts, 1830*, Secs. 1, 2, 6, pp. 90–2.

4. Ibid., Secs. 4, 10, pp. 90–2.

5. Ibid., Secs. 9, p. 92; "An Act to Punish the Crimes Therein Mentioned, and for Other Purposes," Act of March 16, 1830, ibid., Sec. 3, p. 96.

6. Ibid., Secs. 12, 13, p. 94.

The following year, Louisiana lawmakers amended the Act of 1830, allowing resident free persons of color who left the state to return if they owned property in the state, exercised a useful trade, and conducted themselves with the "utmost respect and good order." Fearing rebellious influences, lawmakers only prohibited return of Louisianian free persons of color from the West Indies. Legislators also amended the requirement for a manumitting owner to post bond as a guarantee that a freed slave would leave the state; now if owners proved that they freed slaves for "long, faithful or important service," the slave could remain in Louisiana if the police jury of the parish agreed.[7]

In 1842, lawmakers extended the amnesty provisions in the Act of 1830. Free blacks who entered the state before 1838—not 1825—could stay in Louisiana under certain restrictions. They had to register their names, ages, and places of birth in the mayor's office. If they could prove good character and could give bond for "faithful observance of all the laws of this State relating to free persons of color," they could petition to remain in the state. Failure to obey the laws pertaining to them could result in the revocation of this permission. Hundreds of free blacks took advantage of this act to confirm their legal status in Louisiana. The records of the three New Orleans municipalities and the police juries of other parishes show numerous petitions to remain in the state, almost all of which were granted. Manumissions petitions also contained petitions to remain in Louisiana, and most of those were routinely granted as well.[8]

The Louisiana legislature passed another act in 1842 concerning free people of color entering the state. This act was aimed mainly at free black sailors or crews aboard the many vessels that came into port in New Orleans. It required the captain of each arriving ship to notify the nearest judge or justice of the peace that free blacks made up some of the crew. The judge or justice then issued a warrant for the arrest of the free black sailors and

7. "An Act to Amend an Act Entitled 'An Act to Prevent Free Persons of Color from Entering This State, and for Other Purposes,'" Act of March 25, 1831, *Louisiana Acts, 1831,* Sec. 2, pp. 98–100.

8. "An Act to Amend an Act Approved the Sixteenth March, 1842, Entitled 'An Act More Effectually to Prevent Free Persons of Color from Entering into This State, and for Other Purposes,'" Act of March 22, 1843, *Louisiana Acts, 1842,* pp. 45–6; Lawrence J. Kotlikoff and Anton J. Rupert, "The Manumission of Slaves in New Orleans, 1827–1846," *Southern Studies* 19 (summer 1980): 172–81.

kept them in jail until the ship was ready to leave port, at which point the captain petitioned for their release and paid confinement fees. Furthermore, captains had to post a $500 bond for each free man of color to ensure that jail fees and court costs would be paid. Failure to post this bond resulted in a $1,000 penalty for each person of color detained. If a free person of color returned to Louisiana after having been sent out of the state, he or she could incur a prison term of five years at hard labor. After serving the term, the free black had thirty days to leave the state. Failure to do so resulted in a prison term of life at hard labor.

The 1842 act prohibited hiring or giving lodging to any person illegally in the state, under penalty of $200 for each offense. The act specifically exempted native-born or legally residing free persons of color: "That the provisions of this act shall not be so construed to prevent free negroes or persons of color, who are natives of Louisiana, or who have been residing therein since the first of January eighteen hundred and twenty-five from leaving or returning to this state; *provided,* that they shall not have established their domicile in a free state of the Union." In addition, lawmakers blocked persons from introducing *statu liberi* (those who had acquired the right to freedom at a later date) into the state and prohibited anyone from purchasing them. The act required *statu liberi* already in the state to depart after their time for freedom arrived. After passage of this act, owners wishing to free their slaves might have simply allowed them to live as free, since actually manumitting them would require them to leave.[9]

During the 1840s and early 1850s the New Orleans police only sporadically enforced contravention ordinances, although newspaper editorials and grand jury reports complained of increasing numbers of illegal free blacks in the city. In 1838 the *New Orleans Commercial Bulletin* warned that New Orleans seemed in "danger of begin overrun by this obnoxious class. . . . [A]ll that is wanting is a strict enforcement of the law." An 1855 grand jury stated that "free coloured people continue to visit our city in contravention of our laws, some by ignorance, but the most part through speculative designs to debauch away our slave population to the great injury of the own-

9. "An Act More Effectually to Prevent Free Persons of Color from Entering into This State, and for Other Purposes," Act of March 16, 1842, *Louisiana Acts, 1842,* pp. 308–18; Joe Gray Taylor, *Negro Slavery in Louisiana* (Lafayette: Louisiana Historical Association, 1963), 155.

ers." An 1858 letter to the *Daily Picayune* reported that "free negroes employed on steamers as stewards are nearly all trained and paid to use their influence . . . to prevail upon our servants to abscond. They meet them at Cairo [Illinois], and from that point defy all efforts made to recapture [them]. . . . I lost a valuable man this way, enticed away by the steward of the *Diana*. . . . [A]t the moment I have in my possession a card of his house in Chicago, where he received his colored friends—they paying him well for his trouble of course." An editorial in the *Picayune* in 1858 warned, "The existence of negroes in these different civil conditions [free and slave] in this city, constantly mingling with each other, has become a source of uneasiness. . . . Unless those that have been emancipated, within a few years, prove better qualified for freedom and adopt more the habits and character of the old families of free colored persons, who own property and form a respectable class, their condition must be changed, or the State must be altogether rid of them."[10]

After 1842, city police generally arrested only free people of color illegally in the state who attracted their attention by some inappropriate behavior: drunks, vagrants, prostitutes, thieves, and deserting seamen. Although police seldom arrested a respectable free person of color and demanded proof of resident status, their power to do so was intended to remind free people of color of their status. Free blacks must have been apprehensive almost every time they saw a police officer, knowing that failure to prove their legal status could swiftly force them to leave the state, their families, and their communities, never to return.

Newspaper reports reveal that often those arrested for contravention came to the attention of authorities because of petty criminal acts or what whites considered inappropriate behavior by free persons of color. For example, a free black man named Crick, a British subject who had a white wife, brought attention to himself by allegedly aiding in the abduction of a runaway slave. He had to fight that charge and also the charge that he lived in the state in contravention of the law. Julia Carpentier, a free woman of color and a prostitute who the *Daily Picayune* called "Sweet Julia," successfully proved she had the right to live in the state after being arrested for vagrancy. Catherine, a free woman of color, had to answer to the charge of

10. *New Orleans Commercial Bulletin*, 20 April 1838; *New Orleans Daily Picayune*, 5 July 1855, 13 October 1852, 17 October 1858.

illegally keeping an eating house without a license and being in the state in contravention of the law. In 1858 the *Daily Picayune* reported, "An enterprising young darkey, who gives his name as David Crocket, f.b.c., was arrested yesterday by Officer Pennel, on Circus street, with a box of combs in his possession, supposed to have been stolen, and which he was trying to sell. He was said to have had an illegal pass in his possession, and in addition, he is charged with being in the State in contravention of law." Edward Williams, a free man of color, allegedly stole a pair of shoes from the pilot of the steamboat *Messenger* and found himself charged with the theft and with contravention. Police arrested two free men of color who they found riding around the city in a taxi "aping the fashionable in their dress and manner." They claimed to be stewards aboard a steamboat that came down the Ohio River. The recorder forced them to sign declarations that they would leave the state and not return. The *Picayune* observed, "In this connection we may state that three valuable slaves have lately been run off from their masters in this city, and that it is supposed they have been seduced away by the colored stewards of vessels, who secreted them on board."[11]

At times persons of color who had committed no obvious offense found themselves defending charges of contravention. Perhaps a bad haircut prompted Charles H. Reynolds to complain to a justice of the peace that Joseph Rollins, a free man of color who ran a barbershop in the basement of the Planters' Hotel, resided in the state illegally. Reynolds also charged five or six other free black men working as barbers in the same shop with the same offense. The *Daily Picayune* reported, "Yesterday the well known Goins, Parsons, and five other barbers, all f.m.c., who have for years past smoothed the chins and curled the hair of thousands of our citizens, were brought before Recorder Caldwell, on the charge of being in the State in contravention of the law. Several of these men have been so long in this city, and have for many years kept such famous barbershops, that their arrest excited quite an excitement." No record of their subsequent prosecution exists, and they may have fled the state.[12]

Occasionally police mistakenly charged white people with contravention, as well as those attempting to pass for white as a defense against it. For

11. *New Orleans Daily Picayune*, 20 September 1850, 27 July 1852, 31 May 1853, 17 September, 2 October, 8 November, 29 December 1858; Tansey, "Out-of-State Free Blacks," 376.
12. *New Orleans Daily Picayune*, 4, 8 June 1852.

example, Margaret Wilson, jailed as a person of color for contravention, petitioned for a writ of *habeas corpus*. When she same to court, she proved that her mother was a white woman. Police charged J. M. Brown with the crime of perjury for falsely swearing that his mother was white "in order to elevate his status of being in the state in contravention of the law, and of teaching a school where negroes unlawfully assemble, etc." In 1857 four prostitutes—Margaret Ford, Kate McCarty, Mary Lyons, and Julia Turpy—brutally beat Jane Thomas and then procured her arrest as a free woman of color in the state in contravention of the law. Police locked her up for the night with a woman of color. Thomas obtained a letter from her father in Arkansas proving that she was white, and the recorder immediately dismissed her. The *Daily Picayune* commented, "It is to be hoped that those who were guilty of so great an outrage against her person and status, will be severely dealt with." Finally, in another newspaper article entitled "WHAT IS IN A NAME?" the *Picayune* reported that Louis Thompson, a free man of color in the state in contravention of the law, "thought he had the means to avoid being arrested, [which] was to pass himself off as a white man. But he had reckoned without officer White's sagacity, and was arrested by the latter on Basin street. Certainly, who better than White could know whether a man is white or not?"[13]

Contravention applied even to free persons of color who had been kidnapped and brought into Louisiana as slaves. Mary Ellen, who successfully proved her freedom after being kidnapped from Tennessee and brought to Louisiana as a slave, still had to leave the state within sixty days. The state made an exception in the case of Julia Arbuckle, however. Arbuckle had won her freedom in a New Orleans court in 1849 after having been kidnapped in Missouri and sold as a slave in 1847. Ten years later, officials accused her of contravention because she had been born elsewhere and had come to the state after 1838. Her attorney argued that she could not be in contravention, as she had been brought into the state "forcibly and illegally, and that as she had been declared free by the laws of this State, after great injustice and wrong had been done to her, it would not only be unjust, but cruel, to require her now to leave the State, particularly as the laws of Missouri would

13. Ibid., 29 February, 4 October 1856, 1 February, 3 March 1857, 2 May 1861.

not permit her to go back there." The recorder ordered the case against her discontinued.[14]

An act of 1829 also prohibited any free person of color who had been convicted of a crime in another state from entering Louisiana, on pain of seizure and sale to the highest bidder as a slave for life, with half of the purchase price going to the state and half to the informer. If a person brought a convicted slave felon into the state, the law assessed a fine of no more than $5,000 and no less than $1,000 and a jail sentence of no less than five years. The *Daily Picayune* reported two violations of this act. The first involved a free person of color named Toby, who had been convicted of murder in Milledgeville, Georgia, but pardoned by the governor of that state. The newspaper urged prosecution and expulsion of Toby as soon as possible. Police also arrested Emeline Jones, an Ohio free woman of color who also had been convicted of murder but pardoned by the governor of Ohio. Prosecutions of Toby and Emeline do not appear in the court records; they probably left the state before they could be tried.[15]

Another notorious woman, Sarah Conner, found herself ordered to leave the state within sixty days. Conner, a free woman of color, lived with an unscrupulous slave dealer, Theophilus Freeman, as his concubine. (Freeman sold Solomon Northup into slavery.) The slave dealer had purchased Conner as his slave, but he freed her (claiming that she had purchased herself) when his business dealings went sour and his creditors foreclosed. He then transferred all of his property to her to avoid seizure by his creditors. When brought before the recorder on a charge of contravention, she could not prove that she lived in the state legally, and the recorder ordered her to leave the state within sixty days.[16]

Most free persons of color who were accused of contravention did not stand trial before the First District Court. These cases began in the recorders' courts, where the recorder warned those guilty of contravention to leave the state, usually within sixty days. If they did not do so, the recorder then sent the case to trial before the First District Court. Local newspapers give

14. Ibid., 22 September, 5, 21 November 1857.

15. "An Act Relative to the Introduction of Slaves into This State, and for Other Purposes," Act of January 31, 1829, *Louisiana Acts, 1829*, Sec. 13, p. 48; *New Orleans Daily Picayune*, 19 June 1854, 1 August 1855.

16. *New Orleans Times Picayune*, 15 May 1852.

evidence of many persons of color refusing to leave the state in the allotted time, and the recorder ordering them to stand trial before the criminal court. However, most of these cases do not appear in the district court records, suggesting that the threat of a probable conviction prompted many people to leave the state before trial. For example, Emma White, a free woman of color, went before Recorder Winter, charged with contravention. Winter ordered her to leave Louisiana by April 29, 1853, but she still remained in the city a year later. Winter sent her case to the First District Court, but it never appeared in the court's records. She probably left the state before trial.[17]

In 1852 the Louisiana legislature further tightened the laws concerning free people of color who arrived on steamboats in order to prevent them from freely wandering about the city. The new act provided that free black sailors or crew could avoid being jailed upon arrival by remaining on board their vessels while in port. The captain had to list the name, age, description, and occupation of each free black member of his crew. If a steward had to go ashore to get provisions, the captain had to ask the mayor to issue a passport for the individual crew member. The act provided for the imprisonment of each free black crewman found on shore without a passport and required the captain to pay $1,000 for each violation. The *Daily Picayune* editorialized, "It is well known that this law was passed by the Legislature at a period of excitement, arising from the hostile attitude assumed by the abolitionists of Massachusetts, and other States, whose emissaries inundated the South with publications of an inflammatory character." The editorial questioned the harm of letting free black sailors and cooks on shore, which "inflicts a severe hardship and great injustice upon a useful class of men, whose place cannot properly be supplied by white servants in vessels trading in the Southern latitudes. . . . New Orleans has lost a valuable trade with the British West Indies; almost all of the vessels which came regularly to this port, now go to Baltimore, Philadelphia, or Richmond to purchase their cargoes." A few months later the *Picayune* reported, "The police have been busy in the several districts, hunting up free colored persons who are here without the legal right, and several arrests have been made. All the evils complained of by frequent grand juries, are likely to be eradicated by the

17. Ibid., 5 April, 3 May 1854, 3 July 1855, 23 September 1856, 4, 21 February, 8 September 1857, 2 July 1860.

activity of our consolidated police force." From September 1, 1852, to August 31, 1858, police arrested 429 free persons of color for possession of illegal passes and for remaining in the state in contravention of the law.[18]

Only twenty-seven cases of persistent refusal to leave the state when ordered to do so resulted in trial; most of these ended in conviction and sentence. In many of these cases, the person accused of contravention had committed some additional offense that drew attention to him or herself. For example, charges against George Stevens, a free man of color, asserted that he had insulted John Cushing, a white man, in February 1855. Stevens had been ordered to leave the state in October 1854. By June 1855 he still had not left, and consequently he had to face trial in the First District Court. He pled guilty and received a sentence of one year in the penitentiary at hard labor. The *Daily Picayune* reported in 1859 that Stevens once again faced a charge of contravention, so obviously he either still had not left or had returned after departing. No evidence of prosecution exists, indicating that Stevens either had finally left the state or the prosecutor dropped the charges. Luke Stephany, a free man of color, committed two crimes in two days that surely drew the attention of the police. On June 13, 1855, police arrested him for breaking open a box and stealing a number of silver spoons. Two days later, Stephany assaulted a police officer and attempted to bite and hit him. The recorder sent the case to the First District Court. Although Stephany claimed to have lived in Louisiana before 1825, he could produce no proof of residency, and the judge sentenced him to one year at hard labor in the penitentiary.[19]

18. "An Act to Amend an Act Entitled 'An Act More Effectively to Prevent Free Persons of Color from Entering This State and for Other Purposes,'" Approved the Sixteenth of March, Eighteen Hundred and Forty-Two, Act of March 18, 1852, *Louisiana Acts, 1852,* pp. 193–4; *New Orleans Daily Picayune,* 17 February, 12 June 1852; Robert C. Reinders, "The Decline of the New Orleans Free Negro in the Decade before the Civil War," *Journal of Mississippi History* 24 (January–October 1962): 90.

19. State v. Stevens, f.m.c., No. 10,416, First District Court of New Orleans, 19 June 1855; State v. Stevens, No. 10,417, First District Court of New Orleans, *nolle prosequi,* 24 May 1857; *New Orleans Times Picayune,* 3 August 1859; State v. Stephany, f.m.c., No 10,485, First District Court of New Orleans, 30 June 1855; *New Orleans Daily Picayune,* 13, 15 June 1855. Other cases of contravention include: State v. Martin, f.w.c., No. 299, First District Court of New Orleans, 4 October 1846; State v. Smith, f.m.c., No. 2279, First District Court of New Orleans, 19 May 1848; State v. Eddington, alias Morgan, alias Dutch, f.m.c., No. 3031, First District Court of New Orleans, 20 November 1848; State v. Mills, f.m.c., No. 10,386, First

In 1859 the Louisiana legislature scrapped the passport system and re-quired free black stewards and cooks to go to jail or remain on board their vessel until the ship left port. The captain had to put up a bond for $500 for each person of color who entered the port; violation triggered a civil suit in which officials could seize a captain's vessel. This act set jail fees at 40 cents per person per day. Any free person of color ordered to leave the state had to do so within five days or face a sentence of three to twelve months in prison. Police officers or ordinary citizens who arrested someone in contra-vention would receive a $10 reward. Any free person of color who returned to Louisiana after being ordered to leave the state faced a sentence of five years at hard labor in the penitentiary. Arrests for contravention increased, no doubt motivated by the $10 reward. Between 1853 and 1856, police ar-rested an average of 8.5 free people of color a month for contravention; by 1859 that number had increased to 21.4 a month. From October 1, 1859, to June 1, 1861, police arrested a monthly average of 96.3 free people of color for contravention. Between October 1859 and the end of February 1862, police arrested a total of 2,206 free people of color for contravention, ap-proximately one of every five free persons of color in New Orleans.[20]

The *Daily Picayune* commented on northern response to the Act of 1859, noting that the act had "awakened a terrible clamor from the anti-slavery press. Louisiana is unsparingly denounced as a 'violator of the constitution,' a 'nullifier of the national compact,' and as 'disregardful of commercial and State comity.'" Still, the newspaper defended the act by stating that its ulti-mate goal—to decrease the number of resident free people of color—remained a sound one. Even if an increase in the free black population proved tolerable, the reporter wrote, "we are not disposed to admit into association even with our free men of color, the negro anti-slavery conven-

District Court of New Orleans, 13 April 1855; State v. Henderson, f.m.c., No. 12,723, First District Court of New Orleans, 25 February 1857; *New Orleans Times Picayune,* 11 February 1857; State v. Wilson, f.w.c., No. 12,097, First District Court of New Orleans, 24 April 1856. The *New Orleans Daily Picayune* referred to Henry Eddington as a "great scoundrel and thief." *New Orleans Daily Picayune,* 30 June 1844; Sterkx, *The Free Negro in Antebellum Loui-siana,* 109.

20. "An Act Relative to Free Persons of Color Entering This State from Other States or Foreign Countries," Act of March 15, 1859, *Louisiana Acts, 1859,* pp. 70–2; *New Orleans Daily Picayune,* 15 March, 8 July, 8 September 1859. Tansey, "Out-of-State Free Blacks," 377, 379; Sterkx, *The Free Negro in Antebellum Louisiana,* 116–7.

tionists, slave rescuers, and stealers, mob exciters and law violators, of the North. The United States rejects European paupers and convicts from her shores; Louisiana shuts the door against the free entrance of a worse class of population from the Northern States."[21]

The Act of 1859 did not take effect until September 1, 1859. On August 26, the *Daily Picayune* reported high anxiety in the free black community: "There is great trouble among the colored people just now on account of the late law of the Legislature, which will be in force in a few days. Many have been living in this city for ten or twenty years, who have taken no formal steps to be legally domiciliated [*sic*] here, and now find themselves in contravention, through error or ignorance."[22]

The first arrests under the 1859 law did not involve free black stewards or cooks, but two free black residents of New Orleans, Harriet and Elenora Robinson. Recorder Summers ordered them to leave the state within five days. The *Daily Picayune* noted that the arrests "will be followed by many more." The newspaper reported that the mayor's office had been besieged by a very large number of free people of color demanding to be registered: "Many find themselves in great trouble through their ignorance or neglect. The law of 1843 authorized all free negroes residing in the State previous to 1838 to remain, providing that they would get themselves registered within thirty days following the promulgation of the act. There are hundreds in this city who have been residents for over twenty years, have raised families and acquired property, but who have never complied with that legal formality, and now find themselves in contravention, if the letter of the law is strictly followed." The "Register of Free Coloured Persons" from the mayor's office lists 949 free people of color who registered themselves in 1859 and 1860. Each entry states either that the person of color came into the state before 1838 or had lived in Louisiana from birth.[23]

Six days after the contravention law of 1859 went into effect, police arrested two free men of color, George Logan and John Cook of the steamboat *Elizabeth Hamilton,* and incarcerated them in the parish prison. The *Daily Picayune* noted that the police made many arrests of free people of color in

21. *New Orleans Daily Picayune,* 18 September 1859.

22. Ibid., 23 August 1859.

23. Ibid., 1 September 1859; Mayor's Office, *Register of Free Coloured People, 1840–1863;* Tansey, "Out-of-State Free Blacks," 381.

the first days of September 1859. Logan and Cook were thus not singled out but were part of a larger trend. Within a week, Cook and Logan hired Thomas J. Earhart, the same attorney who had represented the kidnapped Dolly Johnson and Peter Bass in their suit for freedom. In court, Earhart argued the unconstitutionality of the contravention act. The *Daily Picayune* noted, "The question was argued with great ability on both sides and bore directly on the constitutionality of the law. The argument lasted all day." The Fourth District Court upheld the law, and returned the prisoners to jail to await the departure of their ship from port. Three days later, Earhart sued for a writ of *habeas corpus* in the Sixth District Court. He lost, and he appealed to the Supreme Court of Louisiana. The *Picayune* commented, "Ship and steamboat captains and merchants generally, who are connected with the river and the northern trade, are interested in this question, and an early decision from the Supreme Court is eagerly expected." In May 1860, the Supreme Court denied jurisdiction on the grounds that the state constitution of 1852 only allowed the court to hear criminal cases involving sentences of death, life in prison, or fines of over $300. *Habeas corpus* fit none of these categories. Therefore, the high court dismissed the appeal.[24]

As the Supreme Court was mulling over Earhart's appeal, the *Daily Picayune* reported that the New Orleans chief of police was awaiting the ruling of the court to begin enforcing the Act of 1859. Nevertheless, newspaper accounts of arrests of dozens of free people of color appeared even before the judgment of dismissal and continued until the city fell to Union forces in 1862. A typical report appeared in December 1859: "The police throw their net among the suspicious portion of the colored population, and make a large haul. This morning a batch of seven or eight of these luckless individuals were brought before Recorder Monroe by officers Creed and Chalmers who charged them with being in the state in contravention of the law." In 1861 the grand jury reported that a "great many free negroes are residing in the parish and state, in contravention of the law, many having procured false free papers previous to the passage of the law. The attention of the community and Legislature is called to the fact as being greatly prejudicial to the interests of slaveholders." After the Civil War began, the problem of

24. *New Orleans Daily Picayune*, 6, 13, 14, 27 September 1859; State of Louisiana, on relation of Cook et al., v. Keeper of Parish Prison, 15 La. Ann. 347 (1860); Bass and Johnson, f.p.c., v. Chase, No. 14,642, Third District Court of New Orleans, 4 May 1860.

free people of color illegally remaining in the state persisted. In March 1862, the *Daily Picayune* reported "that numerous class of free colored people who don't belong to the city, have no business here since our river trade was nearly stopped, get their living we don't know exactly how, and in time of trouble might become a new cause of danger. Those people are in the State in contravention of the statutes, and would not have been suffered in our midst had they not found a kind of tacit protection in some quarters."[25]

Several persons of color accused of contravention stood trial in 1861 and 1862 before the First District Court. Some seemed resigned to conviction. For example, authorities had ordered Henry Waters, a free man of color, to leave the state sixty days from March 30, 1861. Waters, described as a twenty-two-year-old man with a "yellow complexion, kinky hair," and scars on his face, did not leave in the prescribed time. He stood trial in November 1861 and promptly petitioned the court to allow him to begin serving his sentence, as he had "no intention to take an appeal." Authorities told Hannah Cornelius, a free woman of color, to leave the state in December 1860. The recorder also charged her with harboring and concealing the slave Jane, property of Dr. Bozeman, for some time. Cornelius failed to leave the state as ordered, and the First District Court found her guilty of contravention in July 1861 and sentenced her to one year of hard labor in the state penitentiary. Like Waters, Cornelius said that she had no intention of appealing her conviction. She wrote a letter to the judge stating that she was free and a citizen of Arkansas. She had lived in New Orleans for six years, and she claimed that she had no knowledge of the state's contravention laws. She asked for time to obtain the money to leave the state, as she "knows nothing of the North. . . . I have no friend here to help me and my child except myself." Why would these free people of color have no intention of appealing their convictions? Possibly going to the penitentiary seemed preferable to the uncertainties involved in leaving the state?[26]

25. *New Orleans Daily Picayune,* 7 September, 15 October, 2 December 1859, 12 April, 9 May, 29 June, 27 July, 4 August, 6 October, 9 December 1860, 25 April, 29 June, 1 August 1861, 30 March 1862.

26. State v. Waters, f.m.c., No. 15,523, First District Court of New Orleans, 14 November 1861; *New Orleans Daily Picayune,* 29 June 1861; State v. Cornelius, f.w.c., No. 15,325, First District Court of New Orleans, 2 July 1861; *New Orleans Daily Picayune,* 25 May, 27 June 1861. Samuel Golding, f.m.c., also stated after conviction of contravention that he had no intention to appeal. State v. Golding, f.m.c., No. 15,518, First District Court of New Orleans, 14 November 1861.

In 1862 one sixteen-year-old free woman of color charged with contravention, Cora Celestine Love, alias Tina Vick, managed to prove her birth in New Orleans to a free woman of color. The case dragged on for nearly a year because one of her witnesses no longer lived in Louisiana and the other had gone off to fight in the war. The court finally found her not guilty in January 1862.[27]

The year 1859 marked a turning point in sentiment against free people of color. It had become clear that no law, however draconian, could stop a determined black person from entering the state, nor could the law alone force manumitted slaves to leave. Newspaper editorials stated that free blacks "are not a desirable population and may be made a dangerous one." The Louisiana legislature considered passing a law that would have prohibited free people of color from testifying in court if the plaintiffs or defendants were white, a right they had held since the Louisiana Purchase. The *Daily Picayune* reported that Maryland had considered enslaving all free blacks remaining in the state. Arkansas passed a law enslaving all free blacks who remained in the state a year after passage of the act, although the legislature postponed the act from going into effect until 1863. Because of the Civil War, this statute never actually went into practice. The legislatures of Missouri and Florida also passed free black expulsion laws, but the governors of those states later vetoed these acts. The *Daily Picayune* attributed these extreme measures to the "fanaticism of the North that has induced a gradual change of feeling at the South in regard to free blacks." As their status deteriorated and pressure on them to leave increased, some free people of color felt forced to take desperate and dramatic measures to cope with the increasingly hostile atmosphere. These included leaving the state or, even more drastically, choosing to enslave themselves for life. Only sheer desperation and hopelessness could have induced them to take such steps.[28]

27. State v. Love, alias Vick, f.w.c., No. 15,343, First District Court of New Orleans, 29 January 1862.

28. *New Orleans Daily Picayune,* 18 February, 19 March, 18 June 1859; Berlin, *Slaves without Masters,* 165, 373, 375, 379.

9

DESPERATION AND SELF-ENSLAVEMENT

As the 1850s wore on, free people of color found themselves increasingly despised and feared for their allegedly corrupting influence on slaves. In an 1857 address to the Louisiana legislature, Governor Robert Wickliffe warned, "immediate steps should be taken at this time, by the Legislature, to remove all free negroes who are now in the State. . . . Their association and example has a most pernicious effect upon our slave population." The following year the *New Orleans Daily Picayune* editorialized, "The existence of negroes in these different civil conditions [slave and free] in this city constantly mingling with each other, has become a great source of uneasiness. It can scarcely be doubted that, in a very short period, the Legislature of this State will be compelled to adopt a new policy in regard to our free blacks." The editorial warned that if recently freed free people of color did not prove themselves worthy of freedom, "their condition must be changed, or the State must be altogether rid of them."[1]

Increasing harassment and restriction of free people of color can be seen in an 1858 *habeas corpus* petition. Police arrested Caroline Robertson for being in unlawful assembly with slaves worshiping at her church, the African Methodist Episcopal Church. Recorder Fabre fined her $25 for this offense. Robertson had no money to pay the fine, and the recorder sent her to parish prison. Robertson claimed that she had a "perfect right to assemble in said church or house for divine worship in company with a number of others." The judge of the Fourth District Court denied her petition for *habeas corpus* and returned her to jail. Fabre had based his decision on an 1858 city

1. *New Orleans Daily Picayune,* 20 January 1857, 17 October 1858.

ordinance that cataloged the "dangerous tendency of frequent and numerous assemblages of free persons of color." The ordinance required that every assemblage of free persons of color for worship "shall be under the supervision and control of some recognized white congregation or church located within the limits of the city, to whose discipline and management said congregation or church of persons of color shall be wholly amenable, both as to its spiritual as well as to its temporal affairs." It prohibited slaves and free persons of color from having meetings or delivering sermons without permission of the mayor under penalty of a $100 fine. Before 1858, laws had prohibited persons of color from assembling but had specifically exempted gatherings in a church or at funerals.[2]

In 1848 ten free men of color had formed a private corporation to establish a "place of religious worship and to administer the affairs of the religious body." The act of incorporation allowed them to erect a building suitable for religious worship and to elect a minister. The African Methodist Episcopal Church subsequently built or purchased three churches within the city of New Orleans. In the wake of the 1858 ordinance restricting their assembly, members of the church sued the city of New Orleans in Sixth District Court. The plaintiffs claimed that the ordinance drove away their congregations, prevented church members from attending worship services, which they had done freely since 1847, and confiscated church property; as a result, it was unconstitutional. The church won in the trial court, and the city appealed to the Supreme Court of Louisiana, which reversed the decision. The justices denied the unconstitutionality of the 1858 city ordinance, stating the "African race are strangers to our Constitution, and are the subjects of special and exceptional legislation."[3]

In December 1859, the *Daily Picayune* reported that several southern states, including Arkansas and Missouri, had passed laws forcing all free blacks to leave the state or become enslaved. The *Picayune* noted that 608 free people of color lived in Arkansas and 2,613 in Missouri. Although the Arkansas law never went into effect, only 144 free blacks remained in that state by 1860. As a newspaper article suggested, "The smallness of the num-

2. Robertson, f.w.c., praying for a writ of *habeas corpus*, No. 11,936, Fourth District Court of New Orleans, 11 January 1858; Leovy, ed., *Laws and General Ordinances*, No. 753, p. 258.

3. African Methodist Episcopal Church v. City of New Orleans, No. 6291, 15 La. Ann. 441 (1860).

ber was probably a motive of getting rid of them altogether, and creating at once the total incapacity of the negro to be free at all in the State." The Mississippi House of Representatives passed a similar bill in 1859 by a large majority, but the Mississippi Senate failed to concur. The *Daily Picayune* did not initially think public opinion would support such a policy in Louisiana. An editorial expressed the opinion that no sufficiently dire situation existed in the state to "require the wholesale expatriation of such a large mass of old residents, really an inoffensive and undoubtedly a loyal people." On the same day, the *Picayune* devoted a large column to an article entitled "The Contentment of Blacks," which described "the Potomac to the Nueces . . . [as] entranced with enjoyment. Day and night the sounds of merriment ring forth from plantation negro quarters, and the merry dance never ceases. Luxuries that would light up the faces of many of a Northern laborer smoke on the well filled boards of the slave." However, as one modern historian has argued, pointing out the position of free blacks in New Orleans served as a way to compare their status with their counterparts in the North; thus it actually became an argument in defense of slavery.[4]

Other states passed laws prohibiting manumission or requiring freed blacks to leave the state. Maryland passed an act in 1858 stipulating that a freed slave had to leave the state before a manumission could take effect. The Alabama legislature passed a law prohibiting all manumissions in 1860. Since 1842, Mississippi had a law prohibiting manumission and forbidding free blacks from entering the state. Kentucky prohibited all manumissions and forbade free black immigration into the state in 1860. South Carolina had forbidden manumission since 1841 and had prohibited free blacks from entering the state since 1835. Nonetheless, in 1859 black Charlestonians who had lived as free for decades suddenly faced enslavement when old, previously dormant laws were revived and stringently enforced. Charleston authorities actually went door to door through the free black community, forcing all free people of color to present unquestionable proof of their freedom and enslaving them if they failed to do so. This practice enslaved many blacks from families who had lived as free for several generations; it also

---

4. *New Orleans Daily Picayune*, 12, 24 December 1859, 14 January 1860; "An Act to Prohibit the Emancipation of Slaves," *Arkansas Acts, 1858*, p. 69; "An Act to Remove the Free Negroes and Mulattoes from This State," *Arkansas Acts, 1858*, pp. 175–8; Reinders, "The Decline of the New Orleans Free Negro," 92.

prompted several free persons of color to allow themselves to be sold to trustees, who held them as "nominal slaves." Some even petitioned the legislature for voluntary enslavement. In Texas, the state constitution of 1836 stipulated that free blacks could not reside in Texas without permission. The 1845 Texas constitution required a slave to leave the state before manumission could be complete, and the 1861 constitution prohibited manumission under any circumstances. In North Carolina, free blacks feared deportation or enslavement. The increasingly hostile climate against free people of color had special meaning for those who lived in Louisiana in contravention of the law. If the courts forced them to leave the state, no other southern state would accept them. Faced with going to prison, some sought desperate and dramatic alternatives.[5]

A number of free people of color chose to leave Louisiana permanently in 1859 and 1860. In some rural areas, night-riding bands of armed white

5. Paul Finkelman, "Prelude to the Fourteenth Amendment: Black Legal Rights in the Antebellum North," *Rutgers Law Review* 17 (1986): 479, 481 (note); John Hope Franklin, *The Free Negro in North Carolina, 1790–1860* (Chapel Hill: University of North Carolina Press, 1943), 192, 220; "An Act to Prevent Slaves from Gaining Their Freedom in Certain Cases," Act of March 8, 1858, *Maryland Acts, 1858*, p. 463; "An Act to Amend the Several Acts of This State in Relation to Free Negroes and Mulattoes," Act of February 26, 1842, *Mississippi Acts, 1842*, p. 66; "An Act to Amend the Act Entitled 'An Act to More Effectively Prohibit Free Negroes and Persons of Color from Entering into and Remaining in This State,'" Act of December 4, 1841, *Alabama Acts, 1841*, pp. 11–2; "An Act to Amend the Law in Relation to the Emancipation of Slaves," Act of January 25, 1860, *Alabama Acts, 1860*, p. 28; "An Act to Prevent Emancipated Slaves from Remaining in the State," Act of March 24, 1851, *Kentucky Acts, 1851*, pp. 379–80; "An Act to Aid Removing Free Negroes from This State to Liberia," Act of March 5, 1856, *Kentucky Acts, 1856*, p. 50; "An Act Concerning Free Negroes, Mulattoes, and Emancipation," Act of March 3, 1860, *Kentucky Acts, 1860*, pp. 128–31; "An Act More Effectively to Prevent Free Negroes and Other Persons of Color from Entering This State," Act of December 19, 1835, *South Carolina Acts, 1835*, pp. 34–9; "An Act to Prevent the Emancipation of Slaves," Act of December 17, 1841, *South Carolina Acts, 1841*, pp. 154–5; Michael P. Johnson and James L. Roark, eds., *No Chariot Let Down: Charleston's Free People of Color on the Eve of the Civil War* (Chapel Hill: University of North Carolina Press, 1984), 8; Bernard E. Powers Jr., *Black Charlestonians: A Social History, 1822–1885* (Fayetteville: University of Arkansas Press, 1994), 39, 65; "An Act to Prevent Free People of Color Commonly Known as Free Negroes from Being Brought or Coming into the State of Georgia," Act of December 17, 1859, *Georgia Acts, 1859*, pp. 68–9; Randolph B. Campbell, *An Empire for Slavery: The Peculiar Institution in Texas* (Baton Rouge: Louisiana State University Press, 1989), 110, 112, 207.

men beat free people of color and drove them out of the state, instituting what one historian has termed a "veritable reign of terror." Vigilantes in the Attakapas region killed a number of "free negro criminals," as they called them; other blacks received whippings and banishment from the state. As the borders of other southern states closed against them, some free people of color sought a new life in Haiti. In an 1859 editorial entitled "Negroes and Self-Government," the *Daily Picayune* used Haiti as example of the "incapacity of the negro for self-government." The article touted the unparalleled prosperity of Haiti before the 1790s, when a revolution expelled the white planters and put former slaves and free people of color in control of government. As a result, the article asserted, agriculture and commerce were neglected, livestock was sickly, and the island lacked public roads, bridges, and levees. Despite this gloomy picture, several boatloads of free blacks left Louisiana for Haiti in 1859 and 1860. The Haitian government promised land to each family who moved to the island. Although we cannot know precisely what might have motivated these emigrants, some of them must have come to the despairing conclusion that no future existed for them in Louisiana. Public sentiment against free blacks was so strong in St. Landry Parish that a group of slaveholders sent the legislature a petition demanding legislation that ordered any person of color entering the state, or in the state in contravention of the law, to be sold as a slave. In 1860 the *Picayune* reported that two ships left New Orleans for Haiti with 156 free persons of color from St. Landry Parish. The newspaper estimated that at least five hundred free blacks left for Haiti in 1859 and 1860.[6]

As pessimism about their future increased, a sizeable number of families, perhaps as many as five hundred, left Louisiana for Mexico. The *Daily True Delta* observed that "scarcely a week passes but a large number of free persons leave this port for Hayti or Mexico." Many of the most sensitive and capable leaders of the black community chose to emigrate, worsening the situation for the remaining black community. Yet most free people of color in New Orleans remained in the city. They had strong ties to home, family,

6. Sterkx, *The Free Negro in Antebellum Louisiana,* 114–5, 299–301; *New Orleans Daily Picayune,* 15 January, 23 April 1860; Johnson and Roark, eds., *No Chariot Let Down,* 7, 13. Hundreds of free people of color also left Charleston, South Carolina, for Haiti, Liberia, and Canada because they concluded that their survival demanded emigration.

and friends; whites' hostility was less frightening than the unknown challenges and problems of a new venue. Somewhere else, they feared, might only be worse.[7]

Two days following the passage of the new contravention act, the Louisiana legislature passed an act that showed how thoroughly proslavery logic had conquered the lawmakers. "An Act to Permit Free Persons of African Descent to Select Their Masters and Become Slaves for Life" was essentially a property transaction. It provided that persons wishing to enslave themselves could petition the district court of their parish stating their intention and naming the person to whom they wished to belong. The clerk of the district court then had to post a notice on the courthouse door for thirty days, after which the court would act on the petition. The judge would examine both parties separately, with the district attorney representing the petitioner. If the judge decided that no fraud, collusion, or intimidation existed, the prospective owner was a person of good character, and the act was entirely voluntary on the part of the person seeking to become a slave, the court approved the arrangement. Children under the age of ten followed the condition of their mother and became the property of the new owner. The act required the new owner to pay the expenses associated with the proceedings.[8]

Seven other southern states passed similar laws between 1857 and 1860: Alabama, Florida, Maryland, Kentucky, Tennessee, Texas, and Virginia. South Carolina and Georgia allowed free people of color to enslave themselves by special legislative acts rather than a court proceeding. These acts represented a culmination of the "positive good" theory of slavery—that people of African descent lived happily as slaves and found freedom inconvenient or miserable. The *Daily Picayune* delighted in printing reports of

7. *New Orleans Daily Picayune*, 20 July, 23 June, 10, 14 August 1859, 15 January, 23 April, 28 July, 21 October, 11 November 1860; *Daily True Delta*, 15 January 1860; Mary Gehman, "The Mexico-Louisiana Connection," *Louisiana Cultural Vistas* 11 (winter 2000–01): 68–75; Reinders, "The Decline of the New Orleans Free Negro," 97; Reinders, *End of an Era*, 25. A free black in Charleston, faced with the prospect of leaving, stated, "I feel this is my country and leaving it will come hard." Berlin, *Slaves without Masters*, 165–6, 357. Free blacks in Norfolk preferred to remain in the city rather than leave. Bogger, *Free Blacks in Norfolk*, 37.

8. "An Act to Permit Free Persons of African Descent to Select a Master and Become Slaves for Life," Act of March 17, 1859, *Louisiana Acts, 1859*, pp. 214–5. Morris notes that this act presumed that a property right existed in each person that could be alienated by sale of oneself. Morris, *Southern Slavery and the Law*, 32.

slaves preferring bondage to freedom. In 1850 the paper reported an incident in which Peter, a free man of color, insisted on being sold as a slave. His master had freed him, but the laws of Virginia forbade him to remain in the state for more than twelve months after manumission, and "all the ties which rendered existence desirable, were intimately connected with the place of his birth." So "he entreated that he should be publicly sold to the highest bidder, and Peter secured a good home for life." An 1852 article told of two slaves who had successfully run away for four years to the Cherokee nation. One of them subsequently returned to the home of his master. After being in the free state of Iowa for some time, the paper reported, he "came immediately from that place home." In the same issue the *Picayune* reported that a white man had taken a slave with him to California with the agreement that he would free him at a specified date. When that date came, the slave voluntarily returned to Benton County, "preferring perpetual slavery in Arkansas to freedom in California." Another slave whose master took him to California obtained permission to remain there and try his luck in mining. His efforts met with success, and he returned voluntarily to his owner with a "well-filled purse," preferring "his old home, with its many endearing associations, to the freedom of California, by his voluntary returning." The authorities in New Orleans arrested him for contravention, but they released him when he explained that he planned to return to his master in Mississippi. The article concluded, "The above facts are submitted for the reflection of the Abolitionists of the North." In 1859, the *Picayune* reported that a freed slave named Hannah had requested that her master take her back as a slave, as "she preferred being a slave *and remain in Tennessee, rather than be free in Ohio*" (italics in original).[9]

Another newspaper article noted the departure for New York of thirty-two slaves of the late Elihu Cresswell, a slave trader who left his fifty slaves their freedom in his will. The newspaper reported that the remaining eighteen freed slaves preferred the allure of the "life which experience had taught them to be agreeable and unclouded by care, to the doubtful happiness of less favored regions . . . and the uncertainty of freedom elsewhere." According to an article in *De Bow's Review,* some of Cresswell's former

9. *New Orleans Daily Picayune,* 22 September 1850, 7 February, 8 December 1852, 15 January 1859. In 1837 a seventy-year-old Virginia woman allowed herself to be sold as a slave for $1 to allow her to remain in the state. Bogger, *Free Blacks in Norfolk,* 43.

slaves insisted on returning to New Orleans even if it meant returning to slavery.

In 1859 the *Daily Picayune* reported the departure of the McDonogh slaves for Liberia. Although leaving well supplied, the newspaper noted how sad they looked: "Here was home from childhood; everything around them was connected with pleasant associations of the old times—of happy days spent among their friends, under the protection of a kind master. They are going to a strange land. . . . Will they be happy? If nay, they will be at liberty to go elsewhere, but the doors of their Southern home will be closed against them by the stern arm of the law." An 1850 article reported on a Virginia man who sold himself into slavery because state law forbade free blacks from residing within its borders. Another overtly racist article reported that the slave "Lucky Dick" had won the Havana lottery but had no thought of using the proceeds to purchase what the writer termed a "useless freedom." Lucky Dick stated that he had a good master and as much freedom as he desired, and that his master would care for him when he became old. Another racist testimonial came from a slave who reportedly said, "Africa pretty good for niggers who don't know no other country; but I come here; I learn good many things; I've got a good master, a wife and children, all fat and happy. I work; I eat well, sleep plenty, got good clothes, medicine when I'm sick; never get a whipping. I'd rather die than go back to Africa now; I'm 'merican nigger now."[10]

Nothing could have reinforced proslavery arguments more emphatically than the phenomenon of hundreds of free people of color volunteering to enslave themselves. A Richmond newspaper asserted that voluntary enslavement gave undeniable evidence "in favor of the comfortable and contented condition of the Southern slave." J. D. B. De Bow, editor of *De Bow's Review*, agreed, "The negroes know what their own best interest is." In New Orleans, at least seventeen free persons of color filed petitions to enslave themselves under the terms of the 1859 act. The court records of these cases do not indicate how free people of color selected a master and requested

10. *New Orleans Daily Picayune*, 13 July, 20 September 1852, 9 March 1857; also 18 May 1858, 28 April, 1 May, 25 June 1859. Succession of Cresswell, No. 2423, 8 La. Ann. 122 (1853); U. B. Phillips, *American Negro Slavery: A Survey of the Supply, Employment, and Control of Negro Labor as Determined by the Plantation Regime* (1918; reprint, Baton Rouge: Louisiana State University Press, 1966), 429.

enslavement, although it seems likely that most "voluntary" slaves must have known their soon-to-be-masters well. Could these cases have represented a logical extension of the practice of free blacks bribing whites to claim them as slaves and to free them sometime later, so that they could remain in the state? Could it have been a desperate method to remain in the state when they could not do so as free blacks, even if it meant being treated as slaves? Was self-enslavement simply an arrangement of convenience, or did those who enslaved themselves find themselves actually treated as slaves? The Kentucky law permitting self-enslavement envisioned such a practice and prohibited it. It held that anyone who accepted a free black as a slave but "not with the *bona fide* intention of making him or her a slave" should be fined up to $5,000.[11]

Whatever the arrangement, persons who enslaved themselves stood to lose a significant number of civil rights. Now bound by laws pertaining to slaves, their marriages ceased to exist; they lost the right to testify in court and to enter into contracts. They could neither own nor inherit property. Children born to such women after enslavement became slaves themselves and could be sold away from their mothers after reaching the age of ten. Newly enslaved blacks could only stand trial for criminal acts in special slave tribunals, not in the same courts and under the same rules as whites. They could not own guns or weapons, nor could they be away from their master's property without a pass, and they had to return to it before curfew. Their owner could mortgage or sell them at any time; if the owner fell into debt after the act of enslavement, they could be seized and sold to satisfy creditors. City ordinances prohibited slaves from carrying a cane or stick (under a penalty of twenty-five lashes); they could not attend public bars, purchase liquor, sleep away from their owner's house, "quarrel, yell, curse, or sing obscene songs," insult white persons (again, twenty-five lashes' penalty), or purchase any item worth more than $5. Voluntary enslavement represented a convenient method to get around the state's contravention laws but carried a huge risk. Even if a prospective owner promised not to treat one as a slave, those who enslaved themselves had no way to enforce such a promise,

11. De Bow quoted in Berlin, *Slaves without Masters,* 367; "An Act Concerning Free Negroes, Mulattoes, and Emancipation," Act of March 3, 1860, *Kentucky Acts, 1860,* p. 130; Berlin, *Slaves without Masters,* 263, 367.

since slaves could only initiate suits for freedom—an action courts would find specious after self-enslavement.[12]

Louisiana law considered slaves real estate, and the Act of 1859 required the recording of the transaction enslaving free persons of color in the Office of the Recorder of Mortgages. Despite a thorough search of both the mortgage and conveyance records from March 1859, when the act went into effect, to April 1862, when United States forces captured New Orleans, no such transactions appeared. If these self-enslavements simply represented arrangements of convenience, perhaps the new "owners" purposely did not register them, since doing so would make the persons enslaving themselves saleable property. As with property sales, Louisiana law required sales of slaves to have a clear, traceable title of property. If no such title existed, a sale could not take place. Of course, those accepting free blacks as slaves may have simply neglected to register the transactions in the pre–Civil War crisis.[13]

One historian has argued that advanced age and/or illness motivated free blacks who decided to enslave themselves. Yet the surviving New Orleans district court records indicate only one case in which age or illness was a factor. In 1860, Henry Wilson petitioned to become the slave of William Barrett. In his petition, Wilson described himself as suffering from "infirm health" and therefore desirous of taking advantage of the act permitting him to select a master and enslave himself for life. Barrett stated that he would accept Wilson and comply with the obligations of law. This case lingered on for a year. Finally, the district attorney petitioned the court to dismiss Wilson's petition at his costs, although the record does not reveal a reason for the dismissal. Perhaps humanitarian motives prompted Barrett to volunteer to take on a sick slave. Possibly Wilson's death ended the case. In any event, Wilson's illness suggested fraud, and the transaction did not take place.[14]

Two different historians have asserted that some free people of color,

12. *Civil Code*, Arts. 173–92, pp. 27–30. See *Black Code*, 150–210. For procedure in slave trials, see Judith Kelleher Schafer, "Slaves and Crime: New Orleans, 1846–1862," in *Local Matters: Race, Crime, and Justice in the Nineteenth-Century South*, ed. Christopher Waldrep and Donald Nieman (Athens: University of Georgia Press, 2001), 53–91; Leovy, ed., *Laws and General Ordinances*, 257–62.

13. *Civil Code*, Arts. 2413–7, p. 377.

14. Wilson, f.m.c., praying to become a slave for life, v. State, No. 13,390, Fourth District Court of New Orleans, 24 November 1860.

fearing the outbreak of war between the North and the South, sought a protector because they were the "miserable and wretched victims of a system that was ever pressing down on them with its crushing weight." One of the New Orleans cases might support that contention. A case about which we have little more detailed information indicates that Joseph Thomas, a twenty-nine-year-old free man of color, selected as his master a man "with whom he has been acquainted for many years," indicating that he sought a protector.[15]

Of the remaining fifteen people who sought to enslave themselves, eight seem to have done so because they lived in the state illegally. All of the persons seeking to enslave themselves and all of the selected owners had noncreole names. The remaining cases either did not state when the person came into the state or are so incomplete that we have little but the name and docket number of the case. Several of the Sixth District Court cases have disappeared. Two free blacks attempting to enslave themselves faced prison terms and deportation for convictions for being in the state in contravention of the law. City police arrested Julia Elliot on May 8, 1861, for being illegally in the state. The record states that Elliot was of "bright yellow complexion," had gray eyes, was five feet four inches tall, and was twenty-one years old. After being warned to leave, Elliot had remained in New Orleans; she stood trial in the First District Court for contravention. The jury found her guilty "without leaving their seats," and the judge sentenced her to one year at hard labor in the state penitentiary and expulsion from the state within thirty days of completing her sentence. Elliot then petitioned for arrest of judgment, stating that she desired to become the slave of John D. Lackie. The district attorney argued that the 1859 act allowing persons to enslave themselves did not apply to Elliot because she "was not a good and moral subject." (One wonders why her character mattered when becoming a slave.) Indeed, he said, "criminal proceedings are in process against her in the First District Court. Her present action is only brought to evade said prosecution and the law applicable to her case." Elliot's attorneys filed an appeal to the Supreme Court of Louisiana, but that court closed on May 6,

15. Berlin, *Slaves without Masters,* 367; John Hope Franklin, "The Enslavement of Free Negroes in North Carolina," *Journal of Negro History* 29 (October 1944): 401–28; Thomas, praying to become a slave, v. State, No. 13,318, Fourth District Court of New Orleans, 1 October 1859.

1862, shortly after the city fell to Union forces. The court never heard the appeal, and the end of slavery after the Civil War made the case moot.[16]

The First District Court convicted George Stevens, alias Robertson, of being in the state in contravention of the law in June 1855. The case record describes Stevens, a sailor from Cincinnati, as having a black complexion and black eyes, standing five feet three inches tall, and being thirty-one years old. Stevens had served his sentence of one year in the state penitentiary. Prior to his conviction, he had been warned to leave the state within thirty days, but he had defied that order. Stevens had drawn attention to himself by a conviction for insulting a white person early in 1855. The incident had happened on the steamboat landing near Conti Street. Stevens had called John Cushing a "son of a bitch and [he] has furthermore assaulted and shook his fist in [Cushing's] face." Although the district attorney disposed of the insulting charge with a *nolle prosequi* (literally, "no prosecution"), Stevens did serve time for contravention. Nonetheless he somehow remained in New Orleans after his release from prison. Authorities arrested him for contravention again late in 1861. He filed a petition in January 1862 to enslave himself to James P. Frank, who stated that he would agree to accept him. The following month, the district attorney asked for dismissal of his petition and had him remanded to jail to await sentence for a second conviction of contravention. No record of any subsequent action exists.[17]

Another free man of color, William Gray, age twenty-five, petitioned to become a slave in 1859. Earlier that year, the *Daily Picayune* reported that police had arrested Gray for contravention. The same year, Mary Walker, a twenty-nine-year-old free woman of color, petitioned to enslave herself and

16. *New Orleans Daily Picayune*, 8 May 1861; State v. Elliot, f.w.c., No. 15,514, First District Court of New Orleans, 29 November 1861; Elliot, f.w.c., praying to become a slave, v. State, No. 15,132, Fourth District Court of New Orleans, 26 November 1861. Cases of persons enslaving themselves that have disappeared include: Nells, f.m.c., praying to become a slave, v. State, No. 8647, Sixth District Court of New Orleans, 15 September 1860; Lloyd, f.m.c., praying to become a slave, v. State, No. 8648, Sixth District Court of New Orleans, 15 September 1860; Stewart, f.m.c., praying to become a slave, v. State, No. 9158, Sixth District Court of New Orleans, 13 February 1861; Wells, f.m.c., praying to become a slave, v. State, No. 9593, Sixth District Court of New Orleans, 15 February 1859.

17. State v. Stevens, f.m.c., No. 10,416, First District Court of New Orleans, 23 June 1855; State v. Stevens, f.m.c., No. 10,417, First District Court of New Orleans, 24 May 1855; *New Orleans Daily Picayune*, 3 August 1859; Stevens, f.m.c., praying to become a slave, v. State, No. 16,624, Third District Court of New Orleans, 1 February 1862.

her nine-year-old daughter, Jane, to George W. Whittaker, a "man of good standing and character with whom she had been acquainted for many years." Walker admitted in her petition that she had resided in Louisiana only two years.[18]

One of the most complete existing case records is the petition of Elizabeth Jones to become the slave of John A. Musselman, an attorney. Musselman's son, James, also an attorney, represented Jones in this case. In her petition Jones stated that the Court of Probates in Hamilton County, Ohio, freed her in 1858 in accordance with the will of her late mistress, who died in Louisville, Kentucky, in 1858. After her manumission, Jones came to Louisiana in January 1859. When she discovered that the laws of Louisiana would not permit her to live in the state as a free black, she still wanted to live in New Orleans, and therefore she chose a master who would accept her as a slave. Musselman appeared in court to express his willingness to become the master and owner of Jones. There is no record of objection by the district attorney; presumably the transaction went through.[19]

In 1861 a New York–born free woman of color, Amelia Stone, petitioned to enslave herself to Lucien Adams, the "gallant Recorder of the Garden District." Stone, age twenty-four, lived in Louisiana illegally, having come into the state after 1838. The *Daily Picayune* stated that the reason Stone took this step, "which many other free negroes have taken[,] is that she prefers the liberty, security, and protection of slavery here, to the degradation of free niggerdom among the Abolitionists at the North, with whom she would be obliged to dwell, and in preference to which, she has sought the 'chains' of slavery." Putting the word "chains" in quotations and using the phrase the "liberty of slavery" shows how far the *Picayune* had gone in its proslavery thinking. In noting the self-enslavement of John Wells, the newspaper commented, "Slavery cannot be such a bad thing after all, when we see free men accepting it voluntarily. The negro sometimes understands his own interests better than his would be white friends."[20]

18. Gray, f.m.c., v. State of Louisiana, No. 13,320, Fourth District Court of New Orleans, filed October 1, 1859; *New Orleans Daily Picayune,* 22 January 1859; Walker, f.w.c., praying to become a slave, v. State, No. 13,319, Fourth District Court of New Orleans, filed October 1, 1859. For George Whittaker's obituary, see the *New Orleans Daily Picayune,* 16 November 1862.

19. Jones, f.w.c., praying to become a slave, v. State, No. 13,900, Third District Court of New Orleans, 22 December 1959; *New Orleans Daily Picayune,* 27 January 1860.

20. Stone, praying to select a master, v. State, No. 8597, Sixth District Court of New Orleans, 20 September 1860, 28 August 1861; *New Orleans Daily Picayune,* 30 July 1861, 4 No-

Three other case transcripts give us no clues of motivation for self-enslavement. Emilia Stone enslaved herself to John Haggerty Pope, a pharmacist and one of the founders of the Mystik Krewe of Comus (the oldest and most prestigious Mardi Gras organization). The record notes that Stone paid the court costs of $10.25. Ann Barney enslaved herself to Ann Dickens, the only woman chosen as an owner. A note appears in the record stating that Dickens's husband authorized her to accept Barney as her slave. A third woman, Jane Moore, enslaved herself to a wealthy merchant, Elias Wolfe. The record states only that the court granted her petition and that Wolfe paid the costs of the proceeding.[21]

In 1855, Joseph Johnson drew attention to himself by robbing a store on Carondelet Street of a gold pencil case, a seal, two gold pens, two keys, and $60. When police went to his room, they found it "richly furnished and supplied with a luxuriousness and abundance little to have been expected." When brought before the First District Court, the judge found him in the state in contravention of the law and ordered him to leave the state within sixty days. Somehow, Johnson managed to remain in New Orleans until 1861, when he enslaved himself by notarial act to a police captain, Frederick Hyatt. The act described Johnson as being "of black complexion" and a native of Kentucky, age twenty-six. The notarial act contained the unusual provision that Johnson agreed to pay Hyatt $1,200 if he defaulted on the agreement. Hyatt accepted Johnson as his slave and signed the notarial act.[22]

The guarantee against default might have arisen from news of a free woman of color who planned to enslave herself and then changed her mind. In an article entitled "Breach of Contract," the *Daily Picayune* reported that a white man lodged a complaint in the Second District Recorder's office "of a novel character." A free woman of color, who came from Mobile but had

vember 1860, 30 May 1858. For Lucien Adam's obituary, see the *New Orleans Daily Picayune,* 2 March 1900. Wells, f.m.c., praying to become a slave, v. State, No. 9593, Sixth District Court of New Orleans, 15 September 1859; *New Orleans Daily Picayune,* 16 September 1859.

21. Stone, f.w.c., praying to become a slave, v. State, No. 13,245, Fifth District Court of New Orleans, 7 September 1859; Barney, f.w.c., praying to become a slave, v. State, No. 13,526, Fourth District Court of New Orleans, 18 February 1860; Moore, f.w.c., praying to become a slave, v. State, No. 7589, Sixth District Court of New Orleans, 11 January 1860. For Elias Wolfe's obituary, see the *New Orleans Daily Picayune,* 24 April 1900.

22. Notarial Archives, James Graham, N. P., vol. 21, No. 4909, 20 May 1861; *New Orleans Daily Picayune,* 12, 13, 19 July 1855, 1 July, 11 October 1859. For Hyatt's obituary, see the *New Orleans Daily Picayune,* 17 September 1889.

lived in New Orleans for some years, had realized that she was living in Louisiana in contravention of the law; she had decided to enslave herself to the gentleman who lodged the complaint. Indignantly, he reported that he had taken all the necessary steps to accept her as a slave, but that she had backed out at the last minute and had refused to accept perpetual bondage. The article sarcastically noted that this "philanthropic gentleman, anxious to perform a good deed, wished to make an affidavit before the Recorder, setting forth these facts and praying that the said free woman of color be ordered to become forthwith his slave as per agreement, in order to save her from the trouble and persecution she would be subjected to, for being in contravention." The clerk of court told the "philanthropist" that the woman could not be forced into slavery if she had changed her mind. At this response the man "waxed very warm and thought that justice was not done him, as the woman would certainly choose some other master, and why should he not have the privilege, when *he was the first to suggest to her this way of getting out of difficulty?*" (italics mine). The man raised his voice to such a pitch that the clerk told him that the court was in session in the next room and the recorder might be annoyed by his screaming, firmly pointing out an exit. The disappointed would-be slaveowner took the hint and left, grumbling about city authorities' "injustice" in failing to help him to become a slaveholder.[23]

A New Orleans newspaper gave a detailed account of the trial of John Clifton, a forty-year-old free man of color, who petitioned to become the slave of Green Lee Bumpass. John Clifton first surfaced in the *Daily Picayune* in 1853, when Recorder Genois sentenced him to the chain gang for stealing a bundle of clothing and then offering to pay another free black man to sell the garments. Two year later, Clifton faced trial before the First District Court for contravention. He posted bond to leave the state within sixty days, and the district attorney entered a *nolle prosequi* to end the case. But apparently Clifton never left New Orleans, or if he did, he returned.[24]

Clifton's case to enslave himself is one of those Sixth District Court cases that have disappeared, but the *New Orleans Daily Delta* wrote a detailed

23. *New Orleans Daily Picayune,* 4 September 1859

24. Ibid., 11 January 1855; State v. John Clifton, f.m.c., No. 11,027, First District Court of New Orleans, 25 February 1856. Sterkx states that Clifton was the *only* free person of color to enslave himself, but Sterkx had no access to the records of the district courts of New Orleans. Sterkx, *The Free Negro in Antebellum Louisiana,* 149.

report of the trial and its outcome. The *Delta* article began by reporting that suits for voluntary enslavement made up a "very heavy docket of this class of cases," placing a burden on the district attorney, whom the law required to act as a *amicus curae* (friend of the court) for the person requesting enslavement. Seventeen cases does not suggest a "heavy docket," but the *Delta* delighted in using Clifton's case as proslavery propaganda. It reported that Clifton, who had lived in Louisiana for ten years, stated in his petition:

> Having long since become satisfied that the rights, liberties, and free agency exercised by persons of the African descent, it being the status of your petitioner, is merely theoretical and has no foundation in point of fact. Therefore, your petitioner who was born in the South, and wedded to its institutions, has selected under the act of the legislature approved March the 7th, 1859, for his owner and master Green Lee Bumpass.

Clifton's attorney, Thomas Jefferson Earhart, commented on the petition in typically racist proslavery logic:

> John Clifton is evidently a philosopher. He has the sagacity to perceive and the courage to avow that with a kind and gentle master his *status* as a slave would be preferable to the mockery of freedom with which those seek to delude him, who pretend he can ever sustain himself as the equal of the white man, when nature and circumstances have had him his inferior. John Clifton naturally seeks a protector and guardian, and the law furnishes him one of his own choice, who by acceptance of this guardianship incurs the obligation to protect and support him. Such is the operation of our act of the legislature permitting free people of color to elect [*sic*] their owners and become slaves. [italics in original]

As in much proslavery rhetoric, Earhart's logic defies reason. How could Clifton have been so smart as to earn the term "philosopher" and yet be so "inferior"? Interestingly, Earhart was one of the first to take the oath of allegiance to the United States in 1863. His daughter, Virginia Earhart, married John Ferguson, the judge in the famous "separate but equal" U.S. Supreme Court case of *Plessy v. Ferguson*.[25]

---

25. Clifton, f.m.c., praying to become a slave, v. State, No. 8465, Sixth District Court of New Orleans, 18 May 1860; *New Orleans Daily Delta*, 18 May 1860. Green Lee Bumpass is the same person who testified as to the freedom of Dolly Johnson and Peter Bass in the kidnapping case of Bass and Johnson, f.p.c., v. Chase, No. 14,642, Third District Court of New Orleans, 4 May 1860. Medley, "When Plessy Met Ferguson," 59.

Thomas Jefferson Earhart represented at least four of the persons seeking to enslave themselves. Before entering the legal profession, Earhart had served as assistant quartermaster and storekeeper for the United States Army in the customhouse on Canal Street. In 1850, a federal court found him guilty of embezzling property belonging to the government. The court sentenced him to one year in prison and a fine of $1,000. On June 13, 1853, the Minute Book of the Louisiana Supreme Court showed him as being admitted to the bar. Why the Supreme Court would admit a convicted felon into its membership does not appear in the record. Earhart seems to have made a living mainly by representing low-life characters and slaves. Perhaps people of property and standing would not have trusted him to manage their affairs and did not want to associate with him. In 1856 he represented Dick Diamond, who the *Daily Picayune* termed a "dangerous and suspicious character" and a fugitive from justice. The following year he represented an alleged slave stealer. In 1860, in addition to the four self-enslavement cases, he represented two slaves who sued for their freedom on the basis that they had been kidnapped and held as slaves. In an 1861 case, Earhart sued an Irish woman accused of whipping an Irish man in a domestic dispute. The woman kept contradicting herself in her testimony, and Earhart lost his temper in the courtroom. He "openly denounced the counsel for the accused, calling him a diminutive quadruped of the canine species, and threatened to make smithereens of him. This produced a hiatus in the case, and as soon as his Honor recovered from the electrical shock which went through the courtroom, he fined the belligerent counsel $25 and ordered him to be imprisoned for twenty-four hours."[26]

Most of the seventeen cases give strong clues regarding the motivation for voluntary enslavement. Conceivably some of those seeking enslavement proved unable to support themselves. Or perhaps they chose a particular master because he owned their spouse, parent, or child. If true, these persons must have considered separation from family and community more devastating than being enslaved. Eight of the petitions stated that those enslaving themselves resided in Louisiana illegally; several faced prison and

26. *Cohen's City Directory* (New Orleans: D. Davies, 1849), 60; *New Orleans Daily Picayune*, 21 April 1850; *Minute Book of the Supreme Court of Louisiana*, 11:446, 13 June 1853; *New Orleans Daily Picayune*, 9 November 1856, 23 December 1857, 2 August 1861; Bass and Johnson v. Chase, No. 14,642, Third District Court of New Orleans, 4 May 1860.

deportation under the state's draconian laws prohibiting free people of color from entering the state and ordering the deportation of those who arrived after 1838. These convictions encouraged some free blacks in the city illegally to leave before being apprehended and motivated others to enslave themselves rather than leave family and friends.[27]

Many free persons of color in New Orleans owned considerable amounts of property, but the contravention laws meant that they often had to sell their property at a loss when hurrying to depart. The number of free black holders of real estate declined 32 percent from 1836 to 1860, and the total value of the black real estates went from $2,465,000 to $2,628,000, which was substantially lower than the rising prices of city property. Perhaps self-enslavement proved a way not only to avoid being forced to leave Louisiana, but as an informal way for free blacks to protect their property. If indeed self-enslavement was sometimes an arrangement of convenience, the newly chosen owner could hold the property for the newly enslaved person.[28]

The Civil War and the closing of the New Orleans courts in 1862 halted the process of self-enslavement. We cannot know how these arrangements might have worked out had slavery lasted for several more years, nor can we know how many other free people of color might have opted for enslavement. What we do know is that to some free persons of color, at least a form of slavery, if not a real enslavement, proved a viable and acceptable alternative to leaving family, friends, community, and property. In these instances, free people of color used the law that allowed them to enslave themselves to resist expulsion and exile from their homes. In doing so, they made the great sacrifice of their freedom for their homes and families.

27. For examples of contravention cases, see: State v. Cornelius, f.w.c., No. 15,325, 2 July 1861; State v. Golding, f.m.c., No. 15,518, 8 November 1861; State v. Waters, f.m.c., No. 15,523, 8 November 1861, all in the First District Court of New Orleans.

28. Loren Schweninger, *Black Property Owners in the South, 1790–1915* (Urbana: University of Illinois Press, 1990), 64, 71, 81. David Rankin has made the point that census takers underestimated free black wealth for a variety of reasons. His analysis of black property distribution shows that mulattoes owned 90 percent of free black wealth, most of it in real estate. Nearly half of these property owners were mulatto women. Rankin, "The Forgotten People," 114–5, 118, 121.

EPILOGUE

And the War Came

After Lincoln's election, when secession seemed inevitable, some whites began to question the loyalty of the free black population in New Orleans. A number of the leaders of the free black community sent a letter to the *New Orleans Daily Delta* in which they professed their allegiance to their home state:

> There are certain persons who are disposed to believe and to make others believe—and some will do so from ignorance or mischief—that the free colored population (native) of Louisiana are not well disposed toward her, but this is not so: they love their home, their property, they own slaves, and they are dearly attached to their native land, and they recognize no other country than Louisiana, and care for no other than Louisiana, and are ready to shed their blood for their defense. They have no sympathy for Abolitionism; no love for the North, but they have plenty for Louisiana; and let the hour come, and they will be worthy sons of Louisiana.[1]

When the Civil War began, free men of color issued a call for a meeting to organize themselves into a regiment exclusively of "colored" men called the Native Guards. The *New Orleans Daily Picayune* announced that the "most respectable portion of the colored population" intended to offer their services to the governor "to help repel any enemy who may invade the soil of Louisiana." Nearly two thousand free black men, "representing the flower of the free colored population," met and passed several resolutions. They

1. *New Orleans Daily Delta*, 28 December 1860.

offered their services to local authorities in case of enemy invasion; if allowed to organize themselves into regiments, they expressed their willingness to "take arms at a moment's notice for the defence of their native soil and fight, shoulder to shoulder, with the citizens as their fathers did in 1814." After appointing several men to standing committees, they asked for signatures from volunteers expressing their willingness to serve. Fifteen hundred free black men signed. Reporting on this event, the *Picayune* commented, "What will the Northerners have to say to this?" The paper reported the formation of two other companies composed solely of free colored men, one in New Orleans and one in Jefferson City (immediately upriver of New Orleans).[2]

Economic self-interest provided one motivation for free blacks' willingness to fight for their state. The Native Guards represented the wealthiest and the most educated segment of the Crescent City's free black community. With more than $2 million worth of property in aggregate, their eagerness to defend themselves and their city should come as no surprise. The hope of achieving equality with their white counterparts also strongly motivated them to volunteer to fight for their city. But equality proved elusive, as it became clear that Confederate officials did not plan to supply them with arms or uniforms, or indeed, to assign them to any duties of importance. Their main use to the Confederacy lay in having southern newspapers triumphantly report that free blacks had volunteered to fight for the southern cause.[3]

Shortly after the outbreak of war, the city of New Orleans established a Free Market to help feed the wives and children of white soldiers whose companies fought far away from Louisiana. The free black community supported the Free Market with "Colored Ladies' Fairs," which opened each night, as well as with elaborate dances. In November 1861 the free black community gave a "fancy colored ball" to benefit the Free Market. The *Daily Picayune* commented, "It will be one of the most curious features of this revolution; and we hope to see this reunion well attended. While our volunteers are fighting for our country, it is quite refreshing to see the col-

2. *New Orleans Daily Picayune*, 23, 27 April 1861.

3. James G. Hollandsworth Jr., *The Louisiana Native Guards: The Black Military Experience during the Civil War* (Baton Rouge: Louisiana State University Press, 1995), 2, 4–7, 11; Berlin, *Slaves without Masters*, 387.

ored people dancing for the benefit of the sisters, mothers, daughters and wives left at home by our heroes. What would Lincoln say to this?" *"Darkies Dancing for the Benefit of the Free Market"* proclaimed the accompanying headline. The New Year's Eve ball raised $600 for the Free Market.[4]

Despite their support of their home state, free people of color did not achieve the equality they sought. Although hundreds had left Louisiana for Haiti, Mexico, or elsewhere, eighteen thousand free people of color remained in the state. Humiliation and harassment occasioned solely by their color did not succeed in driving them from their homes. Unable to abandon their community and property, they remained, hoping for better times ahead. Little did they know that emancipation would lower their status, as whites increasingly lumped freed slaves and former free people of color together as one large and highly objectionable part of the state's population. The winning of equal rights for all African Americans would take another one hundred years.[5]

Emancipation in 1864 signaled the end of three great struggles by the New Orleans African American community: the fight to use the courts and the law to become free; the mighty struggle to remain free; and the desperate action of a few to use the law to make themselves slaves rather than face expulsion and exile from their homes and families. After emancipation, New Orleans African Americans enjoyed the consequences of freedom, including autonomy, keeping the fruits of their labor, and freedom from fear of suddenly being snatched into slavery forever.

Now a new and just as lengthy and formidable fight began: a search for acceptance as equals in white society. No longer forced to prove their freedom at every turn, blacks now found themselves relegated to the lowest paying occupations and still harassed by the law if they stepped "out of place." Grinding poverty, subsistence sharecropping, discrimination, and racial prejudice met them at every turn. What they had was their freedom—the most important right next to life itself. The rest—social, economic, political, and racial equality—remained to be won, step by painstaking step.

4. *New Orleans Daily Picayune,* 29 November 1861, 3 January 1862.

5. Sterkx, *The Free Negro in Antebellum Louisiana,* 314–5; Johnson and Roark, eds., *No Chariot Let Down,* 10, 14–5; David C. Rankin, "The Impact of the Civil War on the Free Colored Community of New Orleans," *Perspectives in American History* 11 (1977–78): 379–416.

BIBLIOGRAPHY

CASES

FIRST DISTRICT COURT OF NEW ORLEANS

Adams, alias Napoleon, f.m.c., v. State, Nos. 10,770, 11,084, 28 March 1856 (slave Simon).

Aicard, opposing emancipation of Zabeth and Edward, No. 5192, 17 June 1850.

Aimée, c.w., v. Pluché and Bosquet, No. 1650, 4 May 1848.

Andrinette, f.w.c., v. Maran and Jordan, alias Noble, No. 13,266, 24 December 1859.

Andry v. State, No. 10,793, 7 February 1856 (four slaves, names missing).

Angelina, c.w., v. Parlange, No. 7144, 7 January 1852.

Arsène, alias Cora, f.w.c., v. Pignéguy, Nos. 395, 434, 4 November 1846.

Askew v. State, No. 10,967, 15 February 1856 (slave Hannah).

Aurore, c.w., v. Decuir, No. 1919, 16 October 1848.

Avegno, f.w.c., v. State, No. 10,492, 30 August 1855 (slave Amanda).

Bacchus, f.w.c., v. State, No. 10,788, 5 March 1856 (slave Mary).

Barnett v. State, Nos. 12,006, 12,007, 28 March 1856 (slaves Helene and Maranthe).

Besse, f.m.c., v. State, No. 10,503, 3 December 1855 (slave Nancy).

Boisblanc, f.w.c., v. State, No. 10,956, 3 March 1856 (slave Marie Felicité, alias Evelina).

Bonford, f.w.c., praying for a writ of *habeas corpus,* No. 8653, 14 June 1853.

Brand, f.m.c., v. State, No. 10,783, 4 February 1856 (slave Laurencine).

Brand, f.m.c., v. State, No. 10,797, 7 January 1856 (slave Jean Theophile).

Bussi v. State, No. 10,508, 3 December 1855 (slave Annette).

Charlotte, f.w.c., v. Lizardi and Segur, No. 4933, 1 May 1851.

Claiborne, f.m.c., v. State, No. 10,683, 3 December 1855 (slaves Caroline Claiborne, Henry Claiborne, Pickney, and Jane Wilson).

Couvent, f.m.c., tutor of Mary, c.w., v. Guesnard, Nos. 1634, 1726, 1786, 17 January 1848.

Cruzat v. State, No. 10,723, 21 November 1855 (slave Victoire, alias Mamzelle).

Culbertson v. State, No. 10,776, 28 November 1855 (slave Marion).

D'Apremont v. State, No. 10,812, 3 March 1856 (slaves Sarah and Lewis).

David, praying to be appointed tutor *ad hoc* of François Paillaset, *statu liber*, No. 977, 14 May 1847.

DeGruy, f.w.c., v. State, Nos. 10,769, 11,083, transferred to Sixth District Court of New Orleans, 16 October 1855, 28 March 1856 (slave Francis Moss).

Delpit v. State, No. 10,730, 20 November 1855 (slaves Catiche and her children).

Deschamps v. State, No. 10,770, 4 February 1856 (slave Simon).

Devon v. State, No. 12,005, 28 March 1856 (slave Josephine).

Dewes, testamentary executor, v. State, No. 10,918, 31 January 1856, transferred to Sixth District Court of New Orleans, 14 May 1856 (slaves Zabel and Clem).

Dickerson, f.m.c., v. State, No. 10,732, 20 October 1855 (slaves Charlotte and her children).

Dreyfous v. State, No. 10,792, 5 February 1856 (slave Arthemise).

Ducatel v. State, No. 11,053, transferred to Fifth District Court of New Orleans, 10 April 1856 (slave not named).

Edwards v. State, No. 10,729, 21 November 1855 (slave Joseph Johnson).

Elizabeth, f.w.c., v. State, No. 10,737, 3 December 1855 (slave Mimi, alias Amelia).

Eulalie, f.w.c., v. Blanc, No. 4904, 19 April 1850.

Eulalie, f.w.c., v. Long and Mabry, No. 8668, 26 May 1853.

Everard v. State, No. 11,022, transferred to Fourth District Court of New Orleans, 23 February 1856 (slave Nancy).

Fatjo v. State, No. 10,499, 3 December 1855 (slaves Euphrosine, alias Bribane, and child Antoinette).

Ferman, f.m.c., v. State, No. 10,493, 19 November 1855 (slave François).

Fernandez v. State, No. 10,958, 5 March 1856 (slaves Henry, alias Edward, and Oscar).

Fortin, f.m.c., v. State, No. 10,734, 3 December 1855 (slave Adeline).

Fortin, f.w.c., v. State, No. 10,736, 3 December 1855 (slaves Menos, alias Aimee, and her child Josephine).

Frederick v. State, No. 10,778, 5 March 1856 (slave Pauline).

Galle, f.m.c., v. State, No. 12,051, transferred to Fifth District Court of New Orleans, 10 May 1856 (slaves Juliette and Andella).

Gardère v. State, No. 10,957, 20 February 1856 (slave Agenon Martin).

Gontz v. State, No. 10,777, 5 March 1856 (slave Zemire).

Gras, f.w.c., v. State, No. 11,055, transferred to Fourth District Court of New Orleans, 10 April 1856 (slaves Frances and her two children).

Green, f.m.c., v. State, No. 10,739, 27 March 1856 (slaves Jenny, Ramon, and Stephney).

Hagan v. State, No. 11,082, 12 March 1856 (slaves Lucy Ann Chateaur, her two children, Fredrika and Dolly, and William Loundes).

Haynes, alias Mielkie, f.w.c., v. Forno, Hutchinson, and Hill, curator, No. 7091, 26 December 1851.

Hélène, c.w., v. Blineau, No. 4126, 11 January 1850.

Herminia, f.w.c., and her children, for *habeas corpus*, No. 6512, 3 June 1851.

Holmes, f.w.c., for *habeas corpus*, No. 15,623, 10 December 1861.

In the matter of the slave David, manumitted by Wilson, No. 9715, 11 October 1854.

Irvin v. State, No. 10,789, transferred to Fifth District Court of New Orleans, 16 January 1856 (slave Garrison).

Jacques, wife of David, v. David, No. 5398, 21 October 1851.

Jacquette, f.w.c., v. Lambeth and Harris, No. 8644, 28 June 1853.

Jobert v. State, No. 11,071, transferred to Fourth District Court of New Orleans, 22 April 1856 (slave Adelaide).

John v. State, No. 10,919, transferred to Second District Court of New Orleans, 31 January 1856 (slaves Pelagie, Felix, Maraya, and Marceline).

Johnson, f.m.c., v. Mannel, No. 1707, 27 January 1848.

King, f.m.c., for *habeas corpus*, No. 2266, 17 May 1848.

King, f.m.c., for *habeas corpus*, No. 9591, 8 June 1854.

Labiche, f.m.c., v. State, No. 10,489, 30 August 1855 (slave Marie Louise).

Labiche, f.m.c., v. State, No. 10,490, 3 July 1855 (slave Adele).

Lambert, wife of Laribeau, v. State, No. 10,681, 3 December 1855 (slave Overton).

Lee v. State, No. 10,741, 28 November 1855 (slave Lewis).

Lefebre v. State, No. 10,920, 5 March 1856 (slave Marianne and her child Victor).

Leonora, alias Nora, f.w.c., v. State, transferred to Second District Court of New Orleans, 22 April 1856 (slave not named).

Livaudais v. State, No. 10,772, 20 February 1856 (slaves Louis and Titine).

Liza, f.w.c., v. Puissant, Nos. 5383, 5632, 22 November 1850, 21 December 1850.

Louis, *statu liber,* praying to be emancipated, v. Pedescleaux and Cousins, No. 1453, 30 May 1848.

Louisa, *statu liber,* and Fonvalgne, curator, v. Giggo, No. 6020, 22 March 1851.

Luciani v. State, No. 10,808, 3 December 1856 (slave Lucille).

Lucille, c.w., v. Maspereau, No. 1692, 7 January 1848.

Lusey v. State, No. 10,795, 4 February 1856 (slaves Françoise and children Eugene and Noel).

Magnon v. State, No. 10,502, 8 August 1855 (slaves Marie Ursula and children Cecilia and Josephine).

Malotte, f.w.c., v. Hackett and Newby, No. 2712, 5 March 1849.

Manetta v. State, No. 10,811, 4 February 1856 (slaves Elmire and child Valerin).

Marcelin, f.m.c., v. State, No. 10,491, 3 December 1855 (slave Mirthee).

Marcus, f.w.c., on behalf of Louis, c.m., v. Bacas, f.m.c., No. 1882, 6 January 1849.

Martin v. State, No. 10,787, 19 January 1856 (slaves Mary Ann, Jarod, James Ingraham).

Maynadler v. State, No. 12,052, transferred to Fifth District Court of New Orleans, 19 April 1856 (slave not named).

McCulloch v. State, No. 10,663, 3 December 1855 (slave Harriet).

Milky, c.w., v. Millaudon, No. 1201, 11 November 1847.

Miller, f.w.c., v. State, No. 10,731, 20 November 1855.

Moore, f.m.c., for *habeas corpus*, No. 10,500 (date missing).

Murphy v. State, No. 10,679, 3 December 1855 (slave Cecilia).

Murphy v. State, No. 10,680, 3 December 1855 (slaves Margaret, Caroline, and Milly).

Nautre v. Bonne, f.m.c., No. 7191, 22 April 1852.

Outremont v. State, No. 11,054, transferred to Fourth District Court of New Orleans, 17 April 1856 (slave Phillis).

Pajand v. State, No. 10,733, 24 October 1855 (slave Ryal).

Payne v. Creswell, No. 6532, 6 August 1852.

Peieira v. State, No. 10,678, 3 December 1855 (slave Zulmé).

Perez v. State, No. 10,677, 3 December 1855 (slave Lusida).

Perret v. State, No. 10,686, 3 December 1855 (slave Helene, alias Chouchoute).

Phany, w.c., v. Bouny and Poincy, No. 1421, 3 November 1847.

Poitmineau v. State, No. 11,008, 26 February 1856 (record missing).

Pope, f.w.c., v. Wright, No. 256, 11 February 1847.

Powell v. State, No. 11,032, transferred to Fifth District Court of New Orleans, 10 April 1856 (slave not named).

Prieur v. State, No. 10,508, 3 December 1855 (slave Harriet Rollis).

Robin, f.w.c., v. State, No. 10,796, 7 January 1856 (slave Hannah).

Rogers, f.m.c., v. Guesnard, No. 2362, 8 February 1849.

Ross, testamentary executor of Green, f.m.c., v. State, No. 10,413, 11 November 1855 (slaves Suzan, Henry, Luda, Gardiner).

St. Ours, f.w.c., v. State, No. 10,791, 5 February 1856 (slaves Julien, Leon, and Pauline).

Sally, f.w.c., v. Varney, No. 906, 28 June 1847.

Sarah, c.w., v. Hagan and Guillaume, No. 1898, 11 November 1848.

Sarah Ann, f.w.c., and Charity, f.w.c., et al., v. Atkins, f.w.c., No. 6468, 6 August 1851.

Scanlan v. State, No. 10,504, 3 December 1855 (slaves Clarissa and children Alexander and Lewis).

Schmitt v. State, No. 10,682, 29 November 1855 (slave Damas Bonsignac).

Skipworth v. State, No. 12,169, transferred to Fifth District Court of New Orleans, 16 May 1856 (slave Elsey).

Smith, f.m.c., for *habeas corpus*, No. 2279, 19 August 1848.

Smith v. State, No. 10,767, 21 November 1855 (slave Caroline Johnson).

Soloy v. State, No. 10,746, 3 December 1855 (slaves Suzanne and her three children).

Souri, c.w., v. Vincent, No. 2660, 17 January 1850.

State v. Arbuckle, f.w.c., No. 12,767, 2 June 1857, 5 November 1857.

State v. Arbuckle, f.w.c., No. 14,470, 6 December 1860.

State v. Arbuckle, f.w.c., No. 15,815, 9 May 1862.

State v. Black, f.w.c., No. 1095, 11 June 1847.

State v. Charles, f.m.c., Nos. 1159, 1302, 28 June 1847, 8 July 1847.

State v. Clifton, f.m.c., No. 11,027, 25 February 1856.

State v. Coffee, f.m.c., No. 4244, 20 October 1849.

State v. Cornelius, f.w.c., No. 15,325, 2 July 1861.

State v. David, No. 8160, 18 September 1852.

State v. David, No. 10,384, 12 December 1856.

State v. David, No. 13,188, 26 November 1857.

State v. David, No. 14,304, 18 January 1860.

State v. Discon, f.w.c., No. 15,533, 6 December 1861.

State v. Eddington, alias Morgan, alias Dutch, f.m.c., No. 3031, 20 November 1848.

State v. Eddington, f.m.c., Nos. 3112, 3122, 20 December 1848.

State v. Elliot, f.w.c., No. 15,514, 29 November 1861.

State v. Ettinger, No. 5161, 27 July 1850.

State v. Golding, f.m.c., No. 15,518, 8 November 1861.

State v. Henderson, f.m.c., No. 12,723, 25 February 1857.

State v. Jannings, f.m.c., No. 4910, 6 April 1850.

State v. Love, alias Vick, f.w.c., No. 15,343, 29 January 1862.

State v. Martin, f.w.c., No. 299, 4 October 1846.

State v. McMichael and Miller, No. 13,052, 21 January 1858.

State v. Mills, f.m.c., No. 10,386, 13 April 1855.

State v. Powell, f.w.c., No. 10,876, 19 May 1846.

State v. Puissant, No. 6005, 27 February 1851.

State v. Ritchie, No. 1613, 13 January 1848.

State v. Smith, f.w.c., No. 2279, 19 May 1848.

State v. Smith, f.m.c., No. 10,055, 30 June 1855.

State v. Stephany, f.m.c., No. 10,485, 30 June 1855.

State v. Stevens, f.m.c., No. 10,416, 23 June 1855.

State v. Stevens, f.m.c., No. 10,417, 24 May 1855.

State v. Waters, f.m.c., No. 15,523, 8 November 1861.

State v. Wilson, f.w.c., No. 12,097, 24 April 1856.

Stewart, f.w.c., v. State, No. 10,785, 1 February 1856 (slave William).

Succession of Etienne, f.m.c., No. 7812, 6 February 1849.

Succession of Green, f.m.c., No. 8598, 1 September 1853.

Succession of Hudson, f.w.c., v. Bacas, No. 1882, 22 December 1848.

Succession of Mielkie, No. 7114, 7 July 1849.

Succession of Navarre, No. 4847, 5 April 1850.

Succession of Pigneguy, No. 7053, 3 January 1853.

Suzanne, c.w., v. Warry, No. 3375, 4 April 1849.

Tabé, c.w., v. Vidal, No. 1584, 26 November 1847.

Tremoulet v. State, No. 10,961, transferred to Second District Court of New Orleans, 11 February 1856 (slave Gothon).

Verret v. State, No. 10,933, 16 February 1856 (slave Nicolle).

Walker, f.w.c., v. Succession of Jarvis, No. 9424, 13 February 1856.

Washington, f.m.c., v. State, No. 10,504, 3 December 1855 (slaves Martha Washington and children William and Mathilde).

Washington, f.m.c., v. State, No. 10,807, transferred to Fourth District Court of New
Orleans, 19 January 1856 (slave George Washington).

Widow Abat v. State, No. 11,029, 5 March 1856 (slaves Zélime and Eugène).

Widow Bouny v. State, No. 10,735, 3 December 1855 (slave Gaston Delille).

Widow Clay v. State, No. 10,764, 3 December 1855 (slave Justine).

Widow Duvernay, f.w.c., v. State, No. 10,775, 27 November 1855 (slave Marianne).

SECOND DISTRICT COURT OF NEW ORLEANS

Ann, alias Anna, c.w., v. Durel, No. 1281, 5 March 1857.

Apasie, f.w.c., for *habeas corpus*, No. 849, 29 May 1848.

Arnousse, f.w.c., v. State, No. 10,338, 3 July 1856 (slave not named).

Avegno, f.w.c., v. State, No. 11,106, filed 21 November 1856 (slave Therésa).

Babcock v. State, No. 10,281, 7 May 1856 (slave not named).

Bacas, f.m.c., executor of Beaulieu, f.w.c., v. State, No. 10,217, 3 July 1856 (slave
Chloe).

Bacus, f.m.c., v. State, No. 10,217, 3 July 1856 (slave Theophile).

Barbe, f.w.c., v. State, No. 10,070, 7 May 1856 (slaves Henriette and Coralee).

Barclay, f.w.c., v. Sewell, No. 8019, 25 March 1856.

Bowles v. State, No. 10,369, 3 July 1856 (slave Rosa).

Carmelite, f.w.c., v. Lacaze, No. 4595, 15 December 1851.

Carriere v. State, No. 11,218, 26 December 1856 (slave not named).

Castin, *statu liber,* v. Castin, f.m.c., No. 10,503, 1 June 1857.

Clarkson v. State, No. 10,926, 20 January 1856.

Cox, f.w.c., v. State, No. 9890, 7 May 1856 (slave Vincent).

Cox, f.w.c., v. State, No. 10,056, 7 May 1856 (slave Mary).

Crocker, f.m.c., v. Benoist, f.m.c., and Thompson, No. 1304, 30 October 1848.

David v. Rideau, No. 11,319, 10 March 1857.

Delphine, f.w.c., v. Gillet, No. 7192, 17 May 1855, 18 February 1857.

Dufour, Durand & Co. v. Rideau, No. 10,956, 7 December 1857.

Duria, f.w.c., v. Perez, f.m.c., executor of Nicolaë, No. 17,781, 13 April 1861.

Duvernay, f.w.c., v. State, No. 9824, 13 February 1856 (slave Marianne).

Elisa, *statu liber,* v. Brenan, No. 11,379, 24 February 1857.

Fabre v. State, No. 10,196, 24 June 1856 (slave Elizabeth Belsamine).

Forstall, testamentary executor, v. State, No. 10,042, 7 May 1856 (slaves Eugene and Mathilde).

Fox, f.m.c., v. State, No. 10,153, 2 July 1856 (slave Françoise, alias Peggy).

Glover v. State, No. 10,457, 3 July 1856 (slave Nelly Branch and her children Maria, Churchill, Henrietta, Jones, and Frederick; Kesiah and her children Calvin and Alinda).

Gras, f.w.c., v. State, No. 10,096, 7 May 1856 (slaves Frances and children Jean Anmanciel, Jean Ignace, and Vincent).

Green, f.m.c., v. State, No. 10,466, 3 July 1856 (slaves Ellen, Katy, Juliette, and Mossy).

Grima v. State, No. 11,056, 11 November 1856 (slave Arthermie Anne).

Grima v. State, No. 11,219, 26 December 1856 (slave Justine and child).

Henry v. State, No. 10,152, 2 July 1856 (slave Eliza).

John, f.w.c., v. State, No. 10,097, 24 April 1856 (slave not named).

Lanaux, f.w.c., v. State, No. 10,200, 2 July 1856 (slave Euphrasie, alias Marie Catherine).

Laronde, f.w.c., v. State, No. 10,187, 7 May 1856 (slave Marie Rose, alias Rosella).

Lathrop v. State, No. 10,437, 3 July 1856 (slave John).

Littlejohn, f.w.c., v. State, No. 10,469, 3 July 1856 (slave Patrick).

Love, f.m.c., v. State, No. 10,456, 3 July 1856 (slave Marthe).

Many, f.w.c., v. State, No. 10,470, 2 July 1856 (slave Nelly).

Martin, f.m.c., v. State, No. 11.082, 14 November 1856 (slave Mitchell).

Montreuil v. State, No. 9820, 2 December 1856 (slave Louise).

Naba, f.m.c., v. Derbigny, f.m.c., No. 9252, 7 November 1855 (slave François Naba).

Naba, f.m.c., v. State, No. 9723, 13 February 1856 (slave François Naba).

Pradine, f.w.c., v. State, No. 11,059, 12 November 1856 (slaves Jeanneton and her two children).

Ridell v. Lockwood, No. 10,781, 17 October 1856.

Ross, f.w.c., v. State, No. 10,441, 3 July 1856 (slaves Ellen and her children Alice and Antoine).

Sage v. State, No. 11,010, 7 May 1856 (slaves Nina and daughter Alice).

Simeon, f.w.c., v. State. No. 10,126, 2 July 1856 (slaves Mathilde Rodriguez and two children, Mathilde, alias Palmyre, Simeon and Angelina Simeon).

Simms v. State, No. 11,218, 10 December 1856 (slave not named).

Simonds v. State, No. 10,450, 2 July 1856 (slave Anne).

State v. Marigny, sheriff for *habeas corpus*, No. 9393, 10 October 1855.

Succession of Chappell, No. 7274, 10 April 1854.

Succession of Jacques, widow of Rideau, wife of David, No. 11,427, 28 September 1860.

Tremoulet v. State, No. 10,094, 7 May 1856, 2 July 1856 (slave Gothon).

Vernier, f.w.c., v. State. No. 10,125, 2 July 1856 (slave Hypolite, alias Batallian).

Victoire, f.w.c., v. Ferrand, No. 624, 25 March 1847.

Walker, f.w.c., v. Succession of Jarvis, No. 9424, 13 February 1856.

Weightman v. State, No. 10,452, 3 July 1856 (slave John Reed).

Williams, f.w.c., v. State, No. 10,470, 2 July 1856 (slave Catherine).

Wilson v. State, No. 10,417, 3 July 1856 (slaves Caroline Wilson and two children, Alice Williams and Valentine).

Wood v. State, No. 10,111, 7 May 1856 (slaves Henriette and three children).

Wright v. State, No. 10,202, 3 July 1856 (slave Philis).

Zabelle, f.w.c., v. Dolliole, administrator of Otis, No. 1201, 15 June 1848.

THIRD DISTRICT COURT OF NEW ORLEANS

Bass and Johnson, f.p.c., v. Chase, No. 14,642, 4 May 1860.

Brown, f.m.c., v. Johnson, No. 743, 8 June 1849.

Brown, f.w.c., v. Smith, No. 3555, 13 May 1852.

Charlotte, c.w., v. Cazelar, No. 1078, 14 March 1849.

Denies, f.m.c., v. Nichols and Doré, No. 3845, 8 May 1852.

Duhulcod, alias Myrthé, f.w.c., v. Philippe, f.w.c., administrator of Charles, f.m.c., No. 447, 15 March 1848.

Euphrémie, f.w.c., v. Maran and Jordan, alias Noble, No. 13,231, 24 December 1859.

Florianne, f.w.c., v. Duplessis, f.w.c., No. 15,223, 17 November 1860.

Françoise, f.w.c., v. Pezant, No. 15,013, 16 June 1860.

Johnson, f.m.c., v. Petric, No. 3158, 10 December 1850.

Jones, f.w.c., praying to become a slave, v. State, No. 13,900, 22 December 1859.

Leocarde, f.w.c., v. Cammark, administrator of Blanc, No. 2889, 7 May 1850.

Logan, f.w.c., v. Hickman and Robinson, No. 9470, 20 February 1857, 2 March 1857.

Morrison, f.m.c., v. Townsend and Thomkins, No. 509, 1 July 1848.

Roberts, f.w.c., v. Simmons & Co., No. 14,215, 22 December 1860.

State (Johnson, f.m.c., relator), praying for a writ of *habeas corpus,* No. 14,190, 9 December 1859.

State (relator Taylor, f.m.c.) v. Parker, Nos. 15,566, 15,626, 30 May, 23 November 1859.

Stemphear v. Rideau, No. 11,895, 1856–1859.

Stevens, f.m.c., praying to become a slave, v. State, No. 16,624, 1 February 1862.

Turnbull, f.w.c., v. Turnbull, No. 7953, 22 February 1856.

FOURTH DISTRICT COURT OF NEW ORLEANS

Ajoie, f.w.c., v. Marigny, No. 10,443, 1 December 1856.

Barney, f.w.c., praying to become a slave, v. State, No. 13,526, 18 February 1860.

Bodin v. State, No. 10,227, 31 May 1856 (slave Marie Louise).

Brown, f.w.c., v. Raby, No. 7850, 14 May 1858.

Delphine, f.w.c., for *habeas corpus* of her daughter, v. Davenport, No. 4973, 28 January 1852.

Dubourg v. State, No. 10,011, 8 May 1856 (slave Kitty).

Elliot, f.w.c., praying to become a slave, v. State, No. 15,132, 26 November 1861.

Everard v. State, No. 11,068, 5 May 1856 (slave Nancy Watkins).

Forstall, testamentary executor of Forstall, f.w.c., v. State, No. 9614, 24 January 1856 (slave Mary).

Foster, f.m.c., v. Mish, No. 12,249, 21 February 1858.

Hill v. State, No. 10,106, 5 May 1856 (slave Darcus).

Houston, f.m.c., v. Lapice, No. 3729, 29 November 1851.

Jean Baptiste, praying for his freedom, v. Mix, administrator of Crocker, No. 3347, 27 April 1850.

Johnson, f.w.c., v. State, No. 10,087, 5 May 1856 (slaves Josephine and Caroline).

Lester, f.m.c., v. Preau, No. 7129, 19 December 1853.

Leonora, alias Nora, f.w.c., v. State, No. 10,070, 5 May 1856 (slave Andrew).

Marshall v. Watrigant, No. 5808, 20 December 1853.

Martin, f.w.c., v. State, No. 9588, 24 January 1856 (slaves Mary Ann and John Ingraham).

Montigue, f.m.c., v. Parker, sheriff, No. 13,992, 7 August 1860.

Outremont v. State, No. 10,060, 19 April 1856 (slave Philis).

Rideau v. His Creditors, No. 3980, 19 November 1850.

Robertson, f.w.c., praying for a writ of *habeas corpus,* No. 11,936, 11 January 1858.

Rombald, f.m.c., v. Marigny, No. 10,442, 1 December 1856.

Spear, f.w.c., v. Blanchard, keeper of the police jail, No. 11,451, 12 June 1857.

Sudour, f.w.c., v. Rilleaux, No. 10,738, 12 November 1856.

Thomas, praying to become a slave, v. State, No. 13,318, 1 October 1859.

Walker, f.w.c., praying to become a slave, v. State, No. 13,319, 1 October 1859.

Washington, f.m.c., v. State, No. 9587, 24 January 1856 (slave George Washington).

Webber, f.w.c., v. Howard, No. 4682, 7 November 1851.

Wilson, praying to become a slave for life, v. State, No. 13,390, 24 November 1860.

Young, f.m.c., v. Egan, No. 7462, 12 March 1855.

FIFTH DISTRICT COURT OF NEW ORLEANS

Adonis, f.w.c., v. State, No. 11,278, 18 August 1856 (slaves Augustine and her child Marie Julienne).

Anfoux v. State, No. 11,330, 28 August 1856 (slave Ellen).

Arbuckle, f.w.c., v. Bouny and Talbot, No. 1570, 11 October 1848; No. 2523, 4 June 1849, 22 July 1865.

Belliere, f.w.c., v. State, No. 11,256, 18 August 1856 (slave Lubin).

Belliere, f.w.c., v. State, No. 11,279, 10 July 1856 (slave not named).

Bettinger v. State, No. 11,192, 30 May 1856 (slave Marie Antoinette).

Bracy, f.w.c., v. Lombard, No. 10,968, 5 May 1856.

Brard, f.m.c., v. State, No. 11,073, 8 May 1856 (slave Jean Theophile).

Brewerton v. State, No. 11,314, 18 August 1856 (slave Delia).

Camille, f.w.c., v. Rimassa, No. 10,475, 19 February 1856.

Claude, f.w.c., v. Lombard, agent of Claude, No. 11,344, 12 June 1858.

Cocks v. State, No. 11,129, 27 May 1856 (slave Julia).

Cocks v. State, No. 11,130, 27 May 1856 (slave Eugene Aram Smith).

Constade v. Her Husband, No. 10,707, 9 September 1858.

Connolly and Fox v. State, No. 12, 281, 18 August 1856 (slave Bluford).

Couverse, f.m.c., v. State, No. 11,135, 30 May 1856 (slave Emeline).

Desgarzant v. David, No. 5419, 7 May 1856.

Domer, f.m.c., v. State, No. 11,022, 28 May 1856 (slave William).

Douglas v. State, No. 11,312, 18 August 1856 (slaves Henriette and her children, William, Mary, John, and Alice).

Douglas v. State, No. 11,313, 18 August 1856 (slaves Amelia and her children Henry and Cordelia).

Dowd, f.w.c., v. Stream, No. 9921, 6 May 1856.

Dunbar, f.w.c., v. State, No. 11,311, 25 August 1856 (slave Annah).

Elizabeth, *statu liber*, v. Pellandini, No. 11,321, 9 January 1857.

Galle v. State, No. 10,969, date missing (slaves Angela and Juliette).

Goines, f.m.c., v. State, No. 11,310, 18 August 1856 (slave Marthe).

Guillard v. State, No. 12,294, 25 August 1856 (slave Ascension).

Hagan v. State, No. 11,074, 23 May 1856 (slaves Lucy Ann Chateaur, her two children, Fredrika and Dolly, and William Loundes).

Jobert v. State, No. 11,030, 30 May 1856 (slave Adelaide).

Johns, f.w.c., v. Abadie, executor of Doubéde, No. 10,420, 13 March 1856.

Johnson, f.m.c., v. Steip and the City of New Orleans, No. 8523, 10 April 1857.

Jones, f.m.c., v. Jones, f.w.c., No. 13,086, 23 April 1859.

LeClerc, f.p.c., v. State, No. 12,293, 18 August 1856 (slaves Charlotte and Jules).

LeClerc, f.w.c., v. State, No. 11,295, 18 August 1856 (slaves Marie Rose, Louisa, Mila, Jean, Felix, and Marie Eliska).

Lonsdale v. State, No. 11,452, 21 November 1856.

Louisa, alias Zaza, f.w.c., v. Dorgenois, 25 June 1856.

Marchadie v. State, No. 11,003, 6 May 1856 (slaves Mary and her three children, Gabriel, Henrietta, and Mary).

Marie Emilie, f.w.c., v. Hubbard, f.w.c., No. 11,338, 30 March 1857.

Maynaider v. State, No. 11,020, 30 May 1856 (slaves Becky, Bob, alias Robert, and Helen).

Paine, f.m.c., v. Lambeth, No. 2884, 28 February 1857.

Person v. State, No. 11,201, 30 May 1856 (slave William).

Petron v. State, No. 13,337, filed 26 August 1856 (slaves Josephine and four children).

Powell v. Tate, No. 10,997, 24 May 1856 (slave Emelina).

Ramsay v. State, No. 11,473, 3 December 1856.

Ribe v. State, No. 10,975, 27 May 1856 (slave Boston).

Romero v. State, No. 11,437, 10 November 1856 (slave Elsie).

Rose, *statu liber,* v. Hart, No. 9834, 11 November 1855.

Saizer, wife of Lacaze, v. Her Husband, No. 10,842, 24 March 1856.

Skipworth v. State, No. 11,133, 30 May 1856 (slave Hilsey or Elsay).

Stone, f.w.c., praying to become a slave, v. State, No. 13,245, 7 September 1859.

Tomlarel v. State, No. 11,076, 23 May 1856 (slave Justine).

Tourne v. State, No. 11,113, 30 May 1856 (slave Felicie).

Walker, f.w.c., v. State, No. 11,309, 18 August 1856 (slave Lucinda).

Willard v. State, No. 11,131, 28 May 1856 (slave Willis Perkins).

SIXTH DISTRICT COURT OF NEW ORLEANS

Ann, *statu liber,* v. Brown, No. 3115, 20 August 1855.

Clifton, f.m.c., praying to become a slave, v. State, No. 8465, 18 May 1860.

Jack, alias John Claiborne, *statu liber,* v. Brown, 20 August 1855.

Lloyd, f.m.c., praying to become a slave, v. State, No. 8648, 15 September 1860.

Moore, f.w.c., praying to become a slave, v. State, No. 7589, 11 January 1860.

Nells, f.m.c., praying to become a slave, v. State, No. 8647, 15 September 1860.

Stewart, f.m.c., praying to become a slave, v. State, No. 9158, 13 February 1861.

Stone, f.w.c., praying to select a master, v. State, No. 8597, 20 September 1860, 28 August 1861.

Wells, f.m.c., praying to become a slave, v. State, No. 9593, 15 February 1859.

SUPREME COURT OF LOUISIANA

Adele, f.w.c., v. Beauregard, 1 Mart. (O.S.) 183 (1810).

African Methodist Episcopal Church v. City of New Orleans, No. 6291, 15 La. Ann. 441 (1860).

Andrinette, f.w.c., v. Maran and Jordan, alias Noble, Nos. 6740, 6741, unreported (1865).

Arbuckle, f.w.c., v. Bouny and Talbot, No. 1380, unreported (1849); No. 1632, 5 La. Ann. 699 (1850).

Arsène, alias Cora, f.w.c., v. Pignéguy, No. 459, 2 La. Ann. 620 (1847).

Barclay, f.w.c., v. Sewell, curator, No. 4622, 12 La. Ann. 262 (1857).

Brown, f.w.c., v. Raby, No. 5797, 14 La. Ann. 41 (1859).

Brown, f.w.c., v. Smith and Taylor, No. 2761, 8 La. Ann. 59 (1853).

Carmelite, f.w.c., v. Lacaze, No. 2506, 7 La. Ann. 629 (1852).

Carmouche v. Carmouche, No. 243, 12 La. Ann. 721 (1857).

Claude, f.w.c., v. Lombard, agent of Claude, No. 5909, unreported (1859).

Couvent, f.m.c., tutor of Mary, v. Guesnard, No. 1063, 5 La. Ann. 69 (1850).

Delphine, f.w.c., v. Gillet, No. 4249, 11 La. Ann. 424 (1856); No. 5154, 13 La. Ann. 248 (1858).

Dufour, Durand & Co. v. Rideau, No. 5611, unreported (1858).

Eugénie, f.w.c., v. Préval, No. 99, 2 La. Ann. 180 (1847).

Eulalie, f.w.c., v. Long and Mabry, No. 3227, 9 La. Ann. 9 (1854); No. 3979, 11 La. Ann. 463 (1856).

Euphrémie, f.w.c., v. Maran and Jordan, alias Noble, Nos. 6740, 6741, unreported (1865).

Ex Parte Louis, 3 La. Ann. 467 (1848).

Foster, f.m.c., v. Mish, No. 6344, 15 La. Ann. 199 (1860).

Haynes, alias Mielkie, f.w.c., v. Forno, Hutchinson, and Hill, curator, No. 2850, 8 La. Ann. 35 (1853).

Josephine, f.w.c., v. Poultney, No. 5935, 1 La. Ann. 329 (1846).

Liza, f.w.c., v. Puissant, No. 2326, 7 La. Ann. 80 (1852).

Logan, f.w.c., v. Hickman and Robinson, No. 5736, 14 La. Ann. 300 (1859).

Marie Louise, f.w.c., v. Marot, No. 2748, 8 La. Ann. 475 (1835).

Marshall v. Watrigant, No. 5220, 13 La. Ann. 619 (1858).

Miller v. Belmonti, No. 5623, 11 Rob. 339 (1845).

Morrison, f.w.c., v. White, 16 La. Ann. 100 (1861).

Ridell v. Lockwood, No. 4840, listed as unreported, 13 La. Ann. xiii (1857).

Rogers, f.m.c., v. Guesnard, No. 1507, unreported (1850).

Smith, f.w.c., v. Smith, No. 3314, 13 La. Ann. 441 (1839).

State v. Cecil, 2 Mart. (O.S.) 208 (1812).

State v. Harrison, No. 4464, 11 La. Ann. 722 (1856).

State v. Judge of the First District Court and Tappan, No. 4440, 11 La. Ann. 187 (1856).

State in rel. of Cook v. Keeper of Parish Prison, 15 La. Ann. 347 (1860).

Succession of Cresswell, No. 2423, 8 La. Ann. 122 (1853).

Succession of McDonogh, No. 2416, 7 La. Ann. 472 (1852).

Young, f.m.c., v. Egan, No. 4075, 10 La. Ann. 415 (1855).

UNITED STATES SUPREME COURT

Baron v. Baltimore, 7 Pet. 243 (1833).

Permoli v. City of New Orleans, 3 How. 589 (1845).

Scott v. Sandford, 19 How. (U.S.) 393 (1857).

Strader v. Graham, 10 How. (U.S.) 82 (1851).

OFFICIAL DOCUMENTS

Acts . . . of the Legislative Council of the Territory of Orleans, 1805–11. Cited by year as Orleans Territory Acts.

Acts . . . of the Legislature of the State of Louisiana, 1812–62. Cited by year as Louisiana Acts.

Acts of the Legislatures of the States of Alabama, Arkansas, Georgia, Kentucky, Maryland, Mississippi, and South Carolina, 1835–60. Cited by state and year.

Civil Code of the State of Louisiana. New Orleans: J. C. de St. Romes, 1825.

Cohen's City Directory. New Orleans: D. Davies, 1849.

Conveyance Office Records (New Orleans), 1859–61.

Dart, Benjamin Wall, ed. Constitutions of the State of Louisiana and Selected Federal Laws. Indianapolis: Bobbs-Merrill, 1932.

A Digest of the Civil Laws Now in Force in the Territory of Orleans. 1808. Reprint, Baton Rouge: Claitor's, 1971.

Fifth District Court of New Orleans. Minute Books, 1846–62.

First District Court of New Orleans. Minute Books, 1846–62.

Fourth District Court of New Orleans. *Minute Books, 1846–62.*

Fuqua, James O., ed. *Code of Practice in Civil Cases for the State of Louisiana.* New Orleans: Bloomfield and Steele, 1867.

Journal of the House of Representatives of the State of Louisiana. New Orleans: G. W. Weisse, 1852.

Journal of the House of Representatives of the State of Louisiana. New Orleans: Emile La Sere, 1855.

Leovy, Henry J., ed. *The Laws and General Ordinances of the City of New Orleans.* New Orleans: E. C. Wharton, 1857.

Mayor's Office. *Register of Free Coloured People, 1840–1863.*

New Orleans Notarial Archives, 1861. *James Graham, N.P.*

Official Journal of the House of Representatives of the State of Louisiana: Session of 1857. New Orleans: John Claiborne, 1857.

Official Journal of the Senate of the State of Louisiana: Session of 1858. Baton Rouge: J. M. Taylor, 1858.

Official Reports of the Senate of Louisiana: Session of 1857. New Orleans: John Claiborne, 1857.

Peirce, Levi, Miles Taylor, and William King, eds. *The Consolidation and Revision of the Statutes of the State of a General Nature.* New Orleans: *Bee* Office, 1852.

Report of the House of Representatives of the State of Louisiana. New Orleans: G. W. Weisse, 1852.

Report of the Proceedings of the Convention of the State of Louisiana, 1861. New Orleans: J. O. Nixon, 1861.

Report of the Secretary of State of Louisiana. Baton Rouge: News, 1902.

Report of the Secretary of State of the Census of the State of Louisiana. Baton Rouge: J. M. Taylor, 1859.

Reports of Cases Argued and Determined in the Supreme Court of Louisiana and the Superior Court of the Territory of Orleans. 30 vols. St. Paul, Minn.: West, 1913.

Second District Court of New Orleans. *Minute Books, 1846–62.*

Sixth District Court of New Orleans. *Minute Books, 1853–62.*

Supreme Court of Louisiana. *Minute Books, 1846–62.*

Third District Court of New Orleans. *Minute Books, 1846–62.*

United States Census (Louisiana), 1840–60.

NEWSPAPERS

L'Abeille de la Nouvelle Orléans (New Orleans Bee), 1851.

New Orleans Daily Picayune, April 1846–May 1862.

ARTICLES AND ESSAYS

Baade, Hans. "The Law of Slavery in Spanish Luisiana." In *Louisiana's Legal Heritage*, ed. Edward F. Haas. Pensacola, Fla.: Perdido Bay Press, 1983, 43–77.

Everard, Wayne M. "Louisiana's 'Whig' Constitution Revisited: The Constitution of 1852." In *In Search of Fundamental Law: Louisiana's Constitutions, 1812–1974*, ed. Edward F. Haas and Warren M. Billings. Lafayette: Center for Louisiana Studies, 1993, 37–51.

Finkelman, Paul. "Free Blacks in a Slave Society." In *Articles on American Slavery*, vol. 17, ed. Paul Finkelman. New York: Garland, 1989.

———. "Prelude to the Fourteenth Amendment: Black Legal Rights in the Antebellum North." *Rutgers Law Review* 17 (1986): 415–82.

Foner, Eric. "Rights and the Constitution in Black Life during the Civil War and Reconstruction." *Journal of American History* 74 (December 1987): 863–83.

Franklin, John Hope. "The Enslavement of Free Negroes in North Carolina." *Journal of Negro History* 29 (October 1944): 401–28.

Gehman, Mary. "The Mexico-Louisiana Connection." *Louisiana Cultural Vistas* 11 (winter 2000–01): 68–75.

Hartog, Hendrik. "The Constitution of Aspiration and 'The Rights That Belong to All of Us.'" *Journal of American History* 74 (December 1987): 1013–34.

Kotlikoff, Laurence J., and Anton J. Rupert. "The Manumission of Slaves in New Orleans, 1827–1846." *Southern Studies* 19 (summer 1980): 172–81.

Lachance, Paul. "The 1809 Immigration of Saint-Domingue Refugees to New Orleans: Reception, Integration, and Impact." *Louisiana History* 29 (spring 1988): 109–41.

Matison, Sumner Eliot. "Manumission by Purchase." *Journal of Negro History* 33 (April 1948): 154–67.

Medley, Keith Weldon. "When Plessy Met Ferguson." *Louisiana Cultural Vistas* 7 (winter 1996–97): 52–9.

Rankin, David. "The Impact of the Civil War on the Free Colored Community of New Orleans." *Perspectives in American History* 11 (1977–78): 379–416.

———. "The Tannenbaum Thesis Reconsidered: Slavery and Race Relations in Antebellum Louisiana." *Southern Studies* 18 (spring 1979): 5–31.

Reinders, Robert C. "The Decline of the New Orleans Free Negro in the Decade before the Civil War." *Journal of Mississippi History* 24 (January–October 1962): 88–98.

Schafer, Judith K. "The Immediate Impact of Nat Turner's Insurrection in New Orleans." *Louisiana History* 21 (fall 1980): 361–76.

———. "'Open and Notorious Concubinage': The Emancipation of Slave Mistresses by Will and the Supreme Court of Louisiana." *Louisiana History* 28 (spring 1987): 165–82.

———. "Slaves and Crime: New Orleans, 1846–1862." In *Local Matters: Race, Crime, and Justice in the Nineteenth-Century South,* ed. Christopher Waldrep and Donald Nieman. Athens: University of Georgia Press, 2001, 53–91.

Schweninger, Loren. "Antebellum Free Persons of Color in Postbellum Louisiana." *Louisiana History* 30 (fall 1989): 345–64.

Tansey, Richard. "Out-of-State Free Blacks in Late Antebellum New Orleans." *Louisiana History* 22 (fall 1981): 369–86.

Tregle, Joseph G., Jr. "Creoles and Americans." In *Creole New Orleans: Race and Americanization,* ed. Arnold Hirsch and Joseph Logsdon. Baton Rouge: Louisiana State University Press, 1992, 131–85.

———. "Early New Orleans Society: A Reappraisal." *Journal of Southern History* 17 (February 1952): 20–36.

DISSERTATIONS

Everett, Donald. "Free Persons of Color in New Orleans, 1803–1865." Ph.D. dissertation, Tulane University, 1954.

Howington, Arthur Fletcher. "The Treatment of Slaves and Free Blacks in the State and Local Courts of Tennessee." Ph.D. dissertation, Vanderbilt University, 1982.

Rankin, David. "A Forgotten People: Free People of Color in New Orleans, 1850–1870." Ph.D. dissertation, Johns Hopkins University, 1976.

SECONDARY SOURCES

Berlin, Ira. *Many Thousands Gone: The First Two Centuries of Slavery in North America.* Cambridge, Mass.: Harvard University Press, 1998.

———. *Slaves without Masters: The Free Negro in the Antebellum South.* New York: The New Press, 1974.

Billings, Warren M, and Mark F. Fernandez, eds. *A Law unto Itself: Essays in the New Louisiana Legal History.* Baton Rouge: Louisiana State University Press, 2001.

Black, Henry Campbell, ed. *Black's Law Dictionary.* St. Paul, Minn.: West, 1891.

Blassingame, John. *Black New Orleans, 1860–1880.* Chicago: University of Chicago Press, 1973.

Bogger, Tommy L. *Free Blacks in Norfolk, Virginia, 1790–1860: The Darker Side of Freedom.* Charlottesville: University of Virginia Press, 1997.

Campbell, Randolph B. *An Empire for Slavery: The Peculiar Institution in Texas*. Baton Rouge: Louisiana State University Press, 1989.

Conrad, Glenn R., ed. *Dictionary of Louisiana Biography*. 2 vols. Lafayette: Center for Louisiana Studies, 1988.

De Caro, Frank, ed. *Louisiana Sojourns: Travelers' Tales and Literary Journeys*. Baton Rouge: Louisiana State University Press, 1998.

Fehrenbacher, Don E. *Slavery, Law, and Politics: The Dred Scott Case in Historical Perspective*. New York: Oxford University Press, 1981.

Finkelman, Paul. *Dred Scott v. Sandford: A Brief History with Documents*. Boston: Bedford/St. Martins, 1997.

———. *An Imperfect Union: Slavery, Federalism, and Comity*. Chapel Hill: University of North Carolina Press, 1981.

———. *The Law of Freedom and Bondage: A Casebook*. New York: Oceana Press, 1986.

Franklin, John Hope. *The Free Negro in North Carolina, 1790–1860*. Chapel Hill: University of North Carolina Press, 1943.

Gross, Ariela. *Double Character: Slavery and Mastery in the Antebellum Southern Courtroom*. Princeton: Princeton University Press, 2000.

Hall, A. Oakey. *The Manhattaner in New Orleans; or, Phases of "Crescent City" Life*. 1847. Reprint, Baton Rouge: Louisiana State University Press, 1976.

Hodes, Martha. *White Women, Black Men: Illicit Sex in the Nineteenth-Century South*. New Haven, Conn.: Yale University Press, 1997.

Hollandsworth, James G., Jr. *The Louisiana Native Guards: The Black Military Experience during the Civil War*. Baton Rouge: Louisiana State University Press, 1995.

Johnson, Michael P., and James L. Roark, eds. *No Chariot Let Down: Charleston's Free People of Color on the Eve of the Civil War*. Chapel Hill: University of North Carolina Press, 1984.

Johnson, Walter. *Soul by Soul: Life inside the Antebellum Slave Market*. Cambridge, Mass.: Harvard University Press, 1999.

Jordan, Winthop D. *White over Black: American Attitudes Toward the Negro, 1550–1812*. Chapel Hill: University of North Carolina Press, 1968.

Latrobe, Benjamin H. *Impressions Respecting New Orleans: Diary and Sketches, 1818–1829*. Ed. Samuel Wilson. New York: Columbia University Press, 1951.

Malone, Dumas, ed. *Dictionary of American Biography*. 20 vols. New York: Charles Scribner's Sons, 1933.

Morris, Thomas D. *Southern Slavery and the Law*. Chapel Hill: University of North Carolina Press, 1996.

Nichols, Barry. *An Introduction to Roman Law*. New York: Oxford University Press, 1962.

Northup, Solomon. *Twelve Years a Slave*. Ed. Sue Eakin and Joseph Logsdon. Baton Rouge: Louisiana State University Press, 1968.

Olmsted, Frederick Law. *The Cotton Kingdom: A Traveller's Observations on Cotton and Slavery in the American Slave States*. Ed. Arthur M. Schlesinger Sr. New York: Random House, 1984.

Phillips, U. B. *American Negro Slavery: A Study of the Supply, Employment, and Control of Negro Labor as Determined by the Plantation Regime*. 1918. Reprint, Baton Rouge: Louisiana State University Press, 1966.

Powers, Bernard E. *Black Charlestonians: A Social History, 1822–1885*. Fayetteville: University of Arkansas Press, 1994.

Reinders, Robert C. *End of an Era: New Orleans, 1850–60*. New Orleans: Pelican, 1964.

Remini, Robert V. *Daniel Webster: The Man and His Times*. New York: W. W. Norton, 1997.

Rousey, Dennis C. *Policing the Southern City: New Orleans, 1805–1889*. Baton Rouge: Louisiana State University Press, 1996.

Schafer, Judith Kelleher. *Slavery, the Civil Law, and the Supreme Court of Louisiana*. Baton Rouge: Louisiana State University Press, 1994.

Schweninger, Loren. *Black Property Owners in the South, 1790–1915*. Urbana: University of Illinois Press, 1990.

Stampp, Kenneth. *America in 1857: A Nation on the Brink*. New York: Oxford University Press, 1990.

———. *The Peculiar Institution: Slavery in the Antebellum South*. New York: Knopf, 1956.

Sterkx, H. E. *The Free Negro in Antebellum Louisiana*. Cranberry, N.J.: Associated University Presses, 1972.

Taylor, Joe Gray. *Negro Slavery in Louisiana*. Lafayette: Louisiana Historical Association, 1963.

Urofsky, Melvin, and Paul Finkelman. *A March of Liberty: A Constitutional History of the United States*. 2nd ed. New York: Oxford University Press, 2001.

Wade, Richard. *Slavery in the Cities: The South, 1820–1860*. New York: Oxford University Press, 1964.

Whitman, T. Stephen. *The Price of Freedom: Slavery and Manumission in Baltimore and Early National Maryland*. Lexington: University Press of Kentucky, 1997.

Wilson, Carol. *Freedom at Risk: The Kidnapping of Free Blacks in America, 1790–1865*. Lexington: University Press of Kentucky, 1994.

Wyatt-Brown, Bertram. *Lewis Tappan and the Evangelical War Against Slavery*. Cleveland: Case Western University Press, 1969.

INDEX

Abadie, B., 66

Abadie, executor of Doubéde, Johns, f.w.c., v., 66

Abduction. *See* Kidnapping of free people of color

Abolitionism, 59, 119, 127, 138, 140–1, 151, 157, 163

Adams, alias Napoleon, f.m.c., v. State of Louisiana, 74n4

Adams, Lucien, 157

Adde (slave), 100

Adele (slave), 36, 90

Adele, f.w.c., v. Beauregard, 100–1

Administrators of succession, 36, 37n3, 48–9

Adultery, 52n9

Afferson, G. W., 119

African Americans. *See* Free people of color; Slaves

African colonization, 8–12, 46, 73, 88, 152

African Methodist Episcopal Church, 145–6

African Methodist Episcopal Church v. City of New Orleans, 146

Age requirement for manumission, 4–5, 8, 60

Aimée v. Pluché and Bosquet, 20–1

Ajoie, f.w.c., v. Marigny, 29–30

Alabama, 53, 62–4, 104, 147, 150, 158

Alcohol use. *See* Drunkenness

Allen (slave), 109

American Colonization Society, 10

Amos (slave), 100

Andrinette (f.w.c.), 125

Andry, Aimée, 18

Angelina, c.w., v. Parlange, 37

Ann, alias Anna, c.w., v. Durel, 31–2

Apasie, f.w.c, for habeas corpus, 102

Arbuckle, Julia, 37–8, 119–21, 136–7

Arbuckle, Samuel, 119

Arbuckle, f.w.c., State v., 120–1

Arbuckle, f.w.c., v. Bouny and Talbot, 37–8, 119–20

Arceneaux, François, 8

Arkansas, 85, 136, 144, 146, 151

Arrests. *See* Jail; Police

Arsène, alias Cora, v. Pignéguy, 17–8, 22

Arthur (free child of color), 113

Askew v. State, 73n4

Assaults, 39, 40, 41, 43, 67n10, 108n17, 120, 121, 136, 139, 156

Assembly, unlawful, 109, 145–6

Assumption Parish, 84

Atkins, f.m.c., Sarah Ann, f.w.c., and Charity, f.w.c., et al. v., 49–50

Atkins, Thomas, 49–50

Attakapas, 149

Attorneys: and slaves' freedom suits based on transportation to free soil, 23–7; solicitation of slave clients by, 24, 25, 26, 33, 35, 36; legal fees for, 27, 40, 50, 78n10; for